Praise for *Secret Daughter*

"Cross reaches across the racial divide of America to make sense of her tangled roots . . . in this painful, richly detailed account."
—*Newsweek*

"Cross wonderfully recaptures a child's bewilderment with the adult world—a realm of strange words ('colored' and 'segregated' and 'passing') and inexplicable behavior. . . . Deeply moving, *Secret Daughter* chronicles a complex life buffeted by lies and only partly buffered by love." —*People* (four stars)

"Many passages here crackle with emotion. Cross seems to hold back nothing about her childhood, crafting some of the best parts of the book. Her prose is direct and without flourish, but her vivid anecdotes, often told from a child's perspective, give the story a unique, memorable voice." —*The Cleveland Plain Dealer*

"*Secret Daughter* reads like a novel, a completely engrossing one. . . . I had to keep reminding myself this wasn't fiction. . . . For a young child, such a wrenching experience must have left its mark, and June Cross, in this searing memoir, leaves that mark with the reader." —*St. Louis Post-Dispatch*

"Cross . . . details [her] story in a memoir with equal grace and candor. Her probing and telling of this story opens a rare window on how race takes its toll on the lives of specific people in real but unique situations." —*Black Issues Book Review*

PENGUIN BOOKS

SECRET DAUGHTER

June Cross is a journalist and an award-winning television producer with thirty years of experience in both commercial and public television. Her most recent series, *This Far by Faith: African American Spiritual Journeys*, aired nationally on PBS in 2003. Prior to that, Cross was a producer for PBS's *Frontline*, CBS News, and PBS's *MacNeil/Lehrer NewsHour*. She has won two Emmys, including one for the autobiographical film *Secret Daughter*, which also won an Alfred I. DuPont–Columbia Award for Excellence in Broadcast Journalism. She is currently an associate professor at Columbia University's Graduate School of Journalism. Cross graduated from Harvard University, and lives in Manhattan with her husband, jazz trumpet player Waldron Ricks.

www.pbs.org/wgbh/pages/frontline/shows/secret

SECRET
DAUGHTER

A MIXED-RACE DAUGHTER AND
THE MOTHER WHO GAVE HER AWAY

JUNE CROSS

PENGUIN BOOKS

PENGUIN BOOKS
Published by the Penguin Group
Penguin Group (USA) Inc., 375 Hudson Street, New York, New York 10014, U.S.A.
Penguin Group (Canada), 90 Eglinton Avenue East, Suite 700, Toronto,
Ontario, Canada M4P 2Y3 (a division of Pearson Penguin Canada Inc.)
Penguin Books Ltd, 80 Strand, London WC2R 0RL, England
Penguin Ireland, 25 St Stephen's Green, Dublin 2, Ireland (a division of Penguin Books Ltd)
Penguin Group (Australia), 250 Camberwell Road, Camberwell,
Victoria 3124, Australia (a division of Pearson Australia Group Pty Ltd)
Penguin Books India Pvt Ltd, 11 Community Centre, Panchsheel Park, New Delhi – 110 017, India
Penguin Group (NZ), 67 Apollo Drive, Mairangi Bay, Auckland 1311, New Zealand
(a division of Pearson New Zealand Ltd)
Penguin Books (South Africa) (Pty) Ltd, 24 Sturdee Avenue, Rosebank,
Johannesburg 2196, South Africa

Penguin Books Ltd, Registered Offices:
80 Strand, London WC2R 0RL, England

First published in the United States of America by Viking Penguin,
a member of Penguin Group (USA) Inc. 2006
Published in Penguin Books 2007

10 9 8 7 6 5 4 3 2 1

Page 305 constitutes an extension of this copyright page.

THE LIBRARY OF CONGRESS HAS CATALOGED THE HARDCOVER EDITION AS FOLLOWS:
Cross, June.
Secret daughter : a mixed-race daughter and the mother who gave her away / June Cross.
p. cm.
ISBN 0-670-88555-X (hc.)
ISBN 978-0-14-311211-2 (pbk.)
1. Cross, June—Childhood and youth. 2. Racially mixed people—United States—Biography.
3. Abandoned children—United States—Biography. 4. Racially mixed people—Race identity—
United States. 5. Mothers and daughters—United States—Case studies. 6. United States—
Race relations. 7. Cross, June—Family. 8. Cross family. I. Title.
E185.97.C86A3 2006
973'.040596073009092—dc22
[B]   2005058472

Printed in the United States of America

To my mother,
Norma Catherine Storch,
and
the woman who so lovingly raised me,
Muriel Fortune Bush—
For everything you did

ACKNOWLEDGMENTS

During the years I searched my soul for the words to tell this story, many held my hand and pointed out a path.

Had it not been for my colleagues at *Frontline*, this story might never have been told at all. David Fanning first pulled this story out of me over many long evenings before I even understood why it was important. His careful stewardship, his talent as an editor, and his guidance as a mentor have meant more to me than he will ever know. Michael Sullivan first convinced me that I had a voice as a documentarian. John Baynard, my co-producer, persisted without being pushy; Jean Boucicaut shared my tolerance for ambiguity. Sheila Hairston held my hand. Patti Williamson scoured the country looking for archival material. Mario Valdes researched what must have been the entire genealogical history of the United States as he helped me put the pieces of my tangled family history together.

As I moved from the screen to the written page, Judy Crichton read and reread my drafts, urging me to dig deeper with greater accuracy. Fayre Crossley kept me honest. Francille Wilson offered friendship across the miles as I toiled in the country with only squirrels, deer, and my own fears for company. A'Lelia Bundles, who was first assigned to me as a Big Sister in college, has supported me in ways too many to count over the years and as the publication of this book draws nigh. My two biological sisters, Lynda Gravatt and Candace Herman, displayed great patience as I kept returning to them for details of their lives before we met. My brother, Lary May, who has been a constant ballast, gave me leads and confirmed details. Larry Storch painstakingly explained the good old days of show business and confirmed endless details over the years. My stepmother, Lois Basden, suffered an unending string of queries. My husband, Waldron Ricks, lent the firm support of his shoulder and the shelter of his arms when the task of telling the entire story seemed beyond me. His dedication to artistic excellence inspires me every day.

Others provided a quiet space where, freed from the demands of deadlines and students, I could ply my craft. The Vermont Studio Center gave me a space where I worked on the early drafts. A fellowship at Harvard University's W. E. B. DuBois Institute for African and African American Research allowed me to research my memories through the prism of reality and academic inquiry. Jonnet and Peter Abeles allowed me to use their beautiful Shelter Island home as a sorely needed retreat. Their generosity and friendship meant a great deal to me as I struggled through the final drafts.

Of course, without the great courage displayed by my mother, Norma Catherine, this story could never have been told at all. And without the foundation provided by Muriel Agatha Bush, her husband, Paul, and my extended family of Gregory cousins, aunts, and uncles, I would never have had the fortitude to begin.

My editor at Viking, Wendy Wolf, saw the potential for a book while I was still a television writer. Lucia Watson helped the manuscript mature. Amanda Urban had more faith in me than my early manuscripts justified. Maureen Sugden's careful copyediting saved me from careless mistakes.

Seeing my propensity to lose myself in the stories and dramas of others, years before I even considered telling this story or began writing this book, a fellow Soka Gakkai Buddhist, Kathleen Olesky, posed the question, "If there were a June Cross story, what would it be?"

I have tried to answer as honestly as I can.

CONTENTS

Acknowledgments   *ix*

1. Bedrock   1
2. Formations   14
3. Passages   27
4. Tunnels of Love   44
5. Shelter from the Storm   60
6. The Breck Girl   72
7. Reflections   79
8. Pressure Points   94
9. Seismic Shifts   114
10. Under the Boardwalk   135
11. In Pharaoh's Land   153
12. Paper Cuts   176
13. Women   197
14. Discoveries   207
15. Losing Peggy   227
16. Karma   240
17. Pali   256
18. Norma Desmond   269
19. Reverie   291
20. Mercury   295

SECRET DAUGHTER

1. BEDROCK

I search for my mother's face in the mirror and see a stranger. Her face is toffee-colored and round; her eyes, the eyes of a foreigner, slanted and brown. They are not my mother's eyes: irises of brilliant green, set obliquely in almond-shaped sockets above high cheekbones.

They said I looked exotic, she classic. Together—a bamboo-colored redhead carrying her olive-skinned, curly-haired toddler—together, we seemed alien. Skin fractured our kinship.

When I was young, riding in the supermarket cart's basket, strangers looked from me to her and back again.

"She's so cute! Is she yours?" they'd ask.

"Yes, she's mine," Mommie would answer before turning the basket in another direction. Looking behind her, sometimes I saw their faces turn sour. I learned to recognize the expression well before I knew what it meant.

At night, before she put me to bed, Mommie and I would find our own likenesses. She would ask, "Who's got a perfect little forehead?"

I'd point above my brows.

"You do!" she'd say with a nod. "Who's got a perfect little nose?"

"I do!" I'd say, and she would agree again.

"Who's got perfect little hands?"

"We do!"

We laughed over this, our shared proportions: our hands shaped alike—the pinkie exactly half the length of the ring finger, the index and ring fingers each a half inch shorter than the second digit, our nails shaped the same. Even the arches of our feet arced in the same curve, and our toes, too, had a similar square outline.

My mother was an aspiring actress. We lived in the orbit of show business and its backstage shenanigans, where races mixed out of sight of the public. She had separated from my father, a well-known song-and-dance man, shortly after I was born, in January 1954, six months before the Supreme Court's *Brown v. Board of Education* decision desegregated the country's schools.

By the time I was three, Negroes in Montgomery, Alabama, had forced the city to integrate its city buses. In Manhattan the buses were already integrated, but an immutable social line nevertheless divided the races, even in the Upper West Side building where Mommie and I lived. African-Americans worked there as elevator men but could not rent apartments. The civil-rights movement had not made a dent in our social sphere.

"She looks Chinese," acquaintances guessed, considering the fold of my eyes, the pale olive cast of my skin, my full lips. Oriental-looking, said the middle-aged woman who took care of me much of the time, whom I would come to call "Aunt Peggy."

Aunt Peggy was trying to soothe my feelings—"Oriental-looking" Negro women were considered pretty back then—but I knew I wasn't Oriental. Wrapped in a bright yellow towel after my bath, I contemplated the women in the framed Gauguin prints on our walls: their seal-slick black manes, their knowing smiles. Even as a toddler, I somehow grasped that these women would not have considered me Oriental. My mother liked to call me "Tahitian June," but if I were really Tahitian, why wasn't my hair waist long like theirs?

My skin had not yet fully darkened, and my mother lived in fear that we would be found out.

"She'd pass if it weren't for her hair," I overheard Mommie say one day, and my heart collapsed. I didn't know what she meant by that word "pass," but the tone in her voice sounded the way the faces of the people in the supermarket looked.

I went to the bathroom, climbed atop the toilet seat, and leaned over the sink to explore my short, soft, frizzy curls in the mirror.

My mother's hair fell over her eyes in a bouncy auburn flip that flirted with the world. My hair didn't flip. My curls, soft when they were less than an inch long, frizzed straight out if they grew longer. Mommie made sure they didn't get that long. Cute, Aunt Peggy called my boyish cut. Unusual for a girl, she'd say as she smoothed her own wavy black hair into a French twist. She looked at me in a half-cocked way that meant she didn't really think it was cute, but odd.

In front of the mirror, I tried to pull my hair back with my mother's tortoiseshell comb. The fragile teeth snapped, tangling like splintered tears in my curls.

As far back as I could remember, Mommie traveled. When I was a baby, she took me with her on the plane: by the age of two, I had traveled to Detroit, Las Vegas, and Chicago—I had baby-size spoons and forks as souvenirs. Once I was able to walk, she would announce she had an audition for an acting job or a modeling assignment and, before going, take me to Atlantic City, New Jersey, where she left me with Aunt Peggy and her husband, Uncle Paul.

"I'm visiting Atlantic City, but I really live in New York," I would tell everyone, with my native New Yorker's air of superiority. Moving back and forth between the small seaside town and the big concrete city, I would compare everything, and everything seemed to lead me back to the contours of my face. My mother's lips were primly thin—she wore the stoic expression of a pilgrim. My mouth was broad; my full lips framed a toothy smile. "You have your father's mouth," Aunt Peggy said when I asked her why I didn't look like Mommie. She told me not to smile so broadly—it showed my gums to my disadvantage.

Then I would kneel on a chair in the dining room, balancing my left arm on the credenza against the wall, and look in the large wall mirror. I practiced curbing my smile. Sometimes I made faces at myself and laughed.

"If Norma doesn't want anybody to know who she is, she better not laugh," Paul commented to Peggy one day in his gravelly voice. "That laugh belongs to nobody but Norma."

Norma was my mother's first name. I wondered how my mother's laugh could come from my mouth, which was more like my father's. It had been so long since I'd seen my father that I no longer remembered him. I wondered at laughter's power to make me my mother's daughter. I wondered why my mother didn't want anyone to know who I was. Peggy and Paul seemed to understand the answers to these questions, but when I asked, they would look aside and say offhandedly, "Oh, you'll learn when you're older."

Back in New York, Mommie didn't treat me like a child. When I asked her why my mouth wasn't shaped like hers, she said, "I don't know," and she sounded just as mystified as I was. When I told her that Paul said I laughed just like her, she paused barely a second before answering, "Well, that's because you're around me all the time, and we spend so much time together." Her explanation made it seem as natural as the fact that we shared square toes.

She began teaching me how to read tones of voice and hear intent, even when it seemed at odds with what was said. We would often spend the afternoon at the movies, sometimes catching the same movie several days' running, and afterward she explained how actors used their bodies to convey character: the way Loretta Young swept down a flight of stairs like an aristocrat, how Gloria Swanson's staircase descent at the end of *Sunset Boulevard* made her seem crazy or Katharine Hepburn's in *The Philadelphia Story* made her seem like she didn't care about losing her boyfriend, when she really cared a lot. *Sunset Boulevard* was Mommie's favorite movie; *Gigi*, with Leslie Caron and Maurice Chevalier, became mine. Although I didn't understand the plots of these movies, Mommie had a talent for choosing the one scene that even a four-year-old could grasp, and at home I played my mother's co-star as we reenacted them.

My mother told me stories about her life that seemed as fantastic as any movie star's. She told me she was part Indian, the granddaughter of an outlaw who had ridden with Jesse James's gang. She said she had studied acting with Marlon Brando. She said she had been an Olympic swimmer.

When she told me that her grandpa had performed tricks on horses for Ringling Brothers' circus, I thought she was inventing tales; but that one would turn out, like all her stories, to have a strand of truth.

As a young woman, when telling people the story of my life, I chose my words carefully: "My mother didn't raise me. I was raised in Atlantic City, New Jersey."

Sometimes I'd add, "I was raised by my father's people"—"father's people" being a deliberately vague description that could mean my father's brother and sister, some cousins, or, more generally, the entire dark-hued nation. Depending on the race of the listener and how complicated I wished to make the tale, I described those who raised me as my father's sister, my godmother, or my guardians. Aunt Peggy, who after all was not really my aunt but the guardian in question, preferred the last, but my tongue always stuck on that word—"guardian"—it made me feel like a character in a Dickens novel.

In the vernacular of black America, I was "taken in," or informally adopted.

My mother and I never talked about her decision, how it affected her, the way she saw me and those who looked like me, or how it affected the way I viewed her and those who looked like her. We tried, several times, but it was too painful. She could not look at me—with my wild Afro, wide hips, and Harlem address—and ignore the black woman she saw any more than I could ignore her Upper West Side apartment with the wraparound balcony, her closets full of designer clothes, or her support for Ronald Reagan.

Still, we tried.

"I don't see you as a black woman when I look at you," she protested, almost making me believe her. "I see you as mine, all mine. I don't see Jimmy in you at all."

Jimmy. That was my father, James Cross.

During the thirties and forties, he had made his fame as a comic who danced in a duo called Stump and Stumpy (Jimmy was known as "Big Stump," although he was barely five-eight). Stump and Stumpy were headliners then, during the height of the Jazz Age, playing houses like the Cotton Club and the Paramount Theater, places where blacks could dance onstage but couldn't sit in the audience. When television replaced variety shows in the early fifties, my father's career began a slow nosedive.

My mother had met him backstage at the Paramount in 1949, before television changed show business forever. She saw a talented comic at the height of his powers, and he saw what he later remembered as the most beautiful woman he had ever laid eyes on. They began a relationship that lasted five years.

Aunt Peggy liked to say that she had been the landlord of the apartment where I was conceived, as though she were the biblical Sarah and my mother some kind of Hagar, but as I figure the dates, my mother was already three months pregnant when she and Jimmy moved into the one-bedroom basement apartment at 407 North Indiana Avenue, where Peggy, an elementary-school teacher, and Paul, a county clerk, owned a house.

Jimmy had been appearing at Club Harlem, the premier black nightclub in Atlantic City, for the summer season, and Mommie and Peggy became friendly. After my parents moved out, and as their relationship went downhill, Mommie began leaving me with Peggy and Paul. Those visits got longer and longer, they tell me, until the summer before I started school, when she left me there for good.

That year and the four or five that followed were erased from my memory for a long time. When I asked how I came to live in Atlantic City, Aunt Peggy and Mommie stuck to the same story—they said it had been done gradually, so that I would never know what was going on.

But even at four, I knew that something was amiss. I remember the subtle shift of moving from Mommie's world to Aunt Peggy and Uncle Paul's—from what seemed an unfettered childhood, where I felt treated as an adult and was the center of attention, to a house where children obeyed rules and learned responsibilities. In Atlantic City adults no longer included me in their conversation. If they asked what I thought, it was in the tone reserved for babies. Aunt Peggy and Uncle Paul would sometimes drop their voices low when I entered the room, looking at me with studied nonchalance and frozen smiles when I asked what they were talking about.

The hardest thing was adjusting to the food.

Mommie cooked simply—grilled meat and a steamed vegetable was our usual fare, while Aunt Peggy's food was heavier and spicy. One night she had fixed pork chops with string beans for dinner. The meat was overcooked, the flavoring strange, the string beans a pile of mush occupying a quarter of the plate. Mommie had always said I had to taste everything and show manners when I was a guest. I managed to swallow the meat, but refused the string beans.

Uncle Paul, his voice cracked by emphysema, ordered me to eat my string beans in his Billy Goat Gruff tone.

I refused.

He insisted, and I refused insistently. Aunt Peggy tried to intervene, joking that Uncle Paul had been a corporal in the army and sometimes it seemed he had never left. He cut his hazel eyes at her, warning her to stay out of this. Then he looked back at me.

"You're not leaving this table until you eat your vegetables," he declared.

"I won't, and you can't make me!" I shot back.

The battle lines had been drawn. They wouldn't let me leave, but I could make dinner unpleasant for them. I scraped the string beans from one side of the plate to the other with my fork while kicking the table from underneath with my heavy oxford shoes.

Finally I was sent upstairs, to my room above the kitchen. Mommie had never made me eat food I didn't want. She would never have banished me from the supper table. I stomped on the gray linoleum floor, knowing that the noise would interrupt Peggy and Paul's dinner.

I heard murmuring below—Paul wanted to come upstairs, but Peggy was telling him firmly to let me get it out of my system. I would show them. I dragged my desk chair to the top of the stairs and pushed it down. It rattled down the steps with such a ruckus that it startled even me, but when no one came, I picked up the little pink stool from the night table and sent it down, too. Then all my dolls. And then my books.

A nice-size heap was growing at the foot of the stairs when the phone rang. I could tell from the change in Aunt Peggy's voice after she answered that it was my mother. I redoubled my efforts then, screaming and crying as loud as I could.

After a while Aunt Peggy called me to the phone. I pounded down the stairs, grunting and sobbing as I stepped over the pile of furniture on the landing, drooling, my eyes nearly swollen shut from crying. Taking the phone from Peggy, I poured out the whole story to Mommie. I thought surely she would come on the next bus and save me from these mean people and their nasty food.

Instead she just listened and then quietly said, "You must do as Peggy tells you."

I protested, but she repeated herself and told me to go, immediately, and apologize to Paul. Her quiet voice carried more authority than all of his haranguing. I hung up the phone and did as she said.

Then Aunt Peggy made me carry everything back up the stairs.

In Aunt Peggy's house, I spent hours on my rocking horse, Harry.

Harry had been a present from my mother's then boyfriend, an Italian janitor from the Bronx. I had named him after the singer Harry Belafonte, whose 1956 *Calypso* album had just become the first album ever to sell over a million copies. "Day-O" was one of my favorite songs, not least for its refrain, "Daylight come and me wan' go home."

Peggy and Paul had placed Harry opposite the big upholstered chair where Peggy liked to sit while chatting on the phone. I would pat Harry's neck the way I'd seen the Lone Ranger pat his horse, Silver, on TV, and Harry would come alive. When I spurred his hide, his hollow body answered with a sound as big as the echo across a valley. Away we'd ride, Susannah of the Mounties and Harry, traveling through the Western Territories.

I imagined that I was a girlish Barbara Stanwyck, chasing the bad guys through the crags and gullies in the northern Rocky Mountains. Mother had left me to tend the ranch by myself for a couple of days while she helped the army scout Indians down in Georgia.

Peggy and Paul would watch as I rocked back and forth, oblivious to my surroundings. Once Paul looked at Peggy nervously. "Hey, you think she's all right?" he asked. He said "all right" in the tone you use when you're wondering whether someone's cuckoo.

When I was a teenager, Peggy told me this story with a conspiratorial laugh and a twinkle in her eye, as if the answer might still be in doubt. She recalled approaching me on one particular occasion as I rocked away in my own little world.

"June," she called.

No response.

"June," she called again.

Sitting on Harry in the corner of the dining room, I looked out over a ridge at the morning fog. Gradually, a shape appeared. It was oval, the color of autumn leaves. I strained to make it out and vaguely heard my name. Then the room came into focus, and I found myself looking into Peggy's lean, caramel-colored face. She wore a concerned expression.

"Come on," Aunt Peggy said. "It's time for your bath and to get ready for bed."

Bathing together was a daily ritual for Mommie and me: we luxuriated in a tub of bubbles and giggled over the day's events like two girlfriends having tea.

"We don't have any bubble bath," Aunt Peggy said the first time I asked for my bottle of bubble bath.

"Are you going to get in the tub with me?" I asked.

"No, this is your bath."

"But if it's my bath why can't I have bubbles?" I persisted.

"I told you, we don't have any. Besides, you'll spill them all over the floor and make a mess."

"I don't make a mess in New York," I whined.

"Child, get in that water and stop making such a fuss," Peggy responded, exasperated.

The clear water barely reached my waist. Exposed, my chest and shoulders felt cold. Mommie and I filled the tub chest high in New York, but the water pressure in Atlantic City was so low that filling the giant claw-foot tub would have taken forever. Besides, Aunt Peggy worried about the water bill. I submerged a washcloth in the warm water the way Mommie did to cover herself and leaned back, but the ceramic surface of the tub felt cold against my skin, and I jumped back up, splashing water onto Peggy—thus making the mess she had predicted.

I tried to create bubbles using a bar of Ivory Soap. But instead of bubbles, a scummy film appeared in the water.

"Ush! Dirt! I want to get out!"

"That dirt's from you," Peggy said, handing me a worn wash-cloth. "Here, take some soap and scrub that dirty neck."

"If there were bubbles, there wouldn't be any dirt," I muttered.

Peggy sighed and got down on her knees. She took the washcloth, put some soap on it, and started scrubbing my arms and face and the back of my neck. Her hands were larger than Mommie's, her fingers more slender, her nails longer, filed into ovals, ridged and unpolished. Occasionally a nail poked through the threadbare washcloth and caught my skin, each pinch a reminder that this was not New York, that Mommie wasn't here, and that there were no bubbles.

"Ow!" I said, as Peggy's finger dug inside my ears.

"Did I hurt you? I'll be softer," Peggy said.

Mommie wore no rings, but Peggy wore three on her left hand: a diamond wedding band and engagement ring on her third finger and a jade oval on her pinkie. Now she removed the rings and placed them in the metal soap dish that hooked over the side of the tub. I watched them floating in the soapy water as Peggy attacked the dirt on the back of my neck. The shadow there never disappeared. Mommie told Peggy it was a birthmark, but to Peggy it looked more like caked dirt.

By the time she gave up, that washcloth was worn through.

Mommie came to visit often during those first months I lived in Atlantic City. But she had as much trouble as I did accepting some of the customs in Peggy and Paul's house.

One time we gathered at the gray linoleum dinner table to say grace. Mommie sat across from me, Paul and Peggy across from each other. I sat, head bowed, eyes closed, the way they had taught me.

Paul started grace. Maybe because Mommie was there, he did a longer version, the one that called on the Virgin Mary to bless the food we were about to eat by the grace of Our Lord.

I cocked my head and opened my right eye to peek up at Mommie.

Her head was cocked, too, left eye open, peeking down at me. Her expression said, *You and I both know this is a bunch of poppycock.*

In spite of ourselves, we started to giggle. Paul droned on, barely pausing. When he had finished, he stared down into his plate and remained silent.

Struck by how Mommie's presence had altered the dinner-table dynamics, and still snickering, I glanced at him, then at Peggy, who seemed flustered.

"Er, I don't like that," Peggy said, after a pause, referring to our disrespect of the grace ritual.

Mommie and I just giggled some more.

I liked to compare my life in New York with my life in Atlantic City. Sometimes I kept lists.

Peggy was fifty years old. Mommie was thirty-six. I was four and a half.

New York had big skyscrapers made out of cement. Atlantic City had little houses made out of wood. In New York it took two and a half strides to get from one crack to the next on the sidewalk. In Atlantic City I could do it in one stride.

New York had playgrounds with swings and monkey bars where children could go and play. In Atlantic City you played in the dirt.

There were two kinds of dirt in Atlantic City: the dark earth that Peggy's flowers grew in, and the beige sand at the beach. If I dug deep enough in Peggy's flower bed, which I wasn't supposed to do, dark dirt yielded to beige sand, as if the earth itself had tanned.

The sand at the beach was fine, like sugar. In New York the sand in the playground sandbox was coarse, like the batter of Peggy's fried chicken before she dipped it.

In New York you lived in an apartment high above the streets, where you could look out and see the world.

In Atlantic City you lived in a house and could see only down the block, but everyone at the store knew your name.

I had a hard time figuring out all the different Gods. Peggy's was called Episcopalian. She shared him with her best friend, Aunt Hugh. Paul's was Catholic. He shared his with Italians.

Paul's God had a mommie called Virgin Mary. If you wanted something, you prayed to Virgin Mary, he said, and she talked to God.

Paul's priest talked to God, too, but he did it in a language only he, the Italians, and God could understand—or so Aunt Peggy said.

Mommie didn't trust organized religion. Her friend and my godmother, Mikki in New York, had a God who was Christian Scientist. She was trying to make him be Mommie's God. Mikki told me that her God lived all around me, and on the nights I wanted my dreams to take me back home, I prayed to him. I figured that Paul's God's mommie would be too busy listening to everybody else's prayers, while Peggy's God seemed to live far, far away; too far, it seemed, to even hear the prayers of a child.

At bedtime in Atlantic City, I would put on my pajamas and kneel on the oval green shag rug next to the twin bed against the wall. Aunt Peggy would kneel beside me.

First we did the prayer that my godmother Mikki had taught me:

Father-Mother God,
Loving me—

Guard me when I sleep;
Guide my little feet
Up to Thee.

Then we worked on a longer prayer Peggy was teaching me. She called it the Lord's Prayer. Peggy had shown me a picture of her Lord God in the Bible. He had white hair and a long beard, this God, who had his name hollowed out in a log somewhere, and you had to beg his forgiveness for stepping on it.

Peggy said all these Gods were the same, and I shouldn't try so hard to distinguish them from one another. Sometimes, when I recited my lists of comparisons for her, she would pucker her brows and lips simultaneously, and tell me that I should accept things as they were and stop noticing differences.

So after a while I just kept the lists in my head.

2. FORMATIONS

Peggy drove a 1954 black Cadillac Coupe de Ville, which she had bought used. It was solid, sturdy, and strong, with massive tail fins and a front hood that stretched so far I couldn't see the end of it from the passenger seat. Peggy kept the car parked where she could keep an eye on it, directly across from the picture window in the living room.

Paul didn't like Peggy's Caddy. He called it pretentious and complained that it drove like a truck. He drove a used silver Chevy Impala with powder blue leather seats. Its surface was scarred with fine round grooves from repeated hand waxing. He practically lived in it. He drove an hour each way to his job in Cape May and then, after work, turned the Chevy into a cab for an additional five hours. When he was home, the Impala sat parked in the backyard. Paul liked Chevys because Dinah Shore advertised them on TV. Her show had a commercial that pictured her driving through the Rockies, singing, "See the U.S.A. in your Chevrolet!"

Peggy said if she had to take that long a trip, she'd rather do it in her Caddy. The Cadillac was a classy car. She didn't think either Dinah Shore or the Chevrolets had class. They were common.

Peggy sought class with the eye of a museum curator, and she did her best to imprint me. She kept a canon of those who had class and those who didn't: Jacqueline Kennedy defined class. My mother, Norma, had class, even though she hadn't been as well bred as Mrs. Kennedy. She had learned to dress distinctively and with style.

On the other hand, Sammy Davis Jr., with his greased-down processed hair, gaudy rings, and showy suits, had no class. Peggy said he acted like he had just come into money and didn't know what to do with it. Well-bred people, people like Aunt Hugh, her friend Mrs. Hugh Gregory, turned their noses up at those who acted like that.

My earliest memories of Atlantic City are of the rides Aunt Peggy and I took in her classy black Cadillac Coupe de Ville. I would lie across the passenger seat, my feet toward the door, my head touching her thigh, while Aunt Peggy told me about her life.

She had nicknamed herself Peggy, after a character in Louisa May Alcott's *Little Women*, because she hated her real name, Muriel Agatha. Muriel Agatha Fortune, raised in Flushing, Queens, had been born of gentle means. Her father, Walter, whom she adored, delivered bottled milk in a horse-drawn carriage to the well-to-do residents of Long Island. Her mother had died in childbirth when Peggy was only seven. The baby, a boy, had not survived either, and after their deaths, she said, her father had never treated her the same. He had sent her away to be raised, first by her aunts and then to a boarding school outside Baltimore.

She barely remembered her mother, she said sadly, and her tone made me feel sad, too.

She had wanted to be a model, but "good girls" didn't become models in her day, she said; modeling was associated with loose women. And then there was her deviated eye. She would have liked an operation to fix it, but she was afraid. She had learned photography and wanted to practice photojournalism, but women were discouraged from newspaper work, and in any case the nearest paper that would hire her was in Pittsburgh. She didn't want to move there because she didn't want to leave Paul.

Peggy's own childlessness nestled in her heart like a thorn. Although she wore a cloak of gaiety and spouted funny folk aphorisms, she nurtured her misfortunes. As she got older, she fretted that others made fun of her behind her back. I used to mock her fears, until I found out much later that she had indeed been perceived as an odd duck. As a young teacher in Atlantic City during the 1930s, she had not driven the bodacious Cadillac, but instead pedaled a bicycle to and from school, so that when people spoke of her, they referred to her as "Peggy-Bush-who-rides-the-bike."

She would have found such an appellation demeaning.

The black Cadillac Coupe de Ville left no room for demeaning appellations.

Surrounded on three sides by the ocean, Atlantic City is bounded on the west by lush salt marshes filled with cat-o'-nine-tails, driftwood, rotting boat hulls, and reeds. The bridge that connects the southern part of the island to the mainland constitutes part of the Black Horse Pike, which in those days led to the wealthier parts of town.

A different bridge on the northern side, part of the White Horse Pike, led to the black community, which everyone called the Northside, or the "colored section."

The colored section was really four different neighborhoods: the west side, where the professionals and business owners lived; the inlet, a poorer section to the north; Bungalow Park, another middle-class enclave nestled about the inlet; and Venice Park, which was just then being integrated.

Peggy liked Atlantic City's centrality, its proximity to the major cities in the Northeast. She liked to go to Philly to shop at John Wanamaker's department store, or visit Abraham & Straus in New York; she liked being able to drive to see her husband's family in Washington, D.C., without being so close that they could interfere in her business.

Peggy had been teaching second grade for over twenty years; she had taught parents, siblings, children, cousins, and grandchildren, and she knew more about the private lives of most of Atlantic City's families than the census taker did. She had moved to Atlantic City in 1932, in its heyday, and she delighted in telling me stories about the rich and famous who indulged their peccadilloes and hid their scandals at the seaside resort, including mobsters from Chicago, Philadelphia, and New York who had declared the city neutral territory. William Randolph Hearst built his mistress a mansion off the Black Horse Pike. The remains of the house, a massive terra-cotta ruin, sat amid the overgrown marshland.

At the inlet, where the island ended in a cul-de-sac, we liked to get out of the car. You could walk on the beach from the east side of Atlantic City to the west side in two dozen steps at the inlet. Yards away began the boardwalk, raised four feet above the sand and squared off by an iron banister. Across the street sat a series of two-story wooden row houses, their porches elevated by four wooden steps. This was the end of the island's main street, Atlantic Avenue.

"This is where the Puerto Ricans live," Peggy said.

I giggled at the way she pronounced it: "Porta Rikins" instead of "Puerto Ricans."

Outside the wooden houses, children were playing a street game. Their play made me homesick. I missed my old, run-down neighborhood off Columbus Avenue in New York. Before Lincoln Center was built, the neighborhood had been a seedy section of Manhattan, crowded with working-class families whose children spilled into the streets and onto the basketball courts after school. It was a collection of storefronts with small-business owners who all knew me and Mommie by name. I missed the toy store, crowded to the ceiling with toys Mommie always said we couldn't afford, the liquor store where she went to cash checks, and the dry cleaners who always seemed to lose her clothes. I missed the smell of rotisserie chickens turning in the window, and the *kerthunk* sound that taxicab tires made riding over potholes. I missed the strident voices of the Dominican boys soaring into the night against the rhythm of sirens and the sound of cars traveling down Columbus Avenue.

These Puerto Rican children playing in Atlantic City's inlet seemed less cocky, their language less percussive, their accent more melodious. I ached to play with them.

"Oh, there are plenty of other children for you to play with," Peggy said dismissively.

Atlantic City, like every place else in America, was segregated, not just by race but by ethnicity and, of course, class. Its streets, to anyone who knew them intimately, were signposts to income, culture, and tradition. They marked boundaries not easily crossed.

To the south of the inlet, roughly in the middle of the city, Missouri Avenue divided the white and black neighborhoods. Atlantic Avenue divided the business district—whites to the east (in the hotel district), blacks to the west. Wedged into a narrow strip of Arctic Avenue between Missouri and Mississippi were the Italians. Most Jewish families lived in Margate.

We who lived in Atlantic City used shorthand to describe these fault lines. The Puerto Ricans lived "over" in the inlet. In the opposite direction, "down there" in Ventnor, lived plain old working-class white folks. Most of them were Protestants, but a few Italian Catholics who had worked their way out of the ghetto lived there, too. The rich white folks, most of whom worked in Philadelphia and who came to AC—that's how we who lived there referred to Atlantic City—during the summer season, had summerhouses in communities beyond Ventnor, "up" in Longport, the southernmost tip of the island.

I started taking dance classes at the Jewish Community Center in Margate before I even started school. After class, Peggy liked driving through the white parts of town. She would turn off the main avenue and tour the side streets of Margate and Longport, examining the homes.

She described a dream of a different life in each house. Her own home was a perfectly respectable three-story Folk Victorian, set back from the street twenty yards or so, with a cement walkway and a large lawn. The shingles were painted dark gray, with white stationary shutters. Peggy and Paul rented out the bottom-floor apartment; you reached the upper living quarters via an exterior stairway, set parallel to the street, its fifteen wooden stairs painted gray and decorated in front by a trellis with climbing red roses.

One particular day, when I had gotten used to staying with Peggy and Paul but didn't yet know the city, we passed a gray-and-white house, the same color as the one Peggy and Paul owned, but a true

Victorian, much larger, with a wraparound front porch. A man with sparse white hair combed straight back sat out in a rocking chair. He wore skinny glasses on his nose as he rocked back and forth reading the paper.

Peggy had wanted to be a newspaper photographer, she reminded me as we passed him, but that was a hard profession for a woman.

I looked over at her. Peggy's life seemed, somehow, more limited, more circumscribed, than my mother's. I didn't understand why, but Mommie seemed more adventurous, while Peggy struggled to accustom herself to set boundaries.

We cruised slowly past the fenced-in yards of Longport in the black Coupe de Ville, until we saw a blue-and-red colonial that dwarfed its neighbors.

"Now, that one's *too* big," Peggy said, turning her up nose. "Who would want to rattle around in a big old house like that?"

Another one, she sniffed, looked like the White House, with stately pillars supporting a second-floor deck. Too ostentatious.

Then she pulled to a stop in front of a Tudor-style brick house with a neatly trimmed front lawn, its front door flanked by blue hydrangeas.

"I always like to stop in front of this house," she said with a wistful tone. "I'd love to live in this neighborhood, but they don't allow colored."

I didn't know whether she meant the house or the hydrangeas.

"They don't allow colored what?" I asked.

Peggy inhaled sharply and bit the side of her lip. "Well, that's a way of saying that it's segregated," she explained, exhaling. "Most colored don't make enough money to afford these homes, but even if we did, the neighbors would object. They're afraid we'll make the neighborhood turn."

I thought of a carton of milk sitting in the refrigerator too long, or the scent of old garbage. I tried to imagine the Tudor house with the blue hydrangeas smelling like sour milk.

"Would it stink?" I asked.

She looked at me strangely. "Well, there are some colored like that, that don't know how to keep up their place. And that's the way some whites think all colored are. But there's many colored keep their homes as nice and neat as this one," she said, pointing to the Tudor.

I tried to imagine a box of people the color of Crayola crayons moving in and how pretty soon the neighborhood might turn dark green and brown and begin to smell like old garbage. I wondered how long it would take. A week? A month? A couple of days? And what colors didn't they allow? But before I could ask any more questions, Peggy pulled in to the parking lot of the Dairy Queen, and I was distracted by having to choose between a strawberry and a hot fudge sundae.

The crown jewel of Atlantic City's west side, where the black neighborhood blended into the entrance to the White Horse Pike, belonged to Ralph and Edith Greene. Ralph and Edith both taught at the local colored elementary school, but to look at their house you wouldn't have known teachers lived there. Their home was a palace even by white standards, a newly built, geometrically styled house made of cedar planks, with a huge picture window in front and an A-frame doorway with, appropriately enough, a green door.

Peggy admired the Greenes' "chutzpah," as she called it, in placing so grand a house like a piece of sculpture at the entrance to the Northside. Although the house was too modern for her taste, she liked the statement it made: that colored could buy anything and be just as grand as white people. It was widely believed that Ralph Greene's position as the colored "go-to" person for political patronage had enabled him to buy that house.

A block up the street, in a modest white house with gray shutters and a cement foundation, lived the Weeks family. The mother had worked hard to raise them all, Aunt Peggy said, her voice a mixture of pity and admiration. Peggy had taught several of the six Weeks brothers; three of them now owned a cab company, which they had built from scratch. Down the street from the Weekses lived one of our neighborhood doctors, but Peggy wouldn't go to him because he was too young. Across from him lived the owner of a popular bar and lounge—I would meet his daughter at summer camp.

Forewarned not to repeat what she had told me during our rides in the car, I met Mr. and Mrs. Greene, and Mrs. Weeks, and Dr. Wilson. I also met Mrs. Gambrel—who owned the corner store that sold sundries, candy, and fresh-dipped Breyer's ice cream—and the Italians who owned the grocery store on the corner diagonally across from her. I remember walking with Peggy down the street, my small hand grasped firmly by her long, thin fingers, the tips of her high-heel crocodile shoes, in chronic disrepair, clicking along the sidewalk like taps, arrhythmically scraping the knobby raised ridges of the sidewalk.

On the third corner of the block where we lived sat a house with caramel-colored asphalt shingles. A cement walkway led up to the four short steps to the front door.

"This is Mrs. McKee's house," Aunt Peggy said. "You've been here before, when you were just a baby. You played with Minnie's granddaughter, Regina."

I didn't remember the house or Regina, but then, Peggy said, we had met when I was just three weeks old. Our mommies had been pregnant at the same time.

"Look at that hair!" Mrs. McKee said by way of greeting in her sharp-edge voice. "I guess you'll need some dresses, or nobody will know what you are."

"I'm a girl," I said, annoyed.

Mrs. McKee reached out and ran her fingers roughly through my short, thick curls.

"I guess your mother didn't know what to do with this!" she exclaimed. Then she hooked her bottom lip over her lower teeth, clamped her upper lip against them, and tittered.

She picked me up and stood me on newspapers spread on the dining room table, as though I were a life-size doll. Mrs. McKee sewed clothes for a living. She could copy a dress from *Vogue* just by looking at a picture. Peggy wanted her to make me some new dresses for school.

"Do you know what you want?" Mrs. McKee said to Peggy over

my head, her mouth full of pins. I pouted. Mommie always asked *me* what I wanted.

"Oh, I was thinking something nice and girlish, an organdy maybe, with a little collar and buttons down the front," Peggy said dreamily, looking out the window by Mrs. McKee's staircase.

"Organdy doesn't wear very well. You want her to wear these to school, don't you?" Mrs. McKee said through the pins. She measured me from waist to hip, then turned me around to measure my arms and the distance across the top of my back.

"Well," Peggy said, reconsidering, "maybe a dark organdy will do—or something. Something soft and feminine." She fluttered her right hand for emphasis on the words.

I winced. Soft and feminine meant that I wouldn't be able to do anything except sit still with my ankles crossed and my hands folded in my lap.

"Can't I have a cotton dress?" I asked. Mommie dressed me in cotton because it wore well and she could wash my clothes by hand in the sink.

Mrs. McKee tittered again, this time at Peggy. "I can see you're gonna have a handful trying to control her," she said.

Impatient to get down and play with Regina, I stamped my foot.

"Just hold on a minute. I'm almost through. The dress won't fit if I don't measure you for it," Mrs. McKee said.

I was freed, finally, from the table, and the grown-ups disappeared into the kitchen, leaving Regina and me alone to play.

Regina was a shade lighter than I and thin as a wishbone. Her socks barely stayed up around her ankles. She wore her hair in thick, shoulder-length braids.

"What happened to your hair?" Regina asked.

"Nothing happened to it. My mommie cuts it short." I wished I had longer hair just so I wouldn't have to keep answering this question.

"Where's your mommie?" Regina asked.

"She lives in New York," I answered. "I visit her on vacations.

Where's yours?" Yvette, Regina's mother and Mrs. McKee's daughter, was Aunt Peggy's goddaughter.

"She's at teachers' college, in Glassboro," Regina said, her pride equally strong. "She comes home on weekends."

Thus establishing our mommies' bona fides, we bonded for life.

One day, while I was still trying to make sense out of all my new surroundings, we visited Aunt Peggy's closest friend, Hugh Ella Gregory.

"Hello, Mrs. Gregory," I said, as Peggy had taught me to greet adults.

"You don't have to be so formal," Mrs. Gregory replied in her flute-toned voice. "Now that you're going to be staying here, you can call me Aunt Hugh."

I didn't catch her meaning, but Peggy picked it up right away. "That's not decided yet," she said quickly.

"It's not?" Hugh said, looking up over my head.

Peggy glanced down at me and shook her head slightly, indicating that she did not want to have this conversation in front of "c-h-i-l-d-r-e-n."

Aunt Hugh Gregory offered me some crayons and paper and pointed me toward the living room.

"What do you say?" Peggy prompted.

But I was preoccupied with the earlier exchange. There was something they didn't want me to know. Staying here? At Mrs. Gregory's? For how long? Adults shared a world high above me, filled with signs and secret codes; I had learned that listening, particularly when Peggy was involved, provided more answers than asking direct questions did.

Ensconced with cookies, milk, crayons, and paper in the living room, I took care to sit near the piano next to the open door, where I could hear their conversation. I loved listening to Aunt Hugh's voice. Her soft, lilting tones reminded me of Japanese music and those sweet-smelling flowers Peggy called honeysuckle.

I had recently mastered connecting the four lines that represented the rectangle of a house, and the three that formed the triangle of its roof. I selected brown and red crayons to draw them, gray to make parallel lines for the walkway, and pink for the petunias along the side. I was drawing Peggy's house. I moved the crayons across the page like a whisper, straining to hear the conversation in the kitchen. But Aunt Hugh's voice was so soft that I could make out only a few words.

wishful   adoption   courting   heartbreak
It sounded like a fairy tale.

"Oh, Hugh, I don't think so," Aunt Peggy said, her voice as clear as the yellow circle I drew to represent the sun.

I lifted the crayon from the page and held my breath.

"She'd be better off here," Aunt Hugh said, "but suppose the mother changes her mind and wants her back?"

"I don't think that's going to happen," Peggy said.

I picked up my gray crayon and drew a rectangle standing on its end, the way I drew Mommie's New York house. It wasn't as pretty as Aunt Peggy's—just a shoebox with squares for windows.

"But what if it does, Peggy? You're basing your future on wishful thinking. I think you should insist on a clean break and do a formal adoption."

Between the two houses, bigger than either of them, I drew a figure with orange legs and arms, brown eyes, and then, with my black crayon, I drew a mop of curly black hair.

In my small pink room in Atlantic City, huddled under the big blue blanket Mommie had sent with me from New York, I shivered with fever. The air felt cold on my cheek.

In delirium, I imagined I was a fairy soldier riding a butterfly, sallying forth to fight a horde of enemy fairies riding beetles. The Queen of fairies came to cheer us on. Aside from my mother, the fairy queen was the most beautiful woman I had ever seen.

She floated before me, mounted on a dragonfly steed, her thick, dark, wavy hair pulled back and wrapped in a bun. She had a deep olive complexion, and large, brown almond-shaped eyes, eyes deeper and more compassionate than my mother's. I could not help but stare at her; gradually, I realized that she was no fairy queen, but real, sitting on a chair at the foot of my bed, and that she was spinning out this tale which formed the warp and woof of my dream: how the fairy soldiers attacked the beetles, vanquished them, and saved the beautiful rose people from extinction.

I asked Aunt Peggy who she was.

"You weren't dreaming," she said. "That was Yvonne. She heard you were sick and came to visit you."

"Yvonne?"

"Aunt Hugh's oldest daughter."

I was amazed that someone I didn't even know would visit me and tell me such a wonderful story. Yvonne.

I held her name like a precious jewel. When I started to read, fairy-tale books crowded the shelf by my bed.

The first letters I have from my mother came in envelopes from the Holiday Inn, Augusta, Georgia, near Fort Benning. They are dated 1957, a year or two before I moved to Atlantic City. Mommie told Peggy that she had gotten work in an army film. It was the first time she remembers leaving me with Peggy and Paul.

Stationed in her room at the Holiday Inn, my mother wrote two letters a day, one to me and one to Peggy.

> Dear Peggy,
> Work is progressing at snail's pace. RAIN RAIN RAIN. We drove to Daytona, Florida, to get sun one day—and it was hurricane weather there!!
> Ike [Eisenhower] is here, Mamie, too—and they're both miserable, I understand. Even his presidential powers can't change the atmosphere.
> I have missed June terribly. Knowing she would be with me if I weren't here working has killed some of the joy of this assignment. Well, I should tell the Army to wait. . . .

In the same envelope, she enclosed a letter for me.

> *Dearest Girl,*
> *I've been thinking of you every few hours this week, won-*
> *dering what you're doing and how you are spending your*
> *vacation. Are you having a good time?*
> *The weather here is just terrible—raining every day*
> *and fog, fog, fog. I have reservations on a JET home to-*
> *morrow. I wish you were with me on the flight! Wouldn't*
> *that be fun?*
>
> *xoxoxoxoxo The Lonesome Mommie*

Thirty years later, rereading these letters, I called my mother and read them to her over the phone. She reacted with a silence that warned me there was more to this story.

"There was no modeling assignment," she began, in the flat, nasal tone signaling she had a truth that was hard to tell. "That's what I told Peggy so she wouldn't think ill of me. I had gone to Fort Benning to visit an army colonel I was dating. But he wouldn't accept you. He told me he wouldn't help raise a 'nigger child.' That's what he called you. 'A nigger child.' "

It was my turn to be silent.

A nigger child.

Not Tahitian June. Not exotic. Not Susannah of the Mounties.

I didn't know I was a nigger child, and my mother didn't know how to tell me. So she gave me to Peggy.

Nearly fifty years later, as I excavate these memories, I find the outlines of a scar. I trace its shape, considering the ways in which it restricts my life. Trust eludes me. I never knew how to maintain friendships. I waited until middle age to marry. I never had children.

I bless that scar and call the pain from its hiding place.

3. PASSAGES

Two bus lines made the trip between New York and Atlantic City. Public Service buses carried blue-and-white insignia. Lincoln's were red and yellow. Public Service made the express trip on the hour; Lincoln on the half hour.

Peggy preferred Public Service because they hired more black drivers than Lincoln. I liked Public Service because their buses had plusher seats.

During my first couple of years in school, an adult traveled back and forth with me. Sometimes Mommie came down to get me, sometimes Aunt Peggy took me up, or sometimes a family friend went along. By the time I was in second or third grade, though, Aunt Peggy and Mommie had coordinated a system to allow me to travel by myself. My biweekly departures took on the trappings of ritual. "How-d'y-do," Aunt Peggy would say cheerily to the driver, whether he was black or white and whether she knew him or not, as she boarded behind me. She led me to the seat directly behind the driver and, if he was black, asked his name. Usually she had taught either the driver or someone in his family.

"This is my niece," she'd say in her schoolteacher's voice, whether the driver was black or white. If he was black, she added, "She's traveling to New York, and there will be a woman up there to meet her—a woman of the other persuasion."

If it was a white bus driver, she made eye contact and told him that someone would be meeting this little girl in New York. Then, sitting down next to me, she reminded me that if Mommie wasn't there on time, I was to stay near the driver, but under no circumstances was I to go off anywhere with him.

Once the bus had crossed the White Horse Pike bridge and made its way to the Garden State Parkway, I measured the distance by counting the tolls: the first came forty minutes after we left the bus station, at Toms River; the second, a half hour later, at Barnegat Lighthouse, the midpoint; then six more, about twenty minutes apart, until we finally reached the New Jersey Turnpike and climbed the graffiti-covered granite hill that led down to the mouth of the Lincoln Tunnel, portal to Manhattan, and Mommie.

Sometimes I saw her before she saw me, standing behind the thick glass window that separated the bus tunnel from the passengers at Gate 453, craning her neck as I craned mine, her eyes wide with anticipation, her eyebrows arched as she scanned the rows. Spotting each other, we waved frantically, mouthing a dialogue, me through the window of the bus and she through the glass of the waiting room, silent-movie stars accompanied by the sounds of bus engines, the announcer's voice on the loudspeaker, the conversations of fellow travelers.

"Hel-low-ow" she would shape her mouth to say on her side.

"Hi! Hi!" I would say aloud, jumping up and down, forgetting that she couldn't hear me.

After the bus pulled in, the bus driver would take down my small gray suitcase, covered with decals from places my mother had visited and which I struggled to find on maps: Cincinnati. Memphis. Fort Lauderdale. Hollywood.

I would jump down off the bus and into her arms, wrapping my legs around her.

The bus driver would hand the worn gray suitcase to Mommie, and, with a tip of his cap, our weekend would begin.

My trips to visit Mommie felt like vacation. Atlantic City's black community sheltered its children and valued them, but it exacted responsibility. The adults in the community felt free to discipline me, and I was expected to respect them all, calling them "Mr. or Mrs. So-and-So, or Aunt or Uncle Whoever." I was to speak when spoken to, sit quietly through church services—and eat my vegetables. I was expected to wear dresses and comport myself like a little girl. Sometimes my classmates laughed at my clothes or the Broadway show tunes that I liked—or my short hair.

During my visits with Mommie, we saw movies, played in the park, bought rotisserie chicken and ate it with our hands. We read the letters my older brother, Lary, now in the army's 101st Airborne Division, wrote from Panama. Lary wasn't Jimmy's son—he was born when my mother was just eighteen, long before she came to New York. Still, for five years, my father had been his dad, the only father he had ever known. After I was born, Lary had been my primary caretaker. Even though he was fourteen years older than I, we were very close.

For a long time, Mommie had been afraid that Lary would come to no good. When he was a teenager, their conversations had consisted mostly of yelling on her part and sullen, monosyllabic responses on his. He had spent most of his high-school years on the basketball court, hanging out with his Dominican friends and practicing salsa dancing. He got so good that he won several championships, but he nearly flunked out of high school. Lary had enlisted in the army just before I moved to Atlantic City. Now, Mom said how proud she was that he showed signs of making a man out of himself.

The apartment felt empty without him and his Dominican buddies.

On one particular visit—it must have been the spring when I turned five—my mother suggested that we visit the Museum of Modern Art. "We'll see the originals of what's hanging on our walls," she told me excitedly.

Mommie dressed me in a burgundy corduroy flower-print jumper. She unpacked my white shoes with the daisy-shaped cutouts in the toe and brought out the white polish from where she kept it high in the broom closet. Carefully, she painted over the scuffs on my shoes as I watched intently, inhaling the pungent smell of the polish.

If Mommie was polishing my shoes, that meant the museum visit was really special.

We walked up Sixty-seventh Street to the park. The grass seemed the color of the spring green crayon in my Crayola box. It took fewer paces now to cross the pavement sections of my New York City block. I noted the smooth grain of the Sixty-seventh Street concrete, which was the same color as the silky sand on the beach in Atlantic City. The slope of the black iron grates protecting the trees hit the middle of my shins. So did the short concrete border that lined the walkway of Peggy's yard.

The museum seemed to take up an entire city block. Its windows were even larger than those of the Greenes' house in Atlantic City. Sunlight poured into the white-marble lobby.

Mommie showed me the picture called *Sleeping Gypsy*—her favorite—and then we found Gauguin's *Orana Maria*. I felt slightly disappointed. They looked the same as they did on our living room wall. Mommie wouldn't let me close enough to touch them. Instead she suggested we get a tuna sandwich in the garden.

The garden had a fountain and a series of Giacometti statues that stood about my height. They reminded me of the clay figures we had made in nursery school, except these were fired in bronze. For a while I played a game of hide-and-seek with them.

My mother called me, and when I turned, I saw her sitting at a table with a man the color of the statues. He wore a porkpie hat and a colorfully printed, short-sleeved shirt.

"June, I want you to meet Jimmy," Mommie said in her serious voice. "Jimmy is your father."

Some twenty years later, I would wander into a Harlem club called Showman's and idly mention to an older man at the bar that I was Stump Cross's daughter. That man turned out to be Buster Brown, a well-known tap dancer from Baltimore, and he had been a friend of Jimmy's. Buster recalled how that when I was a toddler, my father and I had been practically inseparable. My mother worked nights as a hatcheck girl at a Fifty-second Street club, and, since my father was rarely working, he looked after me. He had taught me the refrains to a couple of Lena Horne and Judy Garland songs. Buster said I would perform, karaoke-style, on the bar while the jukebox played.

I had no memory of any of it.

So when I met my father that afternoon, at the age of five, in the sculpture garden at the Museum of Modern Art, he was, to me, another stranger with a new appellation attached.

"My, how big you've grown!" he said, taking my hand in his. His sad eyes made his broad smile seem out of place.

"Nice to meet you," I said, as Peggy had taught me to greet adults.

"*Meet* you!?" he exclaimed. "I've known you since you were a little bitty baby!" With that, he laughed more genuinely. Years later Jimmy's friends would tell me that "he wasn't meant to be no kind of father"—that he had been born to go onstage. At that moment, though, in the garden at MoMA, Jimmy seemed born to laugh. The pieces of his face fell into place around a set of big, wide teeth. His laugh was so infectious that I laughed, too.

"Can you snap your fingers?" he asked, snapping his fingers together several times. "Can you? Huh?"

I rubbed my index finger and thumb together.

Jimmy took my hand and placed the third finger and the thumb together.

"Now, don't just rub them," he said. "Push them together so hard that they fall off each other."

I did. For a while it sounded like I was stamping my bare foot against a tile floor. Then I tried it again with my ring finger and heard a little *snap* like a raw string bean breaking.

"There you go!" Jimmy said, as we both laughed with delight. "I never saw anybody snap with their fourth finger, but however it works."

I snapped merrily away with both hands, until Mommie interrupted with a tone as sharp as the snapping sound: "That's enough, now, June."

An awkward silence followed, and I slid away from the table to play with my imaginary friends in Giacometti's garden. From time to time, I looked back at my mother and father talking. I remember wishing this man would leave so Mommie and I could continue our weekend.

I would not see my father again for four years.

By the time we left the museum, I had less than one day to spend with Mommie.

"Will you stop being so glum!" she finally exploded, in the voice she used to tell me Not to Touch, Don't Break, and Stop Doing Things I Wasn't Supposed to Be Doing. "No one likes to be around someone who is whiny and crying all the time. Let's just pretend you're not leaving, and enjoy our time together."

And so we did. We went to Riverside Park. We had grilled cheese sandwiches with vanilla milk shakes at Schrafft's. We went to see a Disney movie.

Time flew by so fast that she had to remind me only an hour was left until the bus departed from Port Authority. I swallowed, and put my little hand in her small one. I compared my clear fingernails to her pink ones to make sure they were still the same shape. At the bus I gave her a big hug, and she gave me the note and the check she always gave me to give to Peggy.

"Bye, Mommie," I said over the roar of the bus engine.

"Bye-bye, sweetheart," she said, her smile pasted on over watery eyes. "You be a good girl and obey Peggy and Paul."

I boarded the bus and sat on the side where I could see her through the window, and we stared at each other, waving, until the bus backed out of sight. As it rolled down Port Authority's coiled spiral and into the Lincoln Tunnel, I sang a song to cheer myself up.

Catch a falling star and
Put it in your pocket,
Save it for a rainy day.

I waited until the bus cleared the Lincoln Tunnel and passed the granite rocks marked with graffiti, and then, only then, did I allow a tear to leak from each of my eyes.

Many years later, after Aunt Peggy died, I found the note she sent back that weekend.

> *Dear Peggy-*
> *Will write a long letter this weekend. June seems so flighty, so like Regina in a way (nervous), not at all her calm self.*
> *We met Jimmy yesterday at the Museum of Modern Art—had lunch together. June seemed unimpressed. I hope I did the right thing by allowing her to meet him. I think once a year is o.k.—Do you?*
> *Otherwise, everything is fine. The extra $25.00 is for the coat—which I adore. I'm going to send out pajamas this week—these are all in bad shape.*
>
> *In a rush—Bye bye—*
> *Norma*

My first day of school was one of the defining moments of my young life. It was September 1959. Alaska and Hawaii had been granted statehood, and I was excited to be entering kindergarten. I wanted to learn how to find all the states on a map, so that I could always know where Mommie was.

I would attend the same school where Peggy herself taught second grade: Indiana Avenue Elementary, one of the two black elementary schools in Atlantic City. The Supreme Court had decreed five years earlier that school systems should begin desegregating "with all deliberate speed." In Atlantic City that had led to a decision to integrate the high school's teaching staff first, then the high school's student body. They would eventually integrate the city's one junior high, but the elementary schools would remain segregated by dint of housing patterns too ingrained for even the Supreme Court to change.

That first day, we arrived an hour early. Peggy took me from classroom to classroom, introducing me to her colleagues. They sported sensible shoes, shin-length dresses, dignified bearings, and neatly pressed hair. Nearly all of them would remember that Peggy introduced me as "my daughter, June," but I clearly remember her saying, "my niece, June, who is coming to stay with me." They must have assumed I was adopted, since everyone knew that Peggy didn't have any biological children; regardless, for the rest of my years in Atlantic City, I was "Mrs. Bush's daughter." At Indiana Avenue School, Peggy was called Mrs. Bush.

We ended our tour at the door of my kindergarten teacher, Edith Dempsey. Peggy had devoted considerable effort to getting me enrolled in this class. She worried about my lack of discipline and thought I needed structure. Edith Dempsey would provide that.

Mrs. Dempsey was the last of a breed: a woman who considered it her duty to socialize as well as educate children. If it takes a village to raise a child, Mrs. Dempsey was the village caretaker. She was a physically structured woman, the large contours of her bust and hips balanced by a small waist and the red bun on the back of her head, her skin the pale color of a watermelon rind.

"Edith, this is June," Mrs. Bush said simply, as if Mrs. Dempsey already knew all about me, which of course she did. She lived a block away from us, across from Gambrel's store.

Then, to me, Peggy said, "June, this is Mrs. Dempsey."

I didn't understand why Peggy called my teacher Edith but I had to call her Mrs. Dempsey. In New York I called all my mother's friends by their first names.

Regina's was the only familiar face I saw among my twenty-two classmates. We tried to sit next to each other.

"Oh, no," Mrs. Dempsey said. "I've been warned about you two." She moved us to opposite ends of the back row.

After being placed in the seats we would occupy all year, each of us stood, introduced ourselves, and stated one thing we knew about any one of the fifty states. If we shimmied or put our fingers in our mouths, we had to start over.

I had learned that lesson by the time my turn came. I stood up tall and declared that although I lived in Atlantic City, I was really from

New York City, the biggest city in the world, in the state of New York, and that I lived with Peggy and Paul and their dog, Sarge.

"You live with *whom*?" Mrs. Dempsey's voice was sharp as a tack.

"With Peggy and Paul?" I said uncertainly.

"Speak in full sentences!" she commanded. "And she's not 'Peggy'! She's 'Aunt Peggy'!"

Her tone of voice made me want to shrink and crawl down my own throat. I sought the safety of my seat, but I wasn't safe, even there.

"DO YOU HEAR ME?!" she demanded. "I SAID, 'SHE'S YOUR AUNT PEGGY!' "

I choked out a thin "Yes."

"YES WHAT?"

"Yes, Mrs. Dempsey." I said it so softly that I scarcely heard myself.

Until that day I thought the differences in the rules between Aunt Peggy and my mother were just that, differences between the two women who were raising me. But that day I realized that I had entered another world. In New York I had been given free rein; in Atlantic City I would be reined in.

Looking back, it's easy to mark the steady progression of what we now call the civil-rights movement. But in 1962, when the headlines described one stalled NAACP court case after another, and as sit-ins, freedom rides, and arrested demonstrators took up more and more time on NBC's *Huntley-Brinkley Report*, every aspect of that movement was up for discussion and debate. Martin Luther King had not yet emerged as the icon he is today. Although he had won in Montgomery, Alabama, and formed a group of progressive ministers willing to challenge racism, he had left Albany, Georgia, before winning desegregation there, and this retreat was viewed as a defeat. At the dinner table, and with friends in our living room, Aunt Peggy and Uncle Paul debated whether King was up to the job of organizing so important a movement. He was so young and untested, Aunt Peggy said. He could talk, but could he convince the right people? Uncle Paul wondered. So many of the old-line ministers in the South seemed unwilling to challenge the status quo. Did the battle for Negro rights belong in the courts or on the streets? Aunt Peggy, who tended toward accommodation, thought that the Student Non-Violent Coordinating Committee, demonstrating in the streets to confront racism, would do more harm than good to the cause. She called them "a bunch of young hotheads."

Uncle Paul had done his army basic training in Texas and served in New Orleans. He said he knew something about the intransigence of those "southern rednecks" as he called them, and he cheered the demonstrators on.

I didn't understand most of these conversations, and most of all I couldn't understand what was meant by the terms "colored" and "rednecks" and "Negro." If the rednecks' necks were red, what color was the rest of them? And why weren't *they* colored if their necks were red? Whoever they were, they were part of "them," but then who was "us"? Aunt Peggy tried to explain it by saying that some people in the South weren't allowed to use the same bathrooms or sit in the fronts of buses, but when I asked why, she just said, "Well, because some people think they're better than other people." She avoided explaining why. When I pressed, she would lighten her voice and say, "Oh, this is adult talk and not for little ears. Go and play." So I would climb the stairs and listen through the gap that extended from the stairwell to the pantry, trying to grasp their meaning through their tone, how they raised their voices, the timbre of their laughs. I heard admiration, anger, and excitement. Trying to sort it all out made me tired. Late at night sometimes I would hear Aunt Peggy talking to Mommie, but even then she was circumspect. "I don't think it's wise for her to think about these things," I overheard her say one time. "It might result in confusion, and with all the other adjustments, I worry it might be too much."

Peggy's Papa lived with us. She said he had worked as a milkman, but that must have been a long, long time before. His skin color reminded me of evaporated milk. In the morning, the stiff gray stubble of his beard stuck my face when he bent to kiss me.

Papa's hazel eyes often looked vacant, as though he were somewhere else, and he smelled musty, like a shirt that's been in the drawer too long. His skin, even lighter than my mother's, had moles and dark spots all over it. He wheezed when he talked, and his breath smelled. At night Aunt Peggy took his teeth out and put them in a glass of water to soak.

Mommie thought Aunt Peggy was awfully brave to bring her father into the house with Paul. Mommie said it might mess up her marriage. But Aunt Peggy said she was going to take care of her father until The End.

In the afternoon, Papa liked to sit in the large Morris chair across from the window in the living room. I was supposed to stay quiet when he sat there. Often, he sat mumbling to himself. I would sit and stare at him staring at nothing, having imaginary conversations.

"Don't stare," Peggy said when she walked in one day and caught me sitting cross-legged on the floor looking at him.

"But what is he doing?" I asked.

"Papa's sick. Be quiet," Peggy admonished me.

One day while Peggy was at the store, Papa got up, put on his sweater and hat, patted me on the head as though I were the dog, and went outside.

"Where's Papa?" Peggy said when she came back.

"Out," I said.

"Out! Where did he go?"

"I don't know. You told me to leave him alone."

Peggy got in her Cadillac and went looking for Papa. We went up Indiana Avenue and down Bachrach Boulevard, across Mediterranean and back up Baltic.

He was nowhere to be found.

Peggy was frantic. "Where could he have gone?" she worried. "He's too weak to walk far."

Finally she called the police. In giving her address and then the description of him—about six feet tall, 150 pounds, hazel eyes, gray hair—she mentioned, "He's light enough to pass. He doesn't look colored."

They found him in the bus station. Maybe he wanted to go home, too.

One Sunday we had just sat down for dinner when the call came. Aunt Peggy answered the phone, then quickly hung up.

"Quick! Quick! There's colored on the Sullivan show!" she yelled, running to turn on the TV set.

Uncle Paul picked up his plate and hurried into the dining room. Even Papa, too weak to hold his plate, pushed back his chair and moved as fast as his spindly legs could carry him.

I left my plate on the table and ran after the adults.

We gathered in the dining room. Paul maneuvered the antenna on our old black-and-white television. Its picture flickered as he attempted to pick up the signal from Philadelphia. The TV sat on top of an older one with a picture tube that had already expired from the effort. Looking up at the grainy image of Ed Sullivan, we heard him announce a name, not one I knew. A rotund man—it might have been Godfrey Cambridge—came out and told jokes, which the adults found funny but I didn't understand.

He was on only a little while, not as long as most of the acts on the Sullivan show, a fact the adults talked about after it was over. Still, they said, at least Ed Sullivan allowed colored on his show. He was one of the few.

I listened to their conversation with growing consternation.

"But you said he was colored!" I burst in finally. "I thought he was going to be purple or green. But it was black and white, just like it always is!"

Uncle Paul looked at Aunt Peggy. Aunt Peggy looked at Papa. Papa looked at me, then down at the floor.

"Well," Aunt Peggy said, "let's go finish eating dinner, and I'll explain it to you later."

I felt as though I had said something wrong, but I didn't know what, and so I was embarrassed. We finished dinner in silence.

When I was ready for bed, Aunt Peggy came up to tuck me in. I said my prayers and lay down on my twin bed next to the wall. Aunt Peggy lay down beside me. She had my children's Bible in her hand.

She opened it and began telling me a story.

"God doesn't always make everything perfect for everybody," she began, opening the Bible to the Book of Exodus. There was a picture of men wearing loincloths working to build a pyramid. "Sometimes he tests people. Once he tested a whole group of people for thousands of years. They were Jews."

"What are Jews?" I asked.

"The Jews believed in one God, while the Egyptians believed in many gods. They were what you call heathens," Peggy answered. "The Jewish people worked as slaves in Egypt from early in the morning until late at night. They didn't get any days off, and they never got paid. They worked for Pharaoh, the king. Their lives were so hard that they sang songs to God, hoping that he would hear their prayers in their music, but he didn't, at least not for a very long time.

"One day Pharaoh's daughter found a baby among the weeds in the river. The baby's mother couldn't care for him, so she had left him there."

I nodded solemnly. I understood that Mommie had left me in Atlantic City because she couldn't take care of me, but at least we still saw each other.

"Pharaoh's daughter named the baby Moses, and she raised him like he was her own baby. When he grew up, he led the slaves out of Egypt, and they became free."

A long time later, she continued, there were slaves in the United States who made up a song about Moses's story.

"Were they Jewish?" I asked.

"No," she said, "they were what we call colored. They came from Africa. But they suffered the same way the Jews had suffered. They were enslaved because they had dark skin, skin like you and me."

I looked at the skin on my forearm, trying to grasp the relationship between me and the Jews who worshipped one god and the slaves with dark skin who had sung the freedom songs, the spirituals Aunt Peggy and I sang together until I fell asleep.

Peggy started singing in her sweet soprano.

> *When Moses was in Egypt land,*
> *Let my people go,*
> *Oppressed so hard they could not stand,*
> *Let my people go.*

"The people who made up that song were called colored people, and they were slaves," Peggy said. "They had other, worse names that people called them, but they were slaves because they were colored. And they made the beautiful songs we call spirituals."

Over many evenings, she would teach me many more spirituals, and gradually I began to understand the kinship between the slaves in Egypt and the slaves in the United States.

Just after Labor Day came summer's grand finale in Atlantic City: the Miss America Pageant, a weeklong festival of pretty girls, invented by the local chamber of commerce to extend the official summer season beyond Labor Day.

The week kicked off with the Miss America Parade. The year I began first grade, Paul bought tickets and we all went.

The only parade I had ever seen was the Macy's Thanksgiving Day Parade, with its giant balloons shaped like Mickey Mouse, Donald Duck, and Popeye. I had felt lost there among the adult kneecaps and giant-size cartoon figures. Even when Mommie picked me up to carry me on her shoulders, I had to crane my neck.

In Atlantic City the contestants paraded on the boardwalk, which was the width of Sixty-seventh Street. Bleachers bounded both sides, giving everyone a view—and a seat. Every organization and business in Atlantic City, from the Elks and the Knife and Fork Inn to the White House Sub Shop and Potler's Furniture Store, had a float. Some had genuine floats with elaborate feathers, while others just festooned a pickup truck with balloons and ribbons. All of them featured a pretty girl dressed in costume. In between the floats were marching bands that came from every high school in New Jersey.

Every year, the floats had seafaring themes: pirates, King Neptune, the prettiest mermaid.

"What's a mermaid?" I asked Aunt Peggy as the Captain Starn's Restaurant float went by. Its pretty girl's legs were covered in green scales, like a fish.

"A mermaid is a girl who's half fish, half human. She lives in the sea," Aunt Peggy said.

"But how does she walk?" I asked.

"She doesn't walk. She swims."

"But how does she breathe?"

"She's a mermaid. She has gills like a fish."

I looked hard at the girl on the float, but I didn't see any gills.

"They're behind her ears, hidden by her hair," Uncle Paul said mischievously.

Paul was the color of beach sand, with hazel eyes that could change color to match the sky or the grass. Peggy said she had fallen in love with his eyes, but it was his voice everyone remembered: a voice abraded by cigarette smoke into an instrument that commanded attention. People said his gravelly voice made him sound like Everett Dirksen, the Republican Senate minority leader, from Illinois.

Sometimes I felt that Uncle Paul and I had never recovered from the incident with the string beans. Paul thought children should be seen and not heard; he thought Mommie had raised me without discipline. Meals were particularly difficult. I liked to sing to my food while squirming in some semblance of a dance. I talked back when he told me to sit still.

Mommie would ask sometimes if it seemed as though he and Peggy were happy, but I never knew how to tell. Uncle Paul worked days as a county clerk in Cape May. It was a job he hated so much, he said, that it drove him to cigarettes. Despite his emphysema, he smoked four to six packs of Salems a day. At night he drove a cab and smoked out of boredom.

Uncle Paul was hard to please. On those rare moments when I did please him, it seemed a great achievement.

He also had an eye for the ladies—Aunt Peggy had saved a *Jet* magazine that had one of his former girlfriends on the cover. Even at the age of six, I found the idea of her saving a magazine with one of her rivals on the cover a bit strange. Nevertheless, where the Miss America pageant was concerned, Uncle Paul was the expert on beauty.

The contestants themselves glided down the boardwalk perched on the trunks of their Chevrolet convertibles. They smiled inexhaustible smiles and waved tirelessly. Peggy and Paul commented on each girl—for "girls" they were called, even though they were young women.

We gave extra cheers for Miss New Jersey, Miss Pennsylvania, Miss New York, and Miss Maryland. Although they were rarely among the prettiest girls, they represented the states closest to ours, and so we cheered for them out of solidarity. The prettiest girls, according to Paul, came from Mississippi, Alabama, North Carolina, and Texas.

We gave them extra cheers for being pretty.

Miss South Carolina went by, wearing a cocktail-length light blue chiffon dress with a flounced skirt and a wrap.

"Now, she looks like she could have some colored in her," Peggy said.

That word again. I turned and looked at Peggy directly. "What's 'colored'?" I asked.

I was sitting to her left, and it seemed her deviating eye bored through me.

"Colored is . . . well, she just looked like she could have some Negro blood in her," Peggy said.

"What's 'Negro'?" I asked.

"We are." Paul came to her rescue from my other side. "Anybody with dark skin—skin that looks tanned. People born with a natural tan. People with really kinky, curly hair like we have, wider lips and noses. That's the way colored people look, and sometimes when we see a white person looking like that, we say they look like they could be colored."

"But they don't like to think of themselves that way," Peggy added, sotto voce, "so we say it behind their backs, lest they think they're getting away with something."

I looked again at Miss South Carolina, but she had already passed us. Miss South Dakota was up next.

Using Paul's description as a reference, I scanned her skin, lips, nose, and hair. Nothing.

"Is Mommie colored?" I asked Paul.

Now it was his turn to pause. "Well . . . there are some colored women who look like your mother. But she's not, no."

I considered this for a while. Why was I colored and Mommie wasn't?

Miss Texas was gliding by. She had a wide smile. Still trying to grasp this idea of what made someone look colored, I asked, "Does she look colored?"

"Well, she's got a wide mouth, but she doesn't look colored. Her lips are too thin."

Aunt Peggy added, in a whisper, "We don't talk about race loudly when we're out in public. It's something we talk about among ourselves. We whisper about it in public or wait until we get home to talk about it."

Silently, I continued examining the contestants and the girls on the floats, making a game out of it, until Miss Wyoming passed, dusk yielded to twilight, and the ocean air filled with a dampness that signaled it was time to go home before we all caught our death of cold.

4. TUNNELS OF LOVE

In the fall of 1946, when she was twenty-four, my mother had spent some time in San Francisco visiting her mother and stepfather. One night they went to a nightclub called the Bal Tavern to see a young comedian, Larry Storch, whose star was rising. They sat at a table down front.

Storch, the grandson of Russian Jews who had fled the pogroms, was a stocky, well-built young man with a head of thick black hair. He had a talent for foreign accents and zany characters: a yogi who got stuck in the lotus position, a Frenchman who threatened to forsake drinking wine, a Japanese merchant who sold cheap paper fans.

After the show Norma sent a note backstage, asking him to come have a drink at the table. He did. They hit it off and spent the next three months living together while he worked in San Francisco.

Norma thought this was it, the "real thing."

Her mother thought she was living in a fool's paradise.

Granny proved to be right. When Norma discovered she was pregnant, Storch said he wanted no part of a wife and family. He wanted her to get an abortion. She refused. He deserted her and went back to New York before the baby was born. My mother named Larry's daughter Candace, but she was never able to provide for her. Candie spent four years in foster care before being put up for adoption when she was five. That was the year before I was born.

Norma didn't see Larry for twelve more years. By then Larry had had his own eponymous TV show, a summer replacement for Jackie Gleason. He had appeared regularly on *The Ed Sullivan Show*.

His navy buddy, the actor Tony Curtis, arranged to hire him in the movie *Who Was That Lady?*, and Hollywood seemed to like what it saw.

Larry's father came from Poland, and his mother's people had fled Kazakhstan, near Mongolia, so he had a vaguely Asian look, which helped him capture ethnic roles. The popular memory has forgotten that not just African-Americans but Indians, Mexicans, and Asians were largely banned from speaking roles in films during Hollywood's golden years. Those ethnic roles went to women and men like Larry Storch. Larry could mimic Chinese. Or Mexican. Or French, Italian, Cuban, or Russian. He knew enough phrases to get by in almost any language and could speak conversationally in four, even though he'd only completed junior high school.

One day when I was in first grade, two albums—*Larry Storch at the Bon Soir*, the club in New York his mother owned, and *Larry Storch Reads Treasure Island*—arrived in the mail. Aunt Peggy told me these albums were by "Mommie's new love interest."

I balked at the thought of yet another unrelated relative. "Will I have to call him 'Uncle Larry'?" I asked Mommie on the phone.

"No, you can call him Larry," she said.

I sighed with relief.

She wrote to Aunt Peggy:

> *After twelve years he has fallen in love with me. I'm just astounded—it's like a dream come true. I've always had a soft spot in my heart for him—even through Jimmy and Dixon, but I just locked it up and pretended it wasn't there. It was sort of like being in love with Clark Gable, you know, when you're Mrs. Jones in Kansas City.*

I first met Larry in 1961, when I was seven. Walking into our apartment on West Sixty-seventh Street, I peered into the living room. There, wedged in a lotus position against the corner of the black sofa, sat a shirtless man with a headful of shiny black hair. He wore blue jeans and black ballet slippers and rolled a cigarette as he watched a Yankees game on the TV.

"Hiya, JuneBug! I'm Larry!" the mop of black hair bellowed. "You like baseball? C'mon and watch the ball game with me!"

I had never watched a baseball game, but he seemed so friendly that I joined him in front of the TV. It was the season of Roger Maris and Mickey Mantle. As we watched, Larry told me their life stories, explained the rules of the game, and described the history of Yankee Stadium. His descriptions seemed so vivid that I asked whether he knew Maris and Mantle personally.

"No, not them, but my brother used to be a batboy for the Yankees," he answered. "That was what I wanted to be. But instead I'm a comedian. Imagine that."

The announcer droned steadily against the roar of the crowd as each player went up to bat. I heard the crack of bat against ball, then the crescendo of the announcer's voice rising in unison with the roar of the crowd. The rhythms had a lulling effect. My mother was napping already, lying in the bedroom with an ice pack against her eyes and forehead—to reduce puffiness, she said.

I wandered between the two of them, observing the rhythms of her deep breathing, watching Larry watch his game, alternately bored with their ritual and fascinated by how comfortable they seemed together, even in separate rooms.

Larry was unlike any other adult I had ever met.

He also liked to watch boxing—or so I remember. He would project fights on a screen against the blank wall in the bathroom with a little eight-millimeter projector. He would sit on the toilet seat while I sat on the bath mat on the floor at his feet and listened while he gave me a running commentary of a welterweight fight he had seen so many times he knew it by heart.

He described the boxers' lives, how they came from hard, tough neighborhoods like he did, where the force of your punch meant more than your score on a school test. Comedians were kids who couldn't fight, he added, so they had learned to protect themselves using jokes.

The way I remember Larry explaining it, comedy, like boxing, was all about timing. The comedian was the boxer, the audience his opponent. Standing in front of an audience, the comic parried with one-liners and bits. You had to bob and weave, know when to jab a heckler and when to duck, when to launch one-liners like upper cuts. If you did it right, you were a champion and the audience rewarded you with applause and laughter.

I didn't know when I met Larry how their battle to win those bouts with the audience bound Larry and my father, Jimmy, together. I didn't know that my father had been a comic or that Jimmy and Larry had been friends, sitting next to one another at a bar on West Fifty-second Street, long before either of them met my mother. The bar was called Charlie's, and it was where show-business people gathered in the days after the war, in those days when Larry's career seemed bright and Jimmy's had already gone as far as it would. They sat at the bar and told lies about their great prospects while drowning their blues in bottles of wine and vodka.

Years later Larry explained to me how easy it was for him to take in another man's child when he began living with Norma in 1960.

"You were Jimmy Cross's daughter," he says. "It was an honor just having you crawl around the house!"

He recalled how malleable my father's face was; my face was like that, too, he said. In fact, when I was a child, Larry said he used my face as his mirror.

We practiced raising first one eyebrow, then the other, then raising an eyebrow while turning down the mouth. Eventually I could lift my eyebrows independently and make different sides of my face do different things, but after a while I tired and just watched while he practiced his faces.

Larry made his own cigarettes. He bought tobacco that came with tissue-thin papers—a blue package with a picture of a sailor and a life preserver on its cover. He used his own tobacco, which was green instead of brown. It had a different smell—sweeter than the tobacco Uncle Paul smoked.

I asked Larry if I could smoke some.

"No, JuneBug, not until you're older," he said, and added that he would give me a whipping if he ever caught me smoking regular cigarettes.

Larry said his handmade cigarettes were better for you than the Salems that Uncle Paul smoked. They expanded your mind, while machine-made cigarettes closed down your lungs and made you unable to think at all.

The next time I saw Uncle Paul lighting up his Salems in Atlantic City, I spoke right up. "Larry smokes cigarettes made from green tobacco. He says his kind is better for you."

Uncle Paul paused just after he inhaled, and he looked at me, smoke rising from his mouth into his nostrils. "Is that so?" he said, exhaling puffs of smoke with every word from his gravelly voice.

"He said the kind he smokes are good for your mind, but the kind you smoke is bad for your lungs."

"Well, I'll have to talk to Peggy about that," Uncle Paul said, without correcting my grammar.

Satisfied that I had contributed to Aunt Peggy's ongoing battle to stop Paul from smoking, I wandered away.

But the next time I visited Mommie, Larry pulled me to one side.

"Now, J.B.," Larry said. "J.B." was his other nickname for me. "This has to be our little secret," he said. "Don't go telling anybody else about these cigarettes."

"Why not?" I said.

"Well, these cigarettes are only for special people. So let's just keep it between you and me, and don't go blabbin' anything about this to Aunt Peggy or Uncle Paul, okay?"

"Okay," I said. And I never breathed another word.

Larry, Mommie, and I trolled the streets searching for Chinese restaurants. Larry was practicing how to talk and hold his face like a Chinaman, as they said then. He planned to audition for the movie version of *Flower Drum Song*, so he was studying Chinese waiters for clues to character.

We'd enter a Chinese restaurant, and after the waiter took our order, Larry arranged his face and tried sounding it out just as the waiter had said it. Mommie expressed delight at every effort, the same way she did when I got good grades.

If Larry got the role, that would mean Hollywood, and Big Money, Aunt Peggy told me later. She seemed as excited as my mother.

During Larry's Chinese phase, Mom embraced all things Chinese. Paper lanterns and porcelain bowls appeared inside our apartment. We ate fried rice with chopsticks. My mother bought a green cheongsam with slits up to her thigh. I wanted one, too, but Aunt Peggy said little girls didn't wear such things.

Back in Atlantic City, I pestered Aunt Peggy and Uncle Paul to take me to a Chinese restaurant. Incongruously enough, the Chinese restaurant in Atlantic City sat in the center of the black nightclub district, at one end of Kentucky Avenue. Its blue neon sign protruded from the building like a triangle, framing the word "Chinese" in pink neon.

The restaurant was a narrow storefront. The vinyl in the booths had cracked; its sharp edges dug into my skin so that I pulled my legs up and folded them underneath me. Uncle Paul complained this was not a ladylike way to sit, but Aunt Peggy intervened.

"Leave the child alone," she begged. "We're out, let's have a pleasant time."

Uncle Paul grumbled and looked down at his menu. He was none too pleased at eating in this "foreign" restaurant. His tastes ran more toward smothered steak and onions with greens on the side.

Aunt Peggy had been surprised when I told her you could get slices of beef with green peppers at a Chinese place. Uncle Paul, steeped in Louisiana culture when he worked as a cook in the army during the war, said he'd try beef with green peppers and onions even if they were Chinese. Looking at the menu, though, they couldn't quite make out which dishes were which, so I explained the menu to them.

After they had ordered, the waiter looked at me and spoke Chinese.

"What?" I said, confused.

He repeated himself.

There was an awkward silence. Finally Peggy spoke up.

"Oh . . . uh, she's not Chinese," she stumbled. "She's . . . uh, colored."

The waiter peered at me more closely, then quickly turned and walked away.

"He thought I was Chinese!" I laughed delightedly after he left. It seemed confirmation of my mother's nickname, "Tahitian June."

"Yes, well, but he's not everybody," Aunt Peggy said tersely, deflating my pride. She didn't want me acting "hincty," as black folks put it—in other words, getting too full of myself by thinking that I could "pass" for anything other than colored.

Yvonne Gregory, Aunt Hugh's oldest child, the one who I had imagined was Queen of the Fairies, had recently married a German air force pilot. In Germany, Aunt Peggy told me, Yvonne "passed" for white, ate at the finest restaurants, and shopped at the couture shops, but back in New York she was still treated as if she were nobody. That had something to do with being "colored" but not looking like it. Aunt Peggy said that being treated as if she were nobody after she had gotten used to being somebody in Germany made Yvonne bitter and resentful.

Aunt Peggy feared the effect these extremes in privilege and prejudice had had on Yvonne, and she worried, too, about the effect my upbringing might have on me.

Once, when I was seven, Mommie had a party in our New York apartment.

I was helping her clean. She was worried. I could tell by the set of her jaw while she dusted. Her teeth clamped so that the lines of her cheekbones formed a parallel with her nose and her chin. It made her look like an Indian. Even before she told me that the party was for Larry's family and for someone called an agent, who, my mother said, would be "very important" to her future with Larry, I knew I should put on my best manners.

I hid all my toys in the giant cardboard toilet-tissue box in the closet and helped dust the TV, the table, and the lamp with a porcelain base shaped like a skinny blue feline that I always thought of as Giacometti Cat.

Then, just before the company came, Mom sat me down and looked me in the eyes as she did when she wanted to ensure I understood something. "I want us to play a game during the party, okay?" she said. I squealed with delight. I loved playing secret games with my mother.

"Why don't you call me 'Aunt Norma,' and I'll tell everyone you're my niece. It will be our private little game, that only you and me will know about."

I had told my mother how Mrs. Dempsey had yelled at me to call Peggy and Paul "Aunt Peggy and Uncle Paul." It bothered me, I confided, because they weren't really my aunt and uncle. Aunt Peggy had suggested that I pretend it was just a game, and so I had.

It was beginning to feel natural.

I'd never played the game with Mommie, but since it was only for the party, I agreed to the rules.

The hors d'oeuvres—pieces of celery stuffed with chive cream cheese—went out, the guests arrived, and the wine flowed from half-gallon jugs. Soon the house filled with adult chatter and laughter and the tinkling of glasses. As usual when I visited Mommie, I was the only child there.

I called Mommie "Aunt Norma" on cue and helped her put the coats on the bed. After they were heaped high, I crawled underneath them, pretending to be an inchworm. I watched a Godzilla movie on TV with the sound off. Then I grew bored and walked around the thighs of the guests, pretending I was Gretel in the forest. I traced a path through the cigarette ashes and alcohol spilled on the carpet.

Maybe, after a while, someone gave me a sip of wine, as my mother's friends sometimes liked to do, or maybe I just grew rambunctious with all the noise and excitement. In the kitchen my mother basted a chicken while she talked.

"Mommie! Mommie!" I called out, wanting to show her something. "Come see!"

She ignored me, finished her conversation, and put down the pot she was working with. She wiped her hands on the half apron she wore over her little black dress. Then she took me by the hand and led me toward the bathroom.

I tried to pull her the other way.

"But, Mommie, I wanted to show you something!"

She quickly and quietly closed the door and sat down on the toilet lid so that we were face-to-face. "Didn't I tell you to call me 'Aunt Norma'?"

I giggled and put my hand over my mouth. I had totally forgotten about our little game.

"This isn't funny!" she hissed.

"I'm sorry, Aunt Mommie—I mean, Aunt Norma," I said, giggling even harder, thinking of the time she and I had giggled ourselves silly while Uncle Paul was trying to say grace. But now, looking into her eyes, I stopped and caught my breath.

I nearly didn't recognize her. Her narrow eyes looked like an evil witch's.

"June, this is very serious!" she said, her voice as sharp as razors. "Larry could lose his job. We could all end up homeless! You won't be able to stay with Peggy and Paul in Atlantic City! Our future depends on this! Do you understand me?"

I tried to back away, but I bumped up against the clothes hamper. Trapped between the toilet and the wall, I responded with a mask of my own—my small voice.

"Yes, Aunt Norma."

When the party was over, after everyone had left, my mother sat down by the side of the bed and apologized for being so harsh.

"I'm sorry I yelled at you," she said, "but this may determine Larry's entire future. This agent could be very important for Larry, to help him get jobs. I didn't want him thinking I'd already been married and had children; it might not reflect well on Larry."

When Mom finally married Larry, his family disowned him. I

thought I was the reason—that my failure to remember the rules
of the game at that party had made his family mad.

Over the years Mom and Larry developed two circles of friends:
those who knew about me and those who didn't. Gradually my visits
began to coincide with those occasions when it was convenient for
me to be seen.

It was around the time that Mommie started anticipating a future
as Mrs. Larry Storch that the stomachaches began.

They would strike just before dinnertime, debilitating, knifelike
cramps that forced me into a fetal position on the sofa, rocking and
moaning in pain. Nothing—not tepid tea with toast, nor warm Coca-
Cola, nor milk of magnesia—eased their intensity, and usually about
ten or fifteen minutes after dinner was served, the cramps dissipated.
Aunt Peggy wondered why I was having these symptoms now. I had
never told her or Uncle Paul about that party, about the game I
had played with Mommie or how bad I had been at playing it. I was
too ashamed. But I had internalized the rules, and I vowed never to
make the mistake of claiming a loved one publicly again.

Soon after the party for Larry's agent, Aunt Peggy's bridge club,
the Wy-Mo-Mays (a sort of acronym for "Wives, Mothers, and
Maidens") held a fashion show. Peggy modeled several outfits, including the finale, a sleeveless red chiffon dress with a boat neckline,
cinched and belted at the waist and flaring to a layered, flouncy
skirt. She would never have worn such a flamboyant dress, but on
the runway she looked fabulous. The shade of red complimented her
complexion. The layered skirt floated around her as she walked. She
looked more like a model than any other woman in the show.

Aunt Peggy's godmother, Daisy, sat next to me. "Doesn't she look
sharp!" Daisy said, as she broke into a series of whoops and hollers.

I had to admit she did, but I didn't know what to do. If I clapped,
would something bad happen to Aunt Peggy because people knew I
knew her? Could we end up homeless, on the street, if everyone
knew I lived with her?

Afraid to risk it, I sat very still, hands folded neatly in my lap, eyes on my shoes. I did nothing to betray that I knew her, nothing that would risk bringing out the Evil Witch in Aunt Peggy.

"Whatsa matter with you? CLAP!" Daisy commanded.

Daisy must not know the rules, I thought.

I continued to stare at my feet as Aunt Peggy came strutting down in the catwalk. In my peripheral vision, I saw the edge of her red dress and the outline of her leg ending in her alligator shoes. My heart swelled with pride as I heard the audience applaud and whistle.

How proud she would be of my restraint!

When it seemed safe, I looked up in time to see her walk away from the audience and disappear behind the curtain.

Afterward, everyone told Aunt Peggy how stunning she looked. As the crowd of her admirers thinned, she sidled up next to me and said in a very, very sad voice, "And my little Juney didn't even clap for me."

I knew instantly that I had made a dreadful mistake.

"I'm sorry," I said. "I didn't know I was supposed to clap for you."

"Supposed to clap! You're not *supposed* to clap. You should feel it in your heart."

"But I—"

"Aw, no buts." She looked at me as if I were a recreant. "At least now I know where I stand with you."

So the rule about not saying that Mommie was Mommie in public did not include saying Aunt Peggy was not Aunt Peggy.

I didn't know *what* to say. All I could do was study the creases in my oxford shoes.

The telegram arrived on a Saturday.

WESTERN UNION   AUGUST 8, 1961
GETTING MARRIED ON TUESDAY. THINK OF US.
LOVE NORMA AND LARRY

After the wedding, Mommie and Aunt Peggy spent long hours on the phone, commiserating about their sudden poverty—Larry had been giving all his money to his mother for safekeeping, and she had seized everything. Aunt Peggy reassured Mommie that at least Larry still had his talent and they could start over. Off the phone, she told me that Larry's mother was being vindictive toward Mom. I was too ashamed to tell her it was all my fault.

I visited Mom and Larry in New York soon after they married.

I cherished the nightly bubble bath I still shared with my mother during these visits. I would sit at the faucet end because I was small, while she lounged in her wide end of the tub. We poured bubbles over our heads. We played peekaboo with the washcloths. We lathered up with Johnson's Baby Soap and made animals out of the bubbles.

One night we were sharing the trivia of our day when Mom looked at me in a serious way and declared, "You know, if you hadn't gotten darker as you grew older, you could have stayed with me. You wouldn't have to live with Peggy."

I looked down at my arm, the brown skin against the white porcelain, the white suds.

"What?" I asked. In the back of my brain, I remembered that word, that word I'd had such difficulty comprehending.

Colored.

"You were light. Light as I am, when you were born. If you had stayed that color, I would never have sent you to live with Peggy. You could have stayed with me."

I kept staring down at my arm.

People born with a natural tan, Paul had said at the Miss America pageant.

I struggled against the comprehension. The color of the crayons at the end of the box.

Really kinky, curly hair.

Reaching up, I touched the tight curls of my hair.

Negro.

The white bubbles dripped from my hand into my eyes. I looked at Mommie watching me.

Thirty years later, when I reminded her of that night, my mother found it hard to believe she could have said such a thing to a child. At the time so did Aunt Peggy and Uncle Paul.

I told Aunt Peggy first, in a matter-of-fact style, giving the information no more meaning than the state of the weather.

Her eyelids fluttered as she looked at me, and her mouth dropped open. "Oh," she said. Her face looked like an ice sculpture ready to crack into a million pieces.

Thinking no more of it, I went upstairs and did some homework. After Uncle Paul got home, I heard murmuring between them. I crept from my bed to the top of the stairs, where the space between the stairwell and the pantry allowed me to eavesdrop.

Uncle Paul was angry. "What kind of a thing is that to say to a little girl?" he demanded in his gruff voice.

As I tiptoed from my eavesdropping spot, the floorboards creaked and their voices lowered. I jumped into bed and pulled the sheets over my head. I had done a bad thing, first by forgetting the rules of the game, and now by telling Aunt Peggy and Uncle Paul that Mommie had noticed I had grown darker.

Early in 1962, Larry and Norma came down to visit me in Atlantic City—the only time that the two of them ever came to visit me there, and the last time Mommie would ever come visit. She wanted to create a new life for herself, and Atlantic City and the house at 407 North Indiana, where she had lived with my father, was baggage she sought to leave behind. Still, Mom and Aunt Peggy talked on the phone at least three times a week, long after Mom no longer visited. Mom looked up to Aunt Peggy. Peggy had graduated college—my mother finished only one year of junior college. Peggy had found a job with security, gotten married, and bought a house. My mother, then thirty-eight, desperately wanted all these things. "I've got one last chance to make it!" she had told Aunt Peggy before leaving me there. And now she wanted to introduce her new husband and get Aunt Peggy's approval.

They arrived late one Saturday morning. I hadn't known they

were coming until they were already on the bus, and I could barely wait to present the Mommie I was always telling my friends about.

Aunt Peggy warned against it. "No one likes a show-off," she said. "You may introduce her to Regina."

Finally they arrived at the house. Mom let us see her wedding photo—even in getting married she had broken the rules, wearing a black cocktail dress (Larry wore his stage suit). She flashed her wedding ring, which Larry had bought from a candy machine at the supermarket. It was plastic, coated with cheap gold paint. The ring didn't matter to her, Aunt Peggy would laughingly observe after they left. What mattered was that piece of paper! My mother, after three children and countless failed relationships, had finally gotten a man to marry her.

I picked up confusing signals from the adults during that visit. Mom seemed solicitous and anxious, while Aunt Peggy seemed strangely quiet. She asked fewer questions than usual, letting Mom do all the talking, responding with a terse Uh-*huh*. Uncle Paul offered Larry a drink, but he drank only red wine and there wasn't any in the house, so Uncle Paul went to the liquor store to get some. Meanwhile, I ran down to Regina's house.

Many years later, my mother would describe her memory of the conversation she and Aunt Peggy had while they were alone. "Peggy, what's the matter?" she remembered asking. "You seem disturbed." She remembered how Peggy looked at her, her eyes welling with tears. "Oh, darlin'," she said, "I'm so happy for you. Paul and I love Larry—and well, I always knew there was a risk that you would take June away one day. It's just that—she has become the child we've always wanted. If she goes to live with you I don't know how I can go on living!"

Mom would remember how she put her arms around Peggy after this outburst. "Oh, Peggy, no," she remembered saying. "I will never take June away. I could never acknowledge her. It would ruin Larry's career. We're going to be traveling a lot now, and she needs to stay with you.

"She will always have two mothers."

Mrs. McKee had made Regina and me matching outfits—red-and-green checked straight-leg pants and tops with a triangle hem. Aunt Peggy suggested that we show Mommie and Larry how we could dance. We put on Chubby Checker's "Let's Twist Again," and away we went, twisting our upper and lower bodies in opposite directions in time to the music, adding variations, picking up on each other's moves and taking them someplace else. Then we put on the record again and added hula hoops.

We each had unique moves—I could do two hula hoops at a time; Regina could kneel and do a back bend while the hula hoop spun within an inch of the floor. "That's George!" Larry said. Since they had returned from their honeymoon on Lake George, "George" was what Larry called anything he liked a lot.

Regina, who would become a runway model and actress, remembers this as the first time any adult ever encouraged her theater talent. I remember it as the moment that began our childhood competition. We always compared who got better grades; who danced better; who had longer, thicker hair; whose mommie was prettier. And so did Aunt Peggy and Mrs. McKee. Sometimes, it seemed, the debates drove a wedge into our friendship.

One day when we were about ten years old, Regina and I were walking home from school with some friends, in heated debate over whose skin was darker. Since absorbing the meaning of "colored," I had learned a lot about the nuances of skin tone. "Mulatto," "quadroon," "octoroon" denoted the fractional proportions of "black" blood in one's veins, but those mixtures yielded wildly variant skin tones. For instance, Regina, who had two black parents, was nearly the same skin color as I was. Those who looked like us were most often called "high yella," although we preferred the more genteel-sounding "café au lait." There were other terms denoting lighter-skinned African-Americans: "zebra," "redbone," "mariny-colored." We called our darker brethren "tar babies," "ink spots," or "shines." In those days the black community was seriously color-struck. Entire conversations revolved around whether our skin tone was more akin to the color of coffee beans or coffee ice cream; to mahogany, ebony, or cut pine; to the blue-black of native Africans or the dull black of a Bakelite telephone. Everything from the church one attended to who one's playmates were depended, to some extent, on these determinations.

On that day, walking home from school, one of our friends peered closely at me and then at Regina and pronounced me the fairer.

"No, I'm darker," I said.

"You're lighter," Regina threw in.

"I am NOT!" I said, almost screaming.

We were a block away from home, and we nearly came to blows. I did not want to be the fairer-skinned. I wanted to be dark: "honey-colored," "chocolate," or "blackberry." If I were fairer, I would be so light as to be almost white—but if I were that light, then I should have been able to pass, and then I should not be living in Atlantic City. I should be in New York with one mother, and I should not then be attending Indiana Avenue school, or living with Aunt Peggy and Uncle Paul, or having Regina for my best friend.

5. SHELTER FROM THE STORM

Described from the ridge of adulthood, my childhood seems impossibly difficult. Yet, no one who knew me in those years remembers a downtrodden little girl, and I don't remember feeling like one. Indeed, my life seemed charmed. I studied piano and dance. I owned a pet miniature schnauzer I named Gigi. My Barbie doll wore hand-sewn fashions copied from *Vogue*. In the home where I grew up with Aunt Peggy and Uncle Paul, I felt surrounded by love and the affirmation that I could achieve anything I dreamed of. Our church reinforced those values and gave me a community that cared about me. At home, piles of *Ebony* magazines documented the success of people like us who had gone before; books by Booker T. Washington and Langston Hughes were displayed next to those by Louisa May Alcott, George Eliot, William Faulkner, and Charles Dickens; recordings by Duke Ellington and Sarah Vaughan nestled in the large record cabinet next to those by Chick Webb (Uncle Paul's favorite) and the McGuire Sisters (Aunt Peggy's).

But it would be Aunt Hugh's children and grandchildren who ultimately defined family values and personal achievement for me.

W. E. B. DuBois, the great black intellectual of the twentieth century, would have referred to the Gregorys as "the talented tenth"— that group he tasked with emancipating the Negro masses. They traced their lineage from the shores of Madagascar to the freedmen's communities of Maryland, from the racetracks and churches of Virginia to the country's finest colleges, and even to its space program.

Mr. Gregory, an acquaintance of DuBois's, was superintendent of Atlantic City's Colored Schools. He had helped Peggy get a job as a teacher shortly after she graduated from Miner Teachers College in 1927. She had joined their church, St. Augustine's Episcopal, even though Paul was a Catholic.

T. M. Gregory had graduated from Harvard in 1910; his brother James Monroe had graduated five years earlier; an uncle of theirs had been the first African-American to graduate from the school of dentistry in 1895.

Aunt Peggy quoted these dates with the reverence due the royal family. Indeed, Thomas Montgomery Gregory looked the part: as fair as DuBois himself, with his wavy hair and cream-colored skin. He had led Harvard's debating team to glory over Yale during his senior year, and he encouraged us all—even the grandchildren, even me—to defend our opinions around the dining room table.

As a young man, "Gum," as everyone called him, had documented Jim Crow segregation for the NAACP magazine, *The Crisis*. Then he become a professor of drama at two different black colleges—first Howard, then Fisk.

It was at Fisk that he met Hugh Ella Hancock, the dark-haired daughter of a tavern owner from Austin, Texas. Hugh Ella was exotic if ever the word had meaning. Eighteen years old and smitten by the dashing professor, she dropped out of school to marry him. Together they raised six children: Peggy had baby-sat them all, and they all claimed her as their godmother. They became my aunts and uncles, and their children became my cousins, playmates, and friends.

As a youngster, I was perhaps closest to Aunt Hugh's second oldest son and his wife. Uncle Hugh and Aunt Sylvia, and their kids, Hugh Jr. and Gina, became my extended family. They also lived in New York, which may explain why I bonded to them so readily.

Uncle Hugh was the fourth child of Aunt Hugh and Uncle Gum. To me he looked like the actor Omar Sharif. He must have been in his late thirties then, balding early, as all the Gregory men did, but with still enough dark hair to set off his dark eyes and mustache.

Sylvia had long, wavy black hair that reflected her Indian ancestry. Yet despite these obvious ethnic mixtures, the family considered themselves 100 percent African-American.

Uncle Hugh had been one of the early black graduates of the University of Chicago Business School. He was also one of the first black corporate marketing executives in America. He made his mark during the early sixties. Back then, Rheingold beer held a wildly popular contest in which consumers elected one pretty girl to be that year's "Miss Rheingold." Black contestants weren't allowed. Uncle Hugh noticed that among New York's black beer drinkers, Schaefer beer sold second to Rheingold. So, he proposed the idea of a "Miss Schaefer" contest in Harlem. Soon, Schaefer overtook Rheingold as the most popular beer among New York's black beer drinkers.

During summer vacation, Uncle Hugh and his family would come spend a week with us in Atlantic City. Our days were spent at the beach, our evenings filled with conversation and joking at the dinner table. Little Hugh, Gina, and I would nag the adults to rent bikes on the boardwalk first thing, then ride the seven miles from one end to the other.

It was a treat for us all. At 6:00 A.M. the air blows off the ocean clean and salty. As we rode, the bicycle tires hummed against the smooth treads of the boardwalk.

"Why don't you come visit us sometime when you're in New York?" Uncle Hugh asked once as we were riding back.

I nearly lost my balance at the thought of it. Looking up, I caught Aunt Peggy shaking her head at Hugh, giving him a warning look.

"What?" he demanded, ignoring her signal. "I'm just asking June, whose company we love, to come visit us during part of the weekend that she spends with her mother in New York."

My belly flipped; the boards wobbled under my wheels. Atlantic City was Aunt Peggy's world, filled with Gregorys; New York was my mother's, filled with her friends and Larry's. I would never become adept at blending the two.

"Well, Norma doesn't get to see her that often," Aunt Peggy said, coming to my rescue, "and their time together is precious. But maybe in the future." Then, with a nod in my direction, she added, "It's up to her."

Aunt Peggy's barbecued chicken wings formed the culinary high-light of these family visits. We ate them with corn on the cob, greens cooked with fatback, and fresh peach cobbler, made with the peaches from the tree out back, for dessert. After dinner we kids re-mained at the table as the adults talked about politics and the state of the race. Then, if it was a nice evening, we piled into Aunt Peggy's Cadillac and drove down to Park Place. It would be around eight o'clock in the evening, the July dusk pink and navy blue and filled with the sounds of crickets and laughter. As the loamy sea breeze filled our nostrils, Uncle Hugh would take us on the rides at the Mil-lion Dollar Pier. My favorite was the Spider, which weaved in and out and up and down, its centrifugal force pushing us to the edge of our seats. Pressed against the corner, swirling around, I felt my senses fill with the smells of salt water, popcorn, cotton candy, and dancing neon lights. Atlantic City seemed like the promised land then, and I was caught in a moment so tactile that there was no family other than this family, no time outside this moment, no Mom-mie that I missed.

By June 1963, the civil-rights movement had come north, and en-tered the timeline of my memory.

The Freedom Rides made the first impression on me. Because I rode the bus so often myself, the idea that people who looked like me had to sit in the back of the bus seemed grossly unfair. I tended to get travel sick, and that sensation was exacerbated when I sat in the rear.

The first Freedom Rides went down Route 40 in Maryland, less than two hours away from Atlantic City. Meanwhile, on Maryland's Eastern Shore, Negroes began demonstrating against segregation. They called it the Cambridge Movement. Whites had fired shots at demonstrators in that seaside town, and, for the first time, the White House had gotten directly involved in negotiating a solution, which the Negroes ultimately rejected.

Aunt Peggy and Uncle Paul argued over the efficacy of the Cambridge Movement and its leader, Gloria Richardson. Aunt Peggy tended to side with President Kennedy, who, embarrassed by demonstrations so close to the nation's capital while he was trying to negotiate a nuclear test-ban treaty with the Russians, had condemned the demonstrators as "people who are just demonstrating because they feel like it."

Uncle Paul, who was raised in Washington and knew the Eastern Shore, said the whites who lived there were a bunch of rednecks. He was glad to see the Negroes finally—as he put it—"acting up."

That June the National Guard moved into Cambridge to quell the demonstrations, the first time martial law was invoked in the civil-rights movement.

They would remain there nearly a year.

The Cambridge Movement, debates over nonviolence, and the legislation that would be the focus of the forthcoming March on Washington were the focus of all dinner-table conversation that July when Uncle Hugh and Aunt Sylvia came to visit.

"I've finally figured out what sin Negroes committed that led to us catching all this hell," Uncle Hugh announced after dinner one night.

We all leaned in closer as he exhaled his cigarette.

"What?" we asked.

"We created white folks," he said.

"Oh, Hugh," Aunt Peggy said, distressed, as laughter burst around the table.

"No, really," he said. "Black Muslims say the white man was created by a mad scientist. Well, I've decided they got part of the story right and part of it wrong. The way I figure it, the Garden of Eden had to have been in Africa, because all the races came from there. It says that in the Bible. Now, if you think about it, all the races except the Caucasian race have color—how could that be?"

He paused for effect, and we waited.

"I've concluded it must have been the Africans who created the white man. Some kind of gene grafting—maybe from pigs, because they have the same color skin as whites do. Africans must have created them to do the work of slaves and made their skin color different so that they could tell them apart. But they must have escaped from bondage, run away to Europe, and ended up colonizing the world."

We glanced at one another dubiously. "See, the Caucasian race had a chance to make a difference," he continued, lighting another cigarette and idly picking up a pencil to sketch something on a napkin. "But have they? No. The white man has messed up the same way the black man did, being greedy and vengeful. So now we Negroes are condemned to live under the heel of the white man until we atone for our mistake of having created a slave race in the first place."

When he finished his history lesson, he slammed down the pencil for emphasis.

The next morning Aunt Peggy found his sketch on the napkin. He had drawn the face of a mustached man wearing a broad-brim hat, looking up to the heavens, his eyes closed, a shower of arrows falling down on his head.

It was a self-portrait.

Aunt Peggy worried about Uncle Hugh—he had already left Schaefer and had just quit a lucrative job as the first black vice president of advertising at Lever Brothers. She laughed ruefully in admiration. "Just walked in, cussed out his boss, and left," she said, shaking her head as though to say, "As if vice presidencies were offered to colored every day."

Aunt Peggy believed you had to put up with a certain amount of foolishness from white people to get anything done, but Uncle Hugh wasn't having any foolishness.

He had graduated valedictorian of his high-school class in 1940—the first colored boy anyone could remember being valedictorian at Atlantic City High School. He joined the prestigious Tuskegee Airmen, but one day he and a buddy took a plane up for a joyride. In a freak accident, his copilot was electrocuted.

Uncle Hugh found himself dishonorably discharged, a punishment his cohorts to this day find harsh. A white pilot, they said, who had done a similar thing would have found himself grounded, maybe held back at promotion, but not dishonorably discharged.

Aunt Peggy said Uncle Hugh nursed in his soul an unrelenting bitterness over how he was treated, one that he never let go.

"I worry you'll become like that," she told me. "Don't get bitter. Just look at the bright side of life."

Most of the time, I did. But occasionally I felt a wall rise between me and the world. As Larry grew more successful, Aunt Peggy's efforts to fill my days with dance classes, piano lessons, school plays, summer camp, tutoring, playmates, and chores only seemed to isolate me more.

My sheer access to such broad experiences and opportunities set me apart from my friends and everyone else I knew in Atlantic City, including Peggy herself.

Adults would ask me what I wanted to be when I grew up, and I would answer a nurse, or a secretary, or maybe a teacher. But in fact I had already heard the call of my vocation: moving back and forth between worlds, eavesdropping on adult conversations; observing how speakers used body language, sometimes unwittingly, to communicate their true meaning; noticing how the same objects or behaviors, even people, were called by different names in different places.

For instance, Mom called the woman who helped her clean each week "the maid," but Aunt Peggy insisted that I refer to "the woman who comes occasionally to help us clean." In Aunt Peggy's house, we addressed and referred to that woman by her proper name, Mrs. Amos.

"All people older than you deserve respect," Aunt Peggy reminded me, "no matter what they do for a living." As I grew older, I came to realize that the living made by most black people older than I was had been so prescribed by race that they were owed that respect. It was payment for their endurance.

As a mature reporter, I would be drawn to the stories of those like Mrs. Calverta Amos. When I was a child, she taught me how to listen. Our friendship, which lasted well into my college years, was a long lesson in the art of the interview. Mrs. Amos did not give up information easily; I had to enter her world. Always, once there, I learned things about myself.

Mrs. Amos was born in Tuscaloosa, Alabama, but something had happened—what, she wouldn't say—when she turned thirteen, and she'd been forced to leave. Her vivid description of waving good-bye to her mother from the back of the train, never to see her again, may have been why I bonded to her—we had both experienced that sadness of leaving our mothers and going off into the world. Mrs. Amos made her way to Memphis, then to Philadelphia, and, after twenty-five years of cleaning other people's houses, to Atlantic City.

If she had survived, I knew I could, too.

Every other Thursday morning, I listened for the syncopated rhythm of her arrival. She suffered from arthritis in her right hip and so came up the stairs one at a time. Once she began work, however, she buried the discomfort by singing a medley of gospel songs and spirituals under her breath. As she breathed those songs, a sparkle entered her eyes and deep dimples formed on her smiling cheeks.

Once I tried to teach her "Whistle While You Work," from the Disney film *Snow White and the Seven Dwarfs.*

"Oh, I know better songs than that," she said, with such certainty that I asked her to teach me one. She taught me several: "How I Got Over," "Take a Closer Walk with Jesus," "His Eye Is on the Sparrow." These were not the staid hymns they sang at St. Augustine's Episcopal Church, where Aunt Peggy took me on Sundays. No, these were the rhythmic gospel songs I heard from the storefront AME church next door where the praise services ran late into the night on Wednesdays and Fridays.

One day Mrs. Amos was vacuuming the hunter green rug in the living room while I watched a movie. It was a Shirley Temple movie, one of my favorites, *The Little Colonel.* My mother had wanted me to be a child star, and I wanted to be Shirley Temple, a little girl who had agency among adults. I asked Mrs. Amos to stop vacuuming so that I could watch the section where Shirley Temple and "Bojangles" dance up and down the stairs.

She scowled. She didn't like to stop in the middle of her day.

"But it's for Shirley Temple!" I pleaded.

With a sigh she turned off the vacuum and sat down in the big armchair to watch it with me.

"Isn't she good?" I prompted.

"I don't know about her, but *he* sure can dance," she said.

I looked at the tall, elegant man who was indeed, now that I paid attention, teaching Shirley Temple the steps.

"Who's he?" I asked.

Mrs. Amos told me that his name was Bill Robinson.

"What a shame that the only way he could make his name is tapping with that little girl," Mrs. Amos said, clucking her tongue. "I never thought too much of *her*."

I reconsidered Mr. Bojangles. I wanted to like him, too, because Mrs. Amos did, but he was just a side player.

"He was a famous, famous dancer among the colored," was all Mrs. Amos said. "But they don't let colored star in movies." She said this in a matter-of-fact way, not in the roundabout way Aunt Peggy would have put it, and I appreciated her openness.

I turned back to the TV, looking at Shirley Temple with new eyes. It was the first time I'd discovered black culture through white references, but it wouldn't be the last. As I grew older, the rock group Blood, Sweat & Tears would lead me to Billie Holiday, Elvis Presley to Jesse Williams, and Chicago to Lightnin' Hopkins.

I would be a college sophomore before I realized how much black artistry formed the foundation of American culture. That morning, as Mrs. Amos resumed her vacuuming, I rose and began practicing, on my own staircase, the routine Shirley Temple and Bojangles Robinson had performed on the movie set. As I recalled the rhythmic patterns, I didn't know that my own father had made his living as a dancer; and I didn't understand how his career had been fettered by the same forces that gave Bill "Bojangles" Robinson recognition only when he danced with a six-year-old child.

I was eight years old and had just started piano lessons. Although I loved the instrument, I sometimes resented the rigor of practicing. For years, playing piano by ear, I had gone to the keys and picked out intervals. It sometimes seemed I could hear the music and see the keys all in the same instant. Now my piano teacher, Mr. Peck, wanted me to think in time signatures, keys, clefs, the correct notes. He didn't want me looking at the keyboard but at the written music; doing so made me feel disconnected from what I played.

Still, music and rhythm transported me. One day while I found myself lost in the music at hand, I vaguely heard Aunt Peggy call my name. I ignored her. The tune included the same notes as "Chopsticks," but at a slower tempo. Instead of flowing up the scale, the melody line resolved into a major second. Mr. Peck wanted me to practice it, working my staccato technique just so: without flopping my wrist, to bounce each finger off the keys so that the notes sounded abbreviated. I was absorbed in the physicality and the notes when Aunt Peggy called my name again.

I turned around.

"Uh, there's someone here to see you," Aunt Peggy said. I could tell by the awkwardness of her phrasing that something was amiss. A man stood just inside the door. He wore a brown-and-white striped sweater with short sleeves, and he smiled at me.

I rose from the piano stool and crossed the room.

"This is your father," Aunt Peggy said.

Father? My father?

I vaguely remembered meeting him in the garden at the Museum of Modern Art, but frankly, the Giacometti statues had had greater impact. What I knew about him was what my mother had told me: that he was no good, that he never contributed a dime to my upbringing, that he was a drunk who beat her and then left us with no money.

Unsure what to do, I shook his hand. It dwarfed mine.

"Nice to meet you," I mumbled.

"What kind of greeting is that?" Aunt Peggy prompted.

"Oh, it's okay," Jimmy said. "You don't remember me, do you?" he asked.

I shook my head no.

"Nice making your recognizance," he quipped.

A piece of my reserve chipped away. I smiled, uncertainly.

"You're learning the piano?" he asked.

"Yes," I said.

"Play me a little something," he urged, smiling.

I smiled back.

Aunt Peggy left us alone and, noiselessly, went into the kitchen.

Because I felt awkward and because the keyboard—despite my artistic shortcomings—was one of my hiding places, I gratefully turned my back and started my major scales. I went through C and G, and then I heard him ask, "Do you know any songs?"

"I'm learning the *Surprise* Symphony," I replied.

"Let's hear it," he said.

I started off gamely but stumbled my way through the end of the piece.

"Well, that was nice. But what can you *really* play?" he asked.

I couldn't *really* play anything. Embarrassed, I looked down at the piano keys.

"I know a song," he said, coming over to sit by me on the bench. The song was "Heart and Soul." He taught me the left hand while he played the right. We made a duet. He encouraged me to find the notes outside the melody.

Then we switched hands. I picked out the melody while Jimmy played the bass line.

"You've got a good ear!" he said.

"My teacher says I have to learn to play with my eyes, not my ears," I said, somewhat sadly.

"Nonsense! The best players all play by ear! Have you heard of Erroll Garner? He plays by ear. Can't read a note."

This was poppycock, my music teacher would respond later. Erroll Garner played popular music, while he was training me to play classical.

Jimmy and I played together for a while. Then, just when it

seemed that I might get to like the presence of this father person, he rose to go.

"Well, I better be getting along," he said.

"Are you coming back?" I asked.

"Oh, I think so," he said.

Peggy materialized from the kitchen. She and Jimmy exchanged some words while I practiced my new song on the piano.

"Good-bye, June," he said as he put on his jacket and left.

"Good-bye, Jimmy," I replied, a good deal more warmly than I had greeted him.

With that, he left, leaving me with the impression, which I carried far into young adulthood, that my father was a musician.

I never forgot how to play "Heart and Soul," but Jimmy never came to see me again.

6. THE BRECK GIRL

As an eight-year-old, what I admired most about Shirley Temple was her hair. I didn't want blond hair, but I coveted those long, bouncy curls. Instead I had hair like Miriam Makeba, the South African singer. My hair made me different. Different not only from Mommie but from my adopted family. Aunt Peggy's chignon formed satin waves as smooth as a flapper's at her temples. My Gregory "cousins" shared that soft, wavy hair, which, though inclined toward frizziness, hung straight down instead of sticking straight out.

My mother, at a loss for how to manage my hair, had always kept it cut short. In those days before girls wore Afros, that meant I was constantly mistaken for a boy. As I grew older, being a girl came to mean having pigtails like all the rest of my classmates.

As I leafed through Aunt Peggy's magazines—issues of *Life* from before I was born, a year's worth of *Woman's Day*—I focused on the ads, particularly the ads for Breck shampoo and conditioner. The Breck girls—pastel sketches of brunettes, blondes, auburn- and black-haired beauties—wore their strands styled in a shoulder-length pageboy that mocked my crew cut. The TV commercials were even worse: the camera, in slow motion, caught models who personifyed the magazine ads, their long hair flaring around their eyes like layers of silk petticoats.

"Be happy with the hair you've got," Aunt Peggy admonished. "Don't waste your time being jealous of what other people have."

But the Breck girls represented beauty and mainstream adulation, and as I grew older, it seemed to be my hair, more than my skin color, that defined me as a black woman; the crinkled curls spoke in the loudest terms possible: you are different, you are not pretty.

This obsession began before I could even read. One afternoon while Aunt Peggy napped, I crept downstairs and pulled her big black patent leather bag from where she stashed it behind the sofa. Reaching inside, I stole three or four dollars in change loose in its depths, then hightailed it down the street to the drugstore.

Inside, I scanned the boxes until I found those with the pastel drawings of the Breck girls with their swinging hair.

I took my purchase to the checkout counter.

The cashier was a black woman. She paused before ringing up my purchase. "You know this won't work on our hair," she said.

"What?" I asked, surprised that my purpose was so transparent.

"This is for white people's hair. It's for hair that's already straight."

"It's not for me. It's for a friend of mine," I said nonchalantly, refusing to concede.

She helped me count out my change, then put the box containing my dream hair into a brown paper bag.

Back home, I tore open the box and tried to make sense of the pictured directions. The pictures showed curler rods. I ignored that. I wanted straight hair, not more curls. I applied the lotion in the bottle the way my mother did the lotion to color her hair, brushing it back so that the perm could do its magical work. Then I tied on a scarf real tight, like I'd seen the neighborhood men with processed hair do.

I waited twenty minutes, then ran to the mirror and removed the scarf.

That perm hadn't done a thing.

As it became obvious that having a ponytail was the object of my existence, Mommie and Peggy discussed letting my hair grow. Mommie consented, reluctantly.

By second grade, my hair had reached two inches or so. One day, Aunt Peggy sat me down in one of the gray vinyl chairs next to her electric stove. Then she pulled out a thick black rubber comb with wide teeth. She began parting, oiling, and braiding, commanding me to hold down first this side, then that, as she combed through the curls. Like Lewis and Clark, we charted the terrain of my virgin hair, in a process that took two hours or more.

Although it was curly at the root, it grew kinkier and frizzier as it got longer. What's more, different textures covered different areas of my head. "Now, here at the front, it's frizzy and wavy," Aunt Peggy noted as she held the roots tight at the base with one hand and pulled the comb through the ends, working her way down. "But, oh, Lord, this interior is kinky as it wants to be. It's almost straight-out nappy."

She meant that the curl was "kinkiest," or tightest, at the crown, practically impossible, even with her wide-toothed comb, to get through.

"Now, you don't have a bad 'kitchen' at all," she commented as she braided thick plaits at the nape of my neck. "If your hair was like this all over, we wouldn't have any problem," she said.

"Ow! What's a 'kitchen'?" I asked as I pulled away from the comb, caught in a tangle.

"Sit up straight or I'll never finish," she said, parting the hair at my nape into more sections. "The 'kitchen' is the hair here on the back of your neck where it gets hot and sweaty. For most colored people, the kitchen is where it gets nappiest. But your hair back there is almost straight. You almost have good hair back here."

Once she finished parting and braiding my hair in seven or eight sections, she produced the straightening comb from the shoe box where she kept it, on the top closet shelf next to the curling iron. She brought a jar of Posner Bergamot from the medicine cabinet and prepared for the second step of my transformation.

Straightening combs terrified me. Once, when I was very little, a Negro baby-sitter my mother had hired determined to make me "presentable" and set about straightening my hair with a hot comb she heated in the flame of the gas stove. Hearing the sizzle as the iron comb hit the oil at the base of my scalp, I imagined that my skin itself was cooking like hamburger, and I screamed in terror. My mother returned in time to rescue me from this torture, but the hot comb seared my memory.

The comb Aunt Peggy had was also made of iron, its handle fashioned of steel concentric circles that led to the teeth. Spaced about an eighth of an inch apart, the teeth themselves were each a quarter inch thick. When heated on Aunt Peggy's electric stove and applied to hair polished with Posner Bergamot, the comb transformed unruly curls into hair shiny as a varnished floor and straight as a pine board.

But the sight of it made me cringe.

Turning the front burner of the electric stove to high, Aunt Peggy set an old folded face towel next to it. She placed the comb so that its iron teeth lay on the burner, its handle on the towel. Then she undid one braided section and parted off a very tiny piece, parking the rubber comb in the loose hair to hold it back. Opening the jar of Posner's, she put a glob on the back of her wrist.

When the straightening comb was hot, she picked it up and wiped it on the face towel. If the towel burned, that meant the comb was too hot. But if it only smoldered, then the comb was ready.

She took a bit of the Posner's and applied it to my newly sectioned hair. I felt heat at the nape of my neck and heard that sizzle that reminded me of meat in a pan.

Trembling, I pulled away.

"Hold still or I'll burn you!" Aunt Peggy warned.

She began again. I smelled my own hair frying and instinctively jumped away.

"I said hold still!"

I managed to sit while she did the "kitchen," but as she moved toward the more tender area near my crown, I cringed and tried once more to wriggle away, holding my right foot tensed in the air as the hot comb tore through tangles. I bent my head and neck to the left and then the right, crying more out of fear than pain.

"Sit still!" Aunt Peggy said. "Don't you want your hair to look long and pretty?"

Of course I did, but what good would pretty hair do me if my scalp was cooked?

After she finished the straightening, there was a third step. For this, Aunt Peggy heated a curling iron and prepared to section each part of my head again, this time to fashion me a head of curls. By now my hair was bone straight, so this part was painless, although there was always the risk of a burned ear or forehead if I moved too quickly.

Finally she finished.

Holding the towel around my shoulders, I ran to the mirror.

Although my scalp was sore, what I saw made me smile with delight. I had a headful of shiny, straight curls.

That weekend, back in New York, I performed "I Enjoy Being a Girl" from *Flower Drum Song* for my mother, tossing my head so that my new curls bounced. At the park I ran straight to the sandbox like a puppy returning to its lost home, delighted that my playmates, who were all little boys, could now see that I was not one of them. Before long I had covered myself with sand and ran under the spouting fountain to wash off. When I returned to my mother, sitting on the park bench, she looked at me and shook her head.

"Well, that's the end of your hair," she said resignedly.

Back in Atlantic City, Aunt Peggy was more demonstrative.

"YOUR HAIR! WHAT HAPPENED TO YOUR HAIR?!"

Thirty seconds in the fountain had drenched it, and it had "gone back" to its original frizzy state. For Aunt Peggy, who had spent three hours straightening and curling, this reversion was unacceptable.

I was not to go into the fountain—or any other water—again, she instructed, without a swimming cap, a shower cap, or something rubber or plastic that would protect my hair. "Water," she told me firmly, "will undo all your dreams of having a ponytail."

I resisted at first, because, by implication, I would no longer be able to swim—no swimming cap kept out all the water. But finally the desire to look like other girls beat out my love of water.

By third grade, my hair reached below my chin. But pressing and curling it took Aunt Peggy four hours every other week, with touchups on Saturday. It was a chore for both of us. She began shopping for a hairdresser.

Aunt Peggy told me that her reason for going down to Delaware

Avenue, over a mile away, when there were plenty of hairdressers nearby, was that she didn't want my hair looking greasy and stiff as a board. But when I went for my first appointment, I discovered she had other considerations.

"Now, don't go answering a lot of questions," she said as we drove. "Some hairdressers get all in your business, asking about where your mother is and why you live with me. Don't answer them. Just say your mother is away traveling, and so you live with your aunt. Don't get into your mother being white and Larry being in the movies and all that, you hear?"

The hairdresser said little when I walked in, just "how d'you do" and "Sit here," and so I sat in a big black leather chair while she wrapped tissue paper around my neck, then tied on a big rubber apron that covered me in the chair. I leaned back against the sink and waited for the worst.

But I was pleasantly surprised as she gently massaged my scalp with her fingers. "Mrs. Bush told me you were tender-headed," she said. "Does this hurt?" I shook my head no.

After the shampoo she massaged some warm olive oil into my hair, then put a rubber cap on my head that plugged into the wall. The cap looked like the kind Amish women wear, except that it was constructed out of two layers of rubber. If I put my hand up, I could feel the coils between them like an electric blanket. I sat, melting under the heat, while the hairdresser watched her soap operas.

I sat for twenty minutes; then she washed my hair again and began to blow it dry.

The dryer looked like a construction crane, except that it was made from gray metal instead of yellow. From its outstretched arm, a nozzle poured hot air down on my head. I gritted my teeth against the heat.

"Too hot?" she asked. "I can turn it down, but the more heat here, the easier the press and curl will be." After she finished straightening it, she asked, "So how do you want it?"

Without batting an eyelash, I answered, "Pulled back and in Shirley Temple curls."

By the time I was twelve, I had a headful of curls Shirley Temple herself might have envied. My mother thought it looked pretty but required too much upkeep. "Don't you get tired of sleeping in curlers every night?" she asked.

The thought had never even occurred to me.

7. REFLECTIONS

H er calls usually came at dinnertime. The black rotary telephone by the upholstered chair in the dining room would ring, and Aunt Peggy, Uncle Paul, and I would wait. One ring, a pause, then a call back—that was the signal.

I would run to the phone to pick up, and the operator's voice would begin, "Hello, this is the operator calling with a person-to-person phone call to Miss June Cross."

I'd been trained to answer this request with, "I'm afraid she's not here at the moment." That meant Mommie would hang up and call back without using the operator—a cheaper rate. If I really wasn't home, Aunt Peggy or Uncle Paul would reply that no one by that name lived there.

After her marriage the phone calls grew less frequent. They were replaced by postcards that arrived almost daily.

May 2   Greece

ΙΟΥΝΟΙΣ (OH-HEE-no-NEH: your name in Greek)

This is the island of Serifos where we were yesterday. This picture cannot begin to show this absolutely fantastic place! The town is built on the very top of the mountain, like people did centuries ago to protect themselves from pirates. You ride up by donkey over winding paths, cobblestones, marble slabs, and then the town is right on the side of the mountain! It looks like a scene from a biblical movie: you go in and out of caves, up rocks—climbing constantly! Sheer drops of thousands of feet! The village is about 200 people, no English spoken at all, no lights (they get up at dawn, go to bed at dark). Everyone rushed out and followed us until we left. It was the most moving experience Larry and I have had. We walked down the mountain—took us two hours!

Love—Ah-dee-o Mom and Larry

By the time my elementary school class began studying western civilization, I already knew about the Acropolis, the Roman Forums, the Temple of Apollo, the oracle at Delphi. Mommie and Larry had been there, had walked the steps of those ancient Greek sites, and Mommie had documented their journey with as many as four postcards a day.

She would remain a traveler all her life. If Aunt Peggy was a curator of class, my mother was its most ardent acquisitor. She had been born, literally, on the wrong side of the railroad tracks, near Blackfoot, Idaho, where her grandfather, a Danish immigrant, worked as a union foreman for the Union Pacific Railroad. Her mother, my Granny, gave birth to her on April 6, 1921.

Granny changed husbands the way other women changed hairstyles—she would have six of them by the time she died. She moved to Long Beach, California, when my mother was nine. There she ran a bookie operation out of her beauty shop. Mom ran the house and escaped to the movies every chance that she got. She loved Mary Pickford and Gloria Swanson, and she dreamed of an acting career.

The facts of my mother's life were tangled in my child's imagination and show-business hyperbole. I thought she was part Native American because in his nightclub act Larry made a joke about his wife being "part Blackfoot Indian, part Irish, and one hundred percent ready to kill me if I look at another woman." I thought she was the daughter of Mormon missionaries. I knew she had excelled as an athlete. She was a junior tennis champ, she said, and was a contender for the U.S. Olympic team in 1942. She swam a mile nearly every day of her life, and she had the long, lean physique of an athlete.

At eighteen she had given birth to my brother, Lary. She refused to let children stand in the way of her dreams; Lary was raised by Granny and in various foster homes while Mom went to acting school in Los Angeles. She wanted to act onstage, and she did, appearing in several productions at the Actors Studio in Los Angeles. That quest for stardom was what brought her to New York in 1950, where she met my father backstage at the Paramount Theater.

My mother was a lifelong student who sought perfection and demanded excellence from herself and those around her. She was extraordinarily glamorous, an extraordinary cook, extraordinarily well mannered, extraordinarily bright. Although she never graduated college, she read voraciously. Even as she neared eighty, word choice was important to her: when in doubt on proper usage, she would call the *New York Times*. She had in her study a framed letter from President Ronald Reagan, not because it was from the president but because it contained seven mistakes of grammar and syntax. She was astounded that the White House would permit such a thing.

She dressed simply, but for effect. She would never admit that she knew how to sew, yet she could judge the craftsmanship of a garment by the width and alignment of its seams. She knew how to distinguish a real Chanel suit from a knockoff and bargained down the price of Wedgwood china at Macy's. Rome was her favorite city, and she shared the passion of the Italians for life itself. She learned to wrap a gele the way women do in Senegal and charged fearlessly through the marketplace maze in Cairo. She claimed she must be a reincarnated Egyptian, because everything there felt familiar to her; she even ate food from the local street vendors without ever getting sick.

While she gallivanted around the world with her new husband, however, I was stuck in a classroom in Atlantic City, New Jersey.

As a student, I was erratic. One quarter I would be graded "excellent," the next quarter only "fair."

"You're not dumb," Aunt Peggy would sigh, exasperated at the appearance of yet another uneven report card. "If you would just concentrate more, you'd be a good student."

Concentration was difficult. Turmoil reigned, within and outside my family circle. It was 1964. President Kennedy had been assassinated the previous fall, Lyndon Johnson was now president, and it seemed as though a civil-rights bill, which the adults around us said would change our world, might finally be passed by Congress. If it passed, colored would be able to stay at the hotels on Pacific Avenue and even buy houses in Margate and Ventnor.

Fortunately, Mommie's postcards invigorated my desultory interest in education, much to Aunt Peggy's relief.

I was ten years old and in Mrs. Cotton's fourth-grade class at Indiana Avenue School.

Mrs. Cotton had graduated with Aunt Peggy in 1933 from the inaugural class at Miner Teachers College in Washington, D.C., the first four-year institution established to train black teachers. I doubt that they were friends there. Aunt Peggy was tall, thin, and fair-skinned, with wavy black hair ("good hair," they would have said in those days), while Mrs. Cotton's skin was darker than a coconut shell, her big, round frame crowned by tightly pressed black curls. Back in the twenties, when Negro strata were determined by "the brown paper bag" test, lighter-skinned Negroes were elevated to a higher social circle than those with darker skins.

But skin color had nothing to do with teaching skills. Mrs. Bush and Mrs. Cotton were both considered among the better teachers at Indiana Avenue School. They were strict disciplinarians but also creative teachers, who would throw out a lesson plan in a minute if a question from a child or the news of the day presented an opportunity for pedagogical improvisation.

Mrs. Cotton liked to eat. She taught us fractions by bringing in sweet-potato pies, which we divided up into halves, fourths, eighths, and sixteenths. A doughnut was a whole, its hole the definition of a

My mother always thought she was too skinny to be considered beautiful. This picture was taken in 1956, two years after I was born.

My father, James "Stump" Cross.

Aunt Peggy graduated from Miner Teacher's College in 1927.

Peggy and Paul on the boardwalk, shortly after they were married. Paul is wearing the Easter suit he took out a two-thousand-dollar loan to buy.

Aunt Peggy took this picture of the Gregory family. All the children considered her to be their godmother. (Back, left to right) Gene, Monty, Uncle Gum, Hugh; (front, left to right) Yvonne, Mignon, Aunt Hugh.

Peggy took the first picture of me and my mother in January 1954.

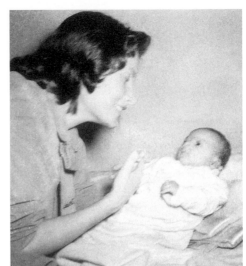

Jimmy, Norma, and Lary, in Peggy and Paul's yard, six months before my birth.

I was never happier than on a playground in Riverside Park—still one of my favorite places.

Peggy and me in her front yard, shortly after I moved to Atlantic City.

Paul and me on the same day.

Peggy took this portrait of Yvonne after she graduated from Howard University.

Mom and I celebrate my fifth birthday.
I had only one friend my age—my
godmother's grandson, Kirk.

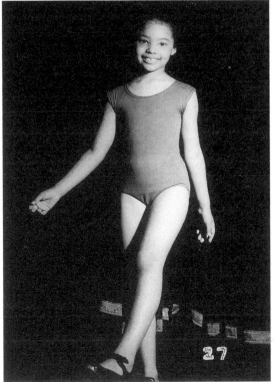

Performing in a tap dance recital
at the Jewish Community Center,
around the time I was eight.

My best friend, Regina, and me, when we were about twelve.

In Atlantic City with Peggy and Paul.

Lary and me in Aunt Peggy's living room.

Celebrating with Mom and Larry when he was a marshal in the Macy's Thanksgiving Day parade.

My confirmation portrait, age thirteen.

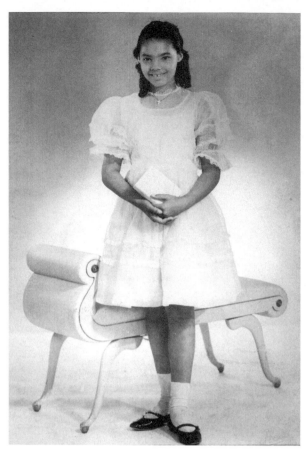

Playing with my pet schnauzer, Gigi. I named her after Leslie Caron's character in my favorite movie.

negative—where the doughnut was not. During social studies her dark, acorn-shaped eyes, which were framed by her black rectangular glasses, darted around the room as she sat at her oak desk holding a straightedge and snapped her wrist in the direction of the hapless soul chosen to answer her questions.

"Brett Johnson, when did the *Mayflower* land at Plymouth Rock?"

Somebody snickered. Brett was a favorite scapegoat that year.

"In 1620," Brett said.

Mrs. Cotton slammed the ruler down on the desk so hard the class jumped. Brett flinched like a dog waiting to be hit.

"How do we answer a question?" she asked.

"In full sentences," Brett answered, compounding his transgression.

Other hands shot up.

"Ooh, ooh, me, Mrs. Cotton! Me! Mrs. Cotton!" we cried in loud whispers.

But Mrs. Cotton wasn't letting Brett off the hook.

"HOW do we answer a question?" she demanded.

Brett looked at the floor, as though his shuffling feet might have the answer.

"*BRETT?*" she demanded more insistently.

"We answer a question in full sentences," he said at last, his voice full of resentment.

"Good. Now. When did the Pilgrims land at Plymouth Rock?"

"The Pilgrims landed at Plymouth Rock in 1620," Brett said. Five arms flopped down, and the class exhaled.

We had been getting drilled on the important dates in American history for weeks: 1492, 1620, 1776. We knew that the Pilgrims had left England seeking religious freedom, that they had landed on Plymouth Rock, that Miles Standish had made friends with the Indians, and that the Indians had helped the Pilgrims celebrate the first Thanksgiving. We had made butter out of curdled milk the way the Pilgrim women did; we'd even had a mock Thanksgiving in our classroom in advance of the holiday so that we could learn what kinds of foods Indians and Englishmen ate. (We decided we preferred real corn to corn pudding.) In the version of history in our textbooks, the Indians had gently given their land away or else sold it for pieces of shiny glass because they didn't know any better.

One morning we were talking about a Tarzan movie that had been on TV the night before. There were just three channels then, and on any given night only one showed anything of interest to fourth-graders. That Tarzan movie had captured our imagination, especially the part where Tarzan beat up the Africans and saved everybody at the end.

"I don't know what you-all laughing 'bout," Ralph Greene's son, Bobby, pointed out. "You African. Your peoples from Africa."

"I am *not* African. I'm *American*," I said. It was very important to me to be on the winning side in the Tarzan movie.

"Me neither," said Brett. "Africans swing on trees and eat people. Africans don't wear no clothes. They wear bones in their noses."

The giant slap of Mrs. Cotton's hands against the blotter of her oak desk made us jump.

"Africans do not swing on trees and eat people!" she sputtered. "This is something they are feeding you on TV. Everybody—sit down! Right now!"

We all dashed back to our seats, thinking that if anybody was in trouble, it was Brett.

"We are going to learn about Africa. Clear your desks. Everybody. NOW."

That meant we were all in trouble. We sat at attention—hands folded, feet pointed straight ahead.

Mrs. Cotton waddled toward her book closet and dug out a stack of timeworn books. They looked old enough to have come over on a ship from Africa. She didn't have a copy for everyone, so we shared.

The book was Carter G. Woodson's *Negro Makers of History*, and it had been published in 1928, five years before Aunt Peggy and Mrs. Cotton graduated from Miner Teachers College.

Mrs. Cotton spent a month teaching us Afro-American history instead of reading, writing, and arithmetic. She said learning who we were was just as important as learning how to count.

We learned that Africans lived in family groups, not in trees; had governments run by chiefs, like the Indians in the United States; and had not worn bones in their noses. We learned that African states, like Zanzibar and Tanganyika, had just declared their independence from European colonizers and joined the United Nations. We learned how to make a grass hut (the base was a circle, and the roof a cone).

We learned that in the wars between Africans, some had been taken prisoner and those prisoners had been sold into slavery in the United States, which explained how we all came to be sitting in Mrs. Cotton's fourth-grade class studying Africa instead of learning arithmetic and science.

I didn't see at the time how understanding this history would allow me to withstand assault from popular stereotypes or how coming to love my heritage would give me a pride of self that could be shaken yet never eliminated. But finally I understood how the slaves who had made up the spirituals Aunt Peggy sang to me at bedtime had come to be slaves. And I understood why the story of the Jews in Egypt had been so important to them—if God had freed the Jews, then one day he would free the colored in the United States.

In 1964 that day seemed to be at hand.

Dear Peggy
An interesting thing happened—if you can call it that!!!
the man who used to manage the liquor store next door
came down to the club where Larry works a couple of
weeks ago. Anyway, he sat with me . . . and told me that
when I first moved in here everybody in the block got up a
petition to have me move. It was started by the people in
this building, then posted in the liquor store and the drug
store for the people in the block to sign. So, they got
about a hundred signatures and presented it to my land-
lord . . . who tore it up!

Isn't that astounding? I was absolutely flabbergasted. I

thought everybody around here liked me and June—I couldn't have been more wrong. So now, of course, the drug store is off limits, as is the liquor store, and a few other people.

Also he said all the negro help around here (the garage attendants, the other man in the liquor store, the grocery delivery boy) were the ones who campaigned the most energetically to get me out. Now what do you make of that? Also he said all of them talked about how they were going to make me, etc., that I could be had. . . . Isn't that disgusting? It just made me sick. I came home and cried and cried. Larry about had a shit fit, he was so enraged. "Small minds! Small minds, Norma! Don't pay any attention to them!" Oh, he was livid!

It still gripes me. I sit and stew about it for an hour or so every day. Now, of course, I'm suspicious of everybody around here. There are only a few tradesmen I can accept wholeheartedly . . . the rest I've changed my entire attitude toward. Where I used to be friendly, chat with everybody, wave hello . . . now I smile to, and that's all. Boy, I tell you, it's not easy being a negro in a white neighborhood. For I'm a negro now, I told that to Larry the other night. I carry all the sensitivity within me, because of June—what she is, I am.

For Negroes the summer of 1964, when I was ten, was the summer of politics. "Politics" that July meant the debate over whether Lyndon Johnson shared John Kennedy's commitment to civil rights and whether he would prove it at the Democratic convention in Atlantic City that August. Colored folks in Mississippi wanted to be delegates at the Democratic National Convention, but the white Mississippi Democrats wouldn't let them.

Uncle Hugh and Uncle Paul thought that the Reverend Martin Luther King should lead a demonstration on the convention floor to make the point that the white Mississippi Democrats ran what amounted to an apartheid regime, but Aunt Peggy thought that kind of rabble-rousing would hurt King's reputation as a nonviolent leader—a conclusion Reverend King himself soon reached.

Election years were especially turbulent in our house. Aunt Peggy voted Republican. She was a Republican because her father had been a Republican. He had voted Republican because Abraham Lincoln had been a Republican, and Lincoln freed the slaves. Uncle Paul voted Democrat because Franklin Roosevelt, who created the New Deal, had been a Democrat.

In 1960, Aunt Peggy had supported Richard Nixon over Kennedy because she felt that Nixon had more experience. After President Kennedy was assassinated, she refused to support Lyndon Johnson. Instead she supported the liberal Republican Nelson Rockefeller. She said she didn't trust Lyndon Johnson as far as she could throw him. He was ruthless and would stoop to anything to get his way. She felt the same way about Bobby Kennedy, although she would change her mind about him after Reverend King's assassination.

Aunt Peggy used Nelson Rockefeller's presidential bid as an object lesson for me. Rockefeller, the governor of New York, had divorced his wife and married a divorcée, Margaretta Murphy—known as "Happy"—a year earlier. Happy, with her class and daring, reminded Aunt Peggy of my mother. I could see the resemblance, although I thought Mommie was prettier.

My mother managed Larry's career. She negotiated with his agents, lobbied for him to get parts, and pushed him when he was reticent to market himself. Peggy said that Mom's ability to do all this depended on her appearing to be "above reproach," as she put it.

Women didn't have the freedom to choose their own destinies in those days; a woman's reputation reflected on her husband, Aunt Peggy said. Aunt Peggy feared that Happy Murphy was going to prove to be Rockefeller's undoing.

Just weeks before the convention, Happy gave birth to a son. The child's arrival seemed to rub Rockefeller's transgression—of leaving his wife for another woman—in the faces of the conservative delegates of the GOP, political commentators said.

"That child will ruin his career," Aunt Peggy announced at dinner one night. And she was right. Arizona senator Barry Goldwater won the nomination overwhelmingly.

I was only ten, but I was struck by the impact of that child on the political order. If Happy's having a baby could destroy Rockefeller's chances for the presidency, I thought, what could my existence do to Larry Storch's career?

The following month the Democrats arrived in Atlantic City.

They occupied the town with signs. Delegates and their families from foreign states displaced locals on the main streets.

Uncle Paul came home and said he'd seen Martin Luther King riding in a rolling chair on the boardwalk. He knew the man pushing the chair, and he had gotten to shake King's hand.

"He's smaller in person than he looks on TV, but he's regular," Paul said.

"Regular" meant somebody who didn't put on a lot of airs and graces. In other words, Martin Luther King in person didn't act like he was the leader of the entire movement to free black people.

On TV the whites in the Mississippi delegation of the Democratic Party were full of themselves, trying to keep the members of the Mississippi Freedom Democratic Party, the colored Democrats from Mississippi, out of the convention.

Aunt Peggy watched the coverage on NBC's *Huntley-Brinkley Report*, sucking her teeth in disgust. Bull Connor, the leader of the Mississippi delegation, was getting away with racism, and Lyndon Johnson was doing nothing to stop him. She said Johnson was so chicken-livered he didn't even have the courage to show up. Instead he had gotten Hubert Humphrey, his vice presidential nominee, to do the dirty work of keeping the colored delegates off the floor.

From Santa Monica, where Larry was filming *Sex and the Single Girl*, Mom sent a postcard after watching Mississippi's lieutenant governor make a lame defense for the status quo:

August 1964   Santa Monica

Dear June
We're watching your city all day now—will you be on
television? Honestly, those delegates from Mississippi are
the most laughable—so ignorant! R. A. Collins leads the
list! He came apart on the stand! Did you watch it?

Love you—
Mom and Larry

On the fourth day of the convention, Aunt Peggy decided to go
down and watch it in person. She took me along.

"I shouldn't be doing this," Aunt Peggy said as we gathered our
sweaters.

"Why?" I asked.

"I don't know. It may end up confusing you."

Demonstrators marched opposite a bust of John Kennedy that
had been dedicated at the start of the convention, four days earlier.
They sang "We Shall Overcome" and "If I Had a Hammer." They
carried signs and marched in the center of an exhibit demonstrating
ways white folks in Mississippi had resisted implementing the Civil
Rights Act. Next to their circle, a charred cross lay on its side. Aunt
Peggy explained that the cross was burned by Ku Klux Klanners on
the lawns of colored folks they considered uppity.

"Why a cross?" I asked. I thought that the cross was a sign of
forgiveness.

"Well, I guess to remind people that if Jesus died on that cross,
you can, too," she said with a grim laugh.

Below the cross lay a blackened and cracked bell. The bell looked
like the Liberty bell, which I had seen in Philadelphia on a school trip.

Next to that stood the burned wreck of a blue Ford station
wagon.

"Those poor boys," she said, shaking her head. "To think of their
mothers and fathers waiting, not knowing what had happened to
them."

The bodies of James Chaney, Andrew Goodman, and Michael Schwerner, three civil-rights workers, had been found just a week earlier; I had read the coverage in *Life* magazine and thought how terrified they must have been as men carrying baseball bats and rifles surrounded their car in the dead of night. Its front windshield and headlights had been shattered. Its tires flattened, the doors dented. I wondered whether they had still been alive when the Klan members destroyed their car—or whether their terror had already ended.

Around me, on the boardwalk, delegates from the Mississippi Freedom Democratic Party carried signs pleading their case, singing "Ain't Gonna Let Nobody Turn Me 'Round." I recognized some of their faces—they were rooming at the Gem, the black-owned hotel near our house, because they weren't allowed to stay in the hotel rooms on the south side of Atlantic City, where the white delegates roomed.

If only you hadn't gotten darker, you could have lived with me, my mother had said.

That day I found the ground from which I would stand to view the world.

Larry and Mom moved from the apartment at 41 West Sixty-seventh to the Lincoln Towers development behind Lincoln Center. Their new apartment faced southwest on the twenty-second floor. It was beautifully sunny, with parquet floors and balconies overlooking the West Side Highway. From the balcony even New Jersey looked pretty.

Larry's change in fortunes had made the new apartment possible. In addition to his nightclub work, he had done two movies with Tony Curtis in 1964; filming of each one lasted about six weeks. But as it is for most entertainers, these spells of work were followed by periods of unemployment.

His downtime allowed me to go to New York and visit them. When I returned, Aunt Peggy peppered me with questions about their lifestyle.

I described how Mom did everything, from paying the bills to negotiating on Larry's behalf, even choosing his clothes. "What does he do all day?" Aunt Peggy asked. I told them that Larry brought Mom a cup of coffee every morning while she was in bed. It had enough cream to make it "exactly the color of Lena Horne."

Aunt Peggy wondered aloud whether my mother followed Larry into the bathroom to wipe his behind.

Whenever Larry got a new job, Mom treated herself to an expedition at Henri Bendel's. Mom loved to take me shopping, and I loved to go. I hated the Villager clothes Aunt Peggy chose for me—the style that today would be epitomized by Talbot's. That was her definition of classic. Mom's classic style was sexier, more flamboyant, and more fashionable. Although they reached consensus on nearly every part of my upbringing, when it came to my wardrobe Aunt Peggy and Mom disagreed; it seemed to be the only arena where Mom challenged Aunt Peggy's authority.

Shopping required dressing for the occasion—underwear nice enough to be seen, clothes that made disrobing easy, socks thin enough to try on shoes. Thus attired, we would bid Larry good-bye and walk south on West End Avenue toward Fifty-seventh street.

"Bendel's epitomizes service," Mom explained as we walked. "The counter girls are so attractive and sweet. This one girl always works with me on the dress floor. She'll have all the best suggestions for color and accessories. You'll be the best-dressed girl in Atlantic City."

We walked arm in arm—the cocoa-colored daughter and her mother with skin like bamboo. Passersby stared. Mom chattered away about the goodies to be found at Bendel's, seemingly oblivious to the looks we drew on the street.

I lived for these shopping trips. Mom and I would fan out across the floors like army scouts, loading our arms with every piece of clothing we saw that struck our fancy. Then we would disappear into the dressing rooms, mixing and matching, trying new accessories, leaving half a day later with several hundred dollars' worth of new clothes.

In the anonymity of the store, I got to call her "Mom" in public. That was the best part of all.

Shopping with my mother was different from shopping with Aunt Peggy. Clerks were instantly solicitous, instead of distantly gracious. Mom knew what she wanted and demanded service; Aunt Peggy chose quietly and carefully. One expected the world to help her; the other half expected to be turned away.

One day Mom and I reached the stately doors of Henri Bendel's at the same moment as an elderly white woman. Even after all these years, I remember her perfectly. She wore a black beret on her steel-blue hair, gold earrings, and a gold brooch with her black-and-white Chanel suit. Over it all she wore a brown mink stole. She was "old money," Aunt Peggy would have said, implying that she spent her money on jewelry and clothes, not on her face. It was deeply lined. Her eye shadow settled in the creases of her eyes. Bags had formed beneath her eyes; she had sagging jowls. She moved slowly and with great effort. Aunt Peggy had taught me to be respectful of elders, and so I paused and opened the door to let her in ahead of us. She entered without saying thank you, but then, Aunt Peggy had also taught me that bad manners were the prerogative of older people.

I was totally unprepared for my mother's reaction. She swept angrily from behind me and confronted me in the open door.

"Never let another person in front of you like that," she hissed.

"What?" I said, taken aback.

"You held the door open for that woman. Don't ever hold the door for anybody!"

I was puzzled by her vehemence. "But Aunt Peggy says I'm supposed to let older people go first," I ventured.

"Well, I don't care what Peggy says. I won't have you accepting second-class treatment."

I felt a tremor in my body, and as I rolled forward on my feet, I felt the aftershock in the pit of my stomach.

We had gone to Bendel's that day to look for a winter coat. Disturbed by the incident at the entrance, I couldn't choose one. My mother wanted something in one of the go-go styles then fashionable—bright colors, rectangular cuts, an above-the-knee length; Aunt Peggy wanted me to find something dark and classy, preferably in a princess style, something Jackie Kennedy would have worn.

My mother thought the princess style would make me look too staid. I agreed with her, but *she* didn't have to live with Aunt Peggy.

"All the girls in the magazines are wearing coats like this," she said, steering me toward a bright red cigarette coat.

Red was too loud for my taste. I knew Aunt Peggy wouldn't like the modified pea coat Mom chose, either. I liked a pencil-thin camel hair but didn't think Aunt Peggy would find it serviceable enough. We must have gone through every coat in the store that day. Finally I chose the safest thing I could find: a maroon car coat with a hood.

When I got back to Atlantic City, though, Aunt Peggy made me return it. "You needed a dress coat," she complained. "You could have gotten *that* style down here!"

She finally had Mrs. McKee make the style she had wanted in the first place: the princess coat with a Jackie Kennedy flavor, in taupe, with chocolate velvet trim around the sleeves and collar.

Mommie and Aunt Peggy both had such strong opinions about my clothes, hair, and personality that my own thoughts got lost in the turbulence.

"How do I know who to listen to?" I would ask Mrs. Amos.

"They both love you and want what's best for you," she would answer, "so you just have to listen to both of them, child, and try to decide for yourself when to do what."

"But how do I know what to do when?"

"You just do it by trial and error, and sooner or later you'll figure it out."

I trusted Mrs. Amos's judgment, but doubted I would ever figure it out.

8. PRESSURE POINTS

Larry Storch wanted to be considered for a starring role. But in the Hollywood of 1964, his face—a face of uncertain ethnicity—limited his career. Hollywood casting agents said Larry didn't look "American" enough for a leading role in a TV series. He looked "too Chinese."

Larry had surgery to get rid of the Mongolian fold over his eyes, which gave him that Chinese look. He hoped that by doing so he might break the glass ceiling that relegated him to cartoon voices and character roles. Afterward he looked more like his Polish father than his Kazakhstani mother. And sure enough, his auditions doubled.

> *Grauman's Chinese Theater   November 5, 1964*
> *Dear June—Are you in the school band yet, Larry wants to know?*
> *He's testing for a pilot today—may have a weekly series next season! A cowboy and Indian type thing—keep your fingers crossed!*
>
> *Love—Mom & Larry*

In February 1965, the black rotary phone rang. Picking up, I heard long-distance static.

"It's Mum!" I called out, even before saying hello. I had taken to calling Mom that since the Beatles invasion. I had just turned eleven. Surely there must be some emergency for her to call without using the coded phone signals. Aunt Peggy came running from the kitchen; her hand, hastily rinsed, smelling of onion and bread crumbs, grabbed the phone. I stood next to her listening to Mom's voice through the receiver.

"Larry's got the series!" I heard her say.

A TV series! Aunt Peggy chatted awhile, then gave me back the phone. I felt as excited as my mother. "So what's the TV series about?"

"It's a comedy with cowboys and Indians—called F Troop. But instead of fighting Indians, they make alliances with the Indians to sell moonshine. Larry's got second billing with Forrest Tucker—do you know him?"

"No."

"Joo-oon," she said, in the exasperated tone she used when I didn't recognize some showbiz tidbit, "he's a big star! He's like John Wayne, only funnier. And Larry's got second billing! Second billing! Isn't that great?"

"That is great," I replied.

By the time I hung up, dinner was ready.

"We'll see if it lasts," Peggy said as she served the plates. "It could all fall through tomorrow. You know how show business is: when you're up, you're up, and when you're not, you're not."

This was Peggy's first and final word about show business. She recited it as if giving thanks not to be in such a fickle enterprise.

Paul just grunted.

F Troop premiered in September 1965, with Larry playing the zany Corporal Agarn. "F Troop" meant "fucked up," and the Indian tribe, the Hakawi, was named after the punch line to an old joke that ended, "Where the heck are we?" The show was anachronistic in its stereotypical depiction of Indians, its doting females—but the white male characters were just as ridiculous: dumb, dumber, and sly.

After its third week on the air, bursting with a secret I could no longer keep, I announced to my fifth-grade class that my stepfather was on TV.

None of them believed me.

For over a year, Aunt Peggy, Uncle Paul, and I had been following the saga of Mom and Larry's house search through their postcards. Mom wanted a house with a story, a history of importance. They looked at one that Mary Pickford had lived in, one whose owner once designed costumes at 20th Century Fox, one with a high gate that reminded Mom of *Sunset Boulevard*.

They finally settled on a place Mom called a Bird (bringing to mind a cockatoo in a cage, although it really was named after an architect named Bird). In a phone call Mom told me the new house had a pool in back with a windmill, and a patio that looked down on North Hollywood. Larry added, with a sense of wonder in his voice, that on a clear day they could see the ocean, on a really clear day Malibu, and little white dots of sailboats. Up the road Stevie Wonder owned a house, although they hadn't seen him yet. At dawn and at dusk, deer came to feed on the apple tree by the carport. At night they heard coyotes howl.

Mom reported that she had killed a rattlesnake—then five—then twelve—right there in the driveway during their first three months. Larry joked that he'd cut a notch in her apron string for each one.

They were living a life of Hollywood dreams: expensive car, big house, designer clothes, paparazzi following them down the street. Meanwhile, in Alabama and Mississippi, black demonstrators trying to register to vote were set upon by police dogs and mowed down by hoses and horses. I watched them—on the brand-new color TV Larry had paid for—with a sense of increasing discomfort. I felt helpless to resolve the contradiction; all I could do was learn to live with it.

In South Central L.A., just down the mountain from my mother's new house, other black Americans watched the images of civil-rights demonstrators, including children, being tossed around like beach balls by the force of fire hoses.

The pressure of their anger would soon reach volcanic force.

I visited my mother's new home for the first time in August 1965. I would spend a month in Los Angeles every summer thereafter, until I graduated from high school.

L.A. looked just like it did on TV: palm trees, blue sky, wide boulevards, manicured lawns, convertibles, and enough pretty houses for Aunt Peggy to imagine spending several lifetimes in.

Mom and Larry's new house was small by Hollywood standards. It was a bungalow covered by brick and cedar shingles, and it had a kitchen and dining area bordered by west-facing bay windows. These yielded to the living area, a bar, and a bedroom that opened onto a modest, guitar-shaped pool. It overlooked the area now known as Beverly Center.

The room I would stay in faced the driveway and the ridge where deer appeared each morning.

"It's the Moroccan room," my mother announced gaily as she led me to the southeastern corner of her new house, nestled in a crag of Nichols Canyon. Mom and Larry had named their Hollywood retreat Dittendorf. They were the duke and duchess. Larry dubbed me the countess.

The Countess of Dittendorf had a room worthy of Scheherazade. Tucked under a sloping roof anchored by a small, round fireplace, my hideaway was not much bigger than my room in Atlantic City— but oh, what a room! One whole wall was mirrored. It reflected the Indian-print bedspread and the matching wallpaper. The colors in the print augured seasonings I had yet to become familiar with: mustard seed, turmeric, green curry. On the wall, candles cast patterned shadows from metal sconces Mom had bought in Marrakesh. A huge waterpipe sat in the small fireplace like a trophy. I imagined lying on the Hollywood bed wearing layers of chiffon, kohl ringing my eyes, gold jewelry dangling from my ears, as I regaled my court with stories.

Aunt Peggy never would have condoned such a room for a little girl, filled as it was with the danger of fire and the hint of debauchery. Not one of my friends, thought the Countess of Dittendorf as she sank into a pile of pillows, could retreat to such a room.

My days were filled with leisurely rituals. At dawn and at dusk,

Larry fed the deer, beckoning them with a whistle and call he had invented. Only he could approach them; Mom and I crouched behind the bamboo shades of the kitchen and watched as they ate their apples, purchased in large bags from the supermarket. In the morning Larry and Mom used the sauna and swam laps in the pool while I drank my orange juice. After they finished, I stretched out on the bed, talking with Mom while she drank her coffee, and then I took my turn in the pool. Larry practiced the saxophone while Mom sunned herself lying in an inversion chair. We had a snack of fruit and yogurt. Then Mom and I went shopping at the Farmers Market.

Ten days after I arrived in Los Angeles in August 1965, police stopped a black motorist in Watts, tried to arrest him, and ignited a riot. Sitting in my mother's living room, watching the riots on TV, I had only to look west, through the sliding glass door, to see smoke rising from the valley below.

Just a year earlier, in Selma, Alabama, television newsmen had been on the front lines with the demonstrators, but now their cameras stayed behind police barricades. From this safety zone, their zoom lenses recorded shaky images of looters chanting "Burn, baby, burn!"

My mother came and stood behind me, watching the explosions of fire that followed Molotov cocktails flying through the store windows that lined 103rd Street in Watts.

"What do they want?" she asked. It was the question of the day, being asked by whites all over America, and even some Negroes. "Why are they burning down their own neighborhood?"

A lifetime of forging relationships with people who weren't my blood relatives, of being with my mother only when she chose, of absorbing the perils of revealing our relationship, informed my answer. "They're angry," I said soberly, "because they're tired of being not wanted by whites. They're stuck in the ghetto because whites won't let us live anywhere else. You don't want us around."

I was only eleven years old. Adults had invented this system. How could she not understand why we were angry?

She fixed me with a long stare, then turned and looked out the window toward the tornado of smoke rising from Watts. High up in the Hollywood Hills, we gazed out the sliding glass doors that lined the patio. I was nearly as tall as she. We stood with our arms around each other's waist—white and black, mother and daughter, observing the smoldering city below.

Three or four nights later, I dreamed for the first time what would become a recurrent dream, that the rioters had moved out of Watts and burned a swath down Wilshire Boulevard and up Fairfax. Nichols Canyon went up in a dry heat, the flames springing from rooftop to rooftop, heralds of a new day. By the time the crowd was nearing my mother's house, the shingled roof was already aflame, the pine timbers showering sparks on the pool deck. Mom and Larry jumped into the pool, as Larry had always said we should if a fire ever got out of control in the canyon. I stayed put, watering down the walls with a hose. Larry called out, "Forget it! Forget the house! Get in the pool!" Instead I went out to the front driveway to wait for the mob. They wore camouflage T-shirts with scuffed jeans, jeans torn at the knees, T-shirts faded and stretched out of shape by too many washings. Their faces were dark and angry, like the faces of people beaten down, coming back for revenge. They carried baseball bats and Coca-Cola bottles stuffed with gasoline-soaked rags, cocktails for the nouveau riche. Their brown skins gleamed in the sunlight as they worked their way to the back of the house where I stood. Confused to see me, they stopped.

"Whatchu doin here?" one of the men at the front demanded to know.

"She's my mother! And he's my stepfather!" I pleaded, as if to say, "These are good white people. Save them!"

"Well, you got to choose!" another brother yelled. "Them or us?"

What I actually did the first time I had the dream, I no longer remember. I've had versions of it where the world closed in on us when I joined Mom and Larry in the pool and held on to them as we braced for the mob's attack. I've had versions of it where I walked away with the mob, possibly in exchange for the lives of those in the pool. What stays with me is the sense of panic, an anxiety that I can only fleetingly capture with words: the feeling that the well-being of the house, of everything I have and everything that my mother and stepfather have worked for, depends on what I say, what choice I make, and whether or not I can convince the rioters to believe me.

When I returned to Atlantic City that September, it seemed the twin tidal waves of the race riots and the black-power movement had left Negroes everywhere adrift. Things long unspoken became celebrated, while others, like minstrelsy and vaudeville, were shoved into the closet. Spirituals became the backdrop for a dance by Alvin Ailey; gospel merged with R&B; everywhere, blacks—for we were, finally, black and proud of it—celebrated the creative conjugation of the verb "to be," the loudness of our laugh, the smell of greens cooking with a slab of fatback; hot pants even celebrated the high curve of our behinds. *Ebony* magazine, the bellwether of the black middle class, published pictures of Joanna LaSane, a model originally from Atlantic City, wearing her cropped hair natural, the way I had when I first moved there, the way women still did in Africa.

LaSane's cover Afro was a seismic event. One of the Gregory cousins, Robin, became the first Howard University homecoming queen to sport an Afro. My old friend Regina sent me a picture of herself, freed from her thick braids, wearing her hair in an eight-inch halo framing her face. It was the most beautiful Afro I'd ever seen. I began to let go of my attachment to the Breck girls.

Regina's mother, Yvette, had remarried and left Atlantic City for Vineland, about a forty-minute drive west. Her new husband, Jim Richardson, an anesthesiologist, had adopted Regina.

"Is Larry going to adopt me?" I asked Aunt Peggy.

"Do you want to be adopted?" she asked, testing me.

I considered my response. Secretly, I seethed that Regina had a father while I lived in limbo, but if I answered yes, would I have to leave all my friends and go live in Hollywood?

"Not really," I answered.

The Richardsons sponsored an art show featuring the work of black artist Robert Threadgill. Such an affair would have been unthinkable just two years earlier; now Threadgill, whose style glorified the folk art of ordinary people, was the latest "new thing."

Aunt Peggy, Uncle Paul, and I drove out for the weekend. Peggy was excited. Such events rarely occurred in Atlantic City; despite the national fascination with black arts, there was no regular outlet for the black intelligentsia in the city. She missed Yvette. I was excited because I would get to see Regina. Paul, however, grumbled all the way at the prospect of having to spend his Sunday afternoon in a suit with a bunch of highfalutin Negroes. He would rather have been fishing.

My black classmates in Atlantic City joked that getting caught in Vineland after dark was like getting caught in Klan country. Vineland was considered the backwoods. Most of its residents ran small family farms, growing vegetables or raising dairy cows. Dr. Richardson was the first black hired at his hospital, and his family was the first well-to-do black family to move into that area.

I had never seen Klan country, and as we drove, I was encouraged to find it filled with green pine trees, and yellow spruce, white birch, and red maple changing their leaves for fall.

Vineland had changed my friend Regina. She was listening to Herman's Hermits, the Animals, and Blood, Sweat & Tears, while I cultivated a taste for groups like Smokey Robinson and the Miracles, the Four Tops, and the Temptations.

We both liked the Beatles, though. I liked Paul. She liked John.

"Don't you like any Motown groups?" I asked her.

"No. I don't like Negroes," she answered.

"What?" I looked at her as if she had grown horns.

"All the Negro kids at school beat me up," she said.

In Klan country?

"They do?" I asked incredulously. For me, the all-black community where we lived in Atlantic City had become a haven; still, it was a truism of the black-power movement that in the rush to embrace all things black, anything "white" was rejected, as if American culture itself could be segregated from the black roots that lay at its foundation.

"Besides," she went on, "I'm not Negro. I'm colored. My Mom is a Negro. And people like my Uncle Fred, they're black."

"Why do the other black kids beat you up?" I asked, too astonished that my friend was being beaten by black students at a mostly white school to question her reinterpretation of her racial identity.

"They say I hang out too much with the white kids, that I'm uppity. But too bad for them. My mother says I shouldn't pay any attention to them, so I don't let them bother me. They're just jealous because my dad is a doctor."

Regina's black classmates, the sons and daughters of laborers and farmworkers, bullied her so much in school that her family finally moved from Vineland to the New York suburb of New Rochelle. I was glad I lived in Atlantic City, where there were enough well-off black families so that having eclectic tastes wasn't such a big deal.

We went into the living room, where the adults—mostly white, some black—stood around drinking wine from expensive glasses. Threadgill's paintings, perched atop the sofa, leaning against the walls, formed a perimeter around the room.

Aunt Peggy bought one of his oil paintings that day, an impressionistic profile of a black field worker, a rag tied around her hair. Her image emerged in relief from a background of brown and rusty orange. Around the lower edges of her collar, dabs of red paint trailed down like threads of blood and tears. But the dignified carriage of her head—that was the point. Something about her reminded me of Mrs. Amos.

Back home I would stare at that painting while I practiced particularly difficult piano passages and wonder what the woman in the picture had found difficult to get right. She looked to be in her thirties, but the shaded layers suggested that she had seen rivers. Sitting there practicing my scales, I wondered what kind of slave I would have been, uneducated, working with my hands dawn until night, being forced to lie down for the master's son. I don't think I would have made it. At least that's what I'd like to think. I'd like to think I'd be one of those who ran away—or died trying.

But another, more pragmatic side—call it my mother's side—warned me not to be so quick to rise up and say I'd be dead and in my grave before I'd be enslaved. Maybe I'd just find the courage to do what I had to do to survive, even if it meant lying with the master's son in order to eat and feed my own children.

I thought about all these things as I stared at the woman's profile and practiced.

For all I know, that's why Aunt Peggy had bought the daggone thing in the first place.

During the year I was in sixth grade, I would walk into the living room and hear Aunt Peggy, on the phone, drop her voice. I knew then she was talking to my mother. I never understood how they arrived at decisions exactly, but they had been spending a lot of time in top-secret discussions lately. Aunt Peggy was worried by my uneven schoolwork.

Mom responded first by writing to me. One letter went:

> I was so pleased with your report card! _Just terrific!_ We are very proud of you! . . . Remember now, speak slowly and distinctly. I think your handwriting is very good— I challenge that D there! And _arithmetic???_ WHAT'S 2 AND 2?

When her written encouragement didn't work, Peggy got back on the phone.

"She seems distracted," I heard her tell my mother one day. "I think we should consider private school."

Aunt Peggy had another consideration about Central Junior High, the public school, which I didn't understand at the time.

It had been eleven years since the Supreme Court had declared that public schools in America should be integrated "with all deliberate speed." Yet the local board of education was even then embroiled in backroom discussions over whether it would agree to integrate the curriculum as well as the classrooms. A group of colored teachers had developed a plan, based on Carter G. Woodson's scholarship, which would integrate Negro history and literature in the high-school lesson plans.

It was roundly defeated by the majority-white board, which simply refused to accept claims of Negro contributions to science and literature as credible.

My class, which finished sixth grade in 1965, would be integrated at Central Junior High School. Seeing what Regina was enduring, Aunt Peggy worried that, given the political climate and the racial tensions that were bound to occur as black and white teenagers encountered one another, my schoolwork might suffer even more.

I don't know how well my mother understood these pressures. She was interested in private school for a different reason. She told Aunt Peggy I was beginning to "sound black." When I asked Aunt Peggy what that meant, she told me that I wasn't talking "slowly and distinctly," that I dropped the endings to my words, slurred words together, talked too fast. This came from not concentrating as I spoke, Aunt Peggy said. She corrected my grammar more often and worked with me to ar-tic-u-late better.

Uncle Paul suggested sending me to Holy Spirit, the local Catholic school, but I engaged my mother's help in quashing this notion; I protested the hourlong commute, while my mother opposed the whole idea of Catholic school, where, she feared, I'd get screwed-up notions about sex. So Aunt Peggy selected a Quaker school, Friends, about a mile away and, just as important, in the opposite direction from the junior high the rest of my friends would be attending.

Aunt Peggy sought to shelter me from racial conflict at Central Junior High School. Instead, I got caught up in being the only black girl in my class at Friends.

Friends had small classes; there were only fourteen students in the entire seventh grade. A construction contractor's son and I turned out to be the only two African-Americans.

On the first day of school, our English teacher, Teacher Pat (we called all our teachers by their first names because Quakers disdain formal titles) told us to rearrange our chairs—colorful plastic seats with writing desks attached—into a circle. I was at one end of the diameter, hidden next to the door, while the contractor's son sat opposite me, closest to the window. We avoided eye contact. Maybe this is how all seventh-graders begin the first day of their school year: diffident, preferring anonymity to ridicule. That's probably why Teacher Pat had arranged us this way in the first place.

She asked us to take turns sharing our heroes or heroines.

Having completed a Negro-history scrapbook for Mrs. Cuff's sixth-grade class the year before, I knew exactly who my heroine was: Mary McLeod Bethune, a personal friend of Eleanor Roosevelt's, who had used her friendship with the first lady to pursue an agenda for higher education for Negroes. Bethune founded an eponymous college in Daytona, Florida, then started a series of girls' schools throughout the South.

The circle named the usual suspects: Marie Curie's name echoed among the girls; John Kennedy and John Glenn resonated among the boys.

In the face of their unanimity, my anxiety increased and my heart beat faster. It tripped my tongue. When the circle came to me, I mumbled, faster than I had intended, "Mary McLeod Bethune."

"Who?" Teacher Pat exclaimed, along with the rest of the class. Their reaction pushed me down in my seat. I looked directly at Teacher Pat. She seemed old enough to have read about Mrs. Bethune in the newspapers.

"Mary McLeod Bethune," I said, a little louder. "She was a Negro educator and—"

"Oh," Teacher Pat said. She turned her head away from me and looked to the next person.

"Okay. Next."

I wanted to tell them that Mrs. Bethune had been educated to be a missionary but had been barred from going to Africa because Presbyterians didn't allow Negro missionaries in the continent; and that Mrs. Bethune had gone on to found three different institutions of higher learning; that she had become Eleanor Roosevelt's good friend and wielded enough influence to make sure that blacks got in on the New Deal; but I never got a chance to say any of that, and it didn't seem that any of my classmates—or Teacher Pat, for that matter—cared.

I resolved not to speak another word in that class. I missed the worn full desks with a space to hide a book of fairy tales, and the wooden chairs with initials carved into them at Indiana Avenue School. I missed my teachers who cared about Mary McLeod Bethune and Marcus Garvey and Benjamin O. Davis. I missed the earthy, ebony smell of my classmates, the scent of Dixie Peach and Posner Bergamot in their hair, their loud, low timbres and staccato speaking rhythms. The people at this new school spoke in modulated tones. They even smelled different: more acrid, foreign.

The first quarter my only "A" came in gym, with the note that "June's natural athletic ability holds her in good stead with her peers." I laughed out loud. At all-black Indiana a year earlier, I had flunked physical education! Aunt Peggy tried to argue that I might have grown more coordinated with the passage of a year, but I knew better. The idea that blacks were somehow "naturally athletic" was one of the oldest stereotypes in the book.

I did speak up in class despite my resolve not to, of course, and eventually Teacher Pat, who had dismissed Mary McLeod Bethune, became one of my favorite teachers. She was the first teacher to encourage me to write. Every day, she read aloud to our class one chapter of Charles Dickens's *Oliver Twist*. Teacher Pat engaged me in the art of storytelling.

I wanted to write a serialized novel, as Dickens had, that appeared in a newspaper every day. But when Teacher Pat described how Dickens had written by candlelight in an unheated attic, wearing cutoff wool gloves to keep his fingers from freezing, my enthusiasm dampened. I didn't want to be a writer so badly that I was willing to starve.

Then, sometime during that fall semester, a *Philadelphia Inquirer* reporter visited the school. As he described his job, I was immediately drawn to the idea of someone's paying me to travel, and having permission to ask questions of strangers and expecting answers. I liked the idea of getting paid to write—and not suffering from frost-bite in an attic while I waited to get paid. From then on, when any-one asked, I said I wanted to work for a newspaper and be a reporter. That summer I attended a journalism program at Glassboro State College. Aunt Peggy said I was still young and likely to change my mind, but I said no, I wouldn't—and I didn't.

While I came to adore Teacher Pat, Teacher Helen, who taught math and social studies, became the bane of my existence. She coun-tenanced neither tardiness nor tomfoolery and, when she noticed one or the other, pierced the offender with a glare of her blue eyes over the tops of her taupe plastic bifocals. Her eyes matched her steel-blue short hair, worn in a crown of curls. She completed her military bearing with slim, fitted skirts hemmed to midcalf and wore plain or ruffled white blouses.

Since second grade, when I had gotten sick during the week that the rest of the class learned subtraction, I had cultivated a fear of math. During one of their first parent-teacher conferences, Teacher Helen told Aunt Peggy that I was "ill-prepared" in this area.

Aunt Peggy came as close to snorting as I ever heard her. "Pffft," she said. "The teachers in math and science at Indiana were so good that students used to be automatically admitted to sophomore level when they got to the high school."

She didn't know that I had spent most of those math and science classes at Indiana surreptitiously reading fairy-tale books. That was why those report cards were so uneven.

Early in our first quarter, Teacher Helen assigned a report about a product manufactured in the United States. I chose carpets. I looked up carpets in my *World Book Encyclopedia* (which Larry Storch had received for making an appearance on *Hollywood Squares*) and clipped magazine ads from the Sunday *Times*. I interviewed the salesmen at the local carpet store on Atlantic Avenue. They ex-plained the different kinds of naps and backing; described the differ-ence between machine-tooled and handmade; showed me quilted,

Persian, and broadloom rugs made in Pennsylvania, just two hours from Atlantic City. I stayed up all night writing the thing and pasted samples of each kind of carpet in my report.

A week later Teacher Helen asked me to stay after school.

As I walked into the classroom, I saw my report on her desk. I swelled with the anticipation of high praise for my outstanding work.

She peered over the edge of her bifocals. "Who wrote your report?" she asked.

My lips parted, but words left my brain. I felt the air whistle through the gap in my front teeth. The roof of my mouth went dry. My stomach clutched.

Who did she think had written it, my dog?

I assured her I had stayed up all night, while in my mind I pasted together probability scenarios. Had I put it together too hastily? Included misspelled words? Sloppy handwriting? Too many scratch-outs?

"Well, who helped you?" she demanded.

Nobody, I said—which was true. I hadn't even shown it to Aunt Peggy.

"Well, when you copy something from someone else, you should say so in the body of your work."

Slowly, I began to realize that she thought I had stolen my words from someone else. "I didn't copy it."

"Where did you get your information?"

I told her I had done it just the way she herself had taught us. I had read the *World Book Encyclopedia* and the *New York Times* ads, then talked to the salesmen at the carpet store; then I had written it all down on note cards and put it in my own sentences.

I could see from her face she didn't believe me. She handed me my report back.

"Needs more original work," she had written on the back in red, along with my grade, a C-minus.

Dejected, I went home and showed Aunt Peggy the paper and explained what had happened.

"I didn't copy it!" I said. To prove it, I retrieved the *World Book* and showed her the pages.

Aunt Peggy didn't think I had copied it either.

She called Teacher Helen and talked to her. Then I tucked my *World Book* under my arm, and we both went in. Teacher Helen asked to see my note cards. Then she asked to see the encyclopedia I'd used as my primary source. She remained adamant that I hadn't changed the language of the *World Book* enough, although she upgraded the paper to a C.

Aunt Peggy told me later that Teacher Helen was expecting too high a level of work from a seventh-grader, and she suspected the reason.

"You're going to meet people like this in life," Aunt Peggy said one evening as we stopped at the White Castle to get a hamburger. "Just do the best you can do and let their criticisms roll off you like so much water off a duck. Don't let it stop you."

She said this with an extra level of meaning in her voice, and even her errant eye seemed focused on me. I understood from her tone that she was giving me a lesson about more than homework.

Go along to get along. Work hard. Be an A student. Blend in. Be cultured, be smart, be witty. Do the race proud.

Aunt Peggy had always told me that because I was colored, I would have to be twice as good to go half as far as whites.

She hadn't told me that some whites would never believe I could be that good.

By the end of *F Troop*'s first season in 1966, Larry had become a public figure. His movie credits included *Sex and the Single Girl* with Natalie Wood and Tony Curtis, *Captain Newman, M.D.* with Gregory Peck, and *The Great Race* with Natalie Wood and Jack Lemmon. Now when I visited them in New York, we went to the best restaurants. The maître d's greeted us with a flourish.

At one steak house, our table turned out to be a booth big enough to seat six, with real leather-upholstered seats instead of the vinyl most restaurants in Atlantic City used. The leather seats embraced a huge round table made of wood, not linoleum.

The maître d' brought a bottle of the best red wine for Mom and Larry and poured me a bottomless glass of iced tea.

"Now J.B., order whatever you want, don't worry about price," Larry assured me.

I felt glad and proud—that is, until a veritable flood of people from places I'd never heard of before began approaching our table, seeking an autograph for their kid or their neighbor and a conversation with Larry. Gracious and polite to everyone as he is, Larry talked with each person, signed autographs, and included a personal note for little Danny or Aunt Sue or Cousin Joe back in Iowa City, Aberdeen, or Duluth. Gradually, Mom and I learned to have our own conversation on the side and leave Larry to the fans.

I ordered steak au poivre, which was served rare. That was the first time I'd had rare steak. I could practically cut it with a fork. Aunt Peggy and Uncle Paul cooked their steak until I had to saw through it with a steak knife.

I wanted to share that meal with Aunt Peggy and Uncle Paul. Mom and I went to Librarie de France on Fifth Avenue and bought a French cookbook so that I could replicate the dish in Atlantic City. Steak au poivre would be the first meal I ever cooked.

Aunt Peggy and I journeyed to the gourmet supermarket in Margate to get the ingredients, including olive oil and red wine vinegar to make salad dressing.

"Isn't Kraft's good enough?" she asked. She was skeptical of these alien ingredients invading her kitchen—whole peppercorns, romaine lettuce, French bread.

As I pressed the peppercorns into the raw meat, I caught Paul and Peggy looking at each other over my head.

"I never heard of putting whole pepper on steak," Peggy said.

"Me neither," Paul agreed.

I showed them the recipe to prove I was on the right track.

Placing the steak in our electric oven, I cooked it eight minutes on one side, eight on the other.

"That meat isn't done!" Peggy cried. They cut into the meat with the temerity I usually brought to Peggy's pan-fried liver. Paul put his piece back into the oven to cook some more, added some Worcester-shire sauce, then declared it was the best steak he had ever eaten.

When, during that summer of 1966, we planned my annual trip to California, Aunt Peggy began searching for a New York beauti-cian who could give me a perm to straighten my hair. Aunt Sylvia observed that my hair texture was similar to many Domincans'—both frizzy and "soft"—so she found a beauty salon in the Bronx.

"Dominicans are good with 'mixed' hair," she assured us.

It was a sojourn. The salon didn't accept appointments, so we took the 5:00 A.M. local bus from Atlantic City to New York's Port Authority bus terminal, then traveled east to Grand Central to catch the number-6 train north to the Bronx in order to be there by 10:00 A.M. on a Saturday.

By then the place was already crowded. Entering the shop was like walking through the portal to another country. We heard the foreign chatter and laughter of Spanish-speaking women. Everyone turned and looked at Aunt Peggy and me. Scanning the place, I no-ticed that none of them had hair just like mine—they all seemed to have the kind of hair that tended toward frizziness but, when pulled back, still looked manageable.

Aunt Peggy tried to explain to the woman at the counter that al-though my hair looked nearly nappy, it was soft and needed some-one who wouldn't put too harsh a chemical in it. We were pointed to the next available beautician. She barely nodded hello.

"Okay, I'm going to walk around, and I'll see you in a couple of hours," Aunt Peggy said, then turned and left with what seemed to be a sigh of relief.

Reluctantly, I entered the booth with its prominent, ominous-looking black porcelain sink. The beautician draped a large rubber bib around me, then began sectioning my hair. She talked in Spanish to her colleague in the next booth the entire time. I exhaled and prayed for the best.

She had what we call heavy-hands. Heavy-hands tear through

tangles, and tender-headed people—like me—fear them the most. At first my cringing had no effect, until she hit a *very* tender spot near the crown of my head. I whined and pulled away.

She stopped. "You tender-headed?" she asked, with an accent that bespoke Harlem, not Santo Domingo.

I nodded yes.

"You should have said so."

I felt very foolish for assuming she didn't speak English.

"Your hair has a really tight curl," she said. "I'm going to have to use the strong relaxer on you."

She left and returned carrying a plastic container about the size of a jumbo margarine tub. As she opened it, the smell of the chemicals burned my nostrils and jump-started my pulse.

She had barely begun when *I* began to complain.

"It burns," I said.

"That's because I used the extra-strength on you. Your hair is really kinky, so you need it," she said.

The burn got worse as she progressed. Then, after she had finished applying the relaxer, I sat for fifteen minutes so that the perm would "take." By then I was sure I would have scabs on my scalp. Mercifully, she washed the straightener out with cool water.

My scalp still tingled after she finished styling my hair in a pageboy. I was not as pleased as I had been, four years earlier, to get Shirley Temple curls. I just wanted to leave that place.

In California two weeks later, though, I jumped into the pool with glee, feeling the water seep into my scalp with an abandon I hadn't felt since I was little. I dove and arced up through the water, slicking my shoulder-length hair back like a seal. Then I shook it free of the water and slicked it back again.

Finally, I was a true Breck girl.

But back in Atlantic City, my hair began falling out.

In clumps.

In wads.

In handfuls.

Aunt Peggy called the salon in the Bronx and complained.

"She had such beautiful hair," she said tearfully, "and now it's all falling out."

"What do you want us to do?" the owner asked. "Put it back? She shouldn't have gone swimming."

In order to save what was left, we cut the remainder to chin level.

I downplayed my own dismay. "It's just hair," I reassured Aunt Peggy. "It will grow back."

Then, one night in late October, I found her sitting at the kitchen table, a Valentine's Day candy box open in front of her. The box was filled with what looked like black cotton candy. It was the remnants of my hair, saved from brushes and combs since my return from California.

"This is all the hair you've lost," she said sadly.

It was as if she had collected the pieces of her own heart, there in that heart-shaped box.

9. SEISMIC SHIFTS

During my annual visit to California in the summer of 1966, the Warner Brothers PR machine decided to assemble the stars of *F Troop* with their families for one giant photo.

I bought a new dress for the occasion: one with a maroon Empire bodice and a skirt color-blocked with a pink and lime green stripe. It was too short by Aunt Peggy's standards, but not fashionable enough by Mom's. She let it go, though, because she was more concerned with my hair. My daily dips in the pool had left it dry and frizzy. Mom's heated curlers weren't hot enough to make my hair hold a curl, and neither of us had any idea how to find a good black hairdresser in L.A. So I found some pink sponge rollers at the drugstore and sat in the sauna wearing them long enough for my hair to hold a limp flip.

We arrived at the Warner Brothers studio in Burbank on a sunny late morning and drove through the massive gates I had seen in so many movies. Parking the new burgundy Mercedes coupe at one end of the lot, Mom and I walked what seemed like a mile, past a mass of windowless warehouses, all painted the same sandy hue.

Inside, it took my eyes a while to adjust to the dark. Then I saw, about thirty yards away, the shell of the show's Fort Courage and a line of false storefronts, propped up by giant two-by-fours.

We found Larry sitting in his costume red longjohns, off to one side. "You're lucky you came this afternoon," he said. "This morning we were filming out in the Valley. It was a hundred and ten degrees in the shade."

How they withstood that heat, I don't know. Maybe they didn't. Maybe that's why they so often spent lunchtime knocking back pitchers of cold margaritas in the Mexican joint across the street.

I watched as some technicians copied the script in huge block letters onto three-by-four-foot poster boards.

"What're you doing?" I asked one of them.

"We're making idiot cards so they can read the words," he answered. "They usually come back from lunch too looped to remember the lines."

When the director finally called a wrap and the assistant director declared a lunch break, the set relaxed. Set dressers appeared from the shadows, working to finish the saloon stage, where the families would be posed.

My brother Lary arrived.

Lary and I were getting to know one another again. He was thirty years old, had finished his tour in the army, graduated from George Washington University, gotten married, gotten divorced, and was now doing graduate work in film history at UCLA. That summer he had introduced me to his friends, to Bob Dylan, and to *Invisible Man* by Ralph Ellison. We had zoomed around Los Angeles's freeways on his motor scooter. We went to Disneyland and were refused admittance—not because I was black and he white but because the amusement park had a policy against admitting men with facial hair, and he sported a beard!

For the *F Troop* picture, he shaved.

The *F Troop* families didn't socialize together; in fact, they had never met before. The set designers arranged us as though we were just another prop: secondary stars and their families on the end, major stars and their families in the middle. Larry and Forrest Tucker, who played the scheming Sergeant O'Rourke, and Ken Berry, who as Captain Parmenter played the straight guy to the two comics in the show, disappeared into the Mexican restaurant for their liquid lunch.

They returned less than an hour later, and when Mom caught sight of Larry's alcohol-flushed face, she looked angry. The cameraman captured her expression, a mask of Nordic severity, in the first group shot.

Then the photographer took portraits of each family. He put my brother and Mom behind Larry, who sat in a chair holding his beaten-down hat to his chest, and me on a little footstool by his right knee.

My mother must have realized she'd have a lot of explaining to do when those pictures became public. As for me . . . well, I was just twelve, and consumed by the heady excitement of my first visit to the set of a Hollywood TV show. I was oblivious.

Back in Atlantic City two months later, the phone rang with Mom's signal, interrupting dinner.

"There's going to be a magazine article about us!" she announced.

"Really?" I said, excited but trying my best to sound nonchalant. "Where?"

"Well, that picture they took—the publicity department saw it, and someone asked who was that Negro girl, so I told them you were our adopted daughter, that you had grown up across the hall from us in New York City. . . ."

She went on about how my fictitious mother had been beaten by her husband and used to leave me with her and Larry—but I couldn't really absorb what she was saying. Having me call her "Aunt Norma" was one thing, but her disavowing me altogether felt as though I were being erased. I made an excuse to give the phone to Aunt Peggy and got up and stood in the living room, watching the sunset and the darkness overtake the house across the street.

"I'm not sure that's such a good idea, Norma," I heard Aunt Peggy say behind me. "Suppose some reporter comes here and tries to find her?"

They talked a long time. It was the first of several long conversations about how to handle the anticipated fallout from the article: how to coordinate our stories, how best to hide any evidence that contradicted the story my mother had invented. Aunt Peggy worried out loud that my father and his friends might emerge from the woodwork to blackmail Mom and Larry for money. I thought then that her paranoia had reached new depths.

The article, in a magazine I remember as *TV Screen* or something like that, came out three months later: LARRY STORCH: WHY I ADOPTED A NEGRO GIRL, the headline read. Inside was the photograph taken that day at Warner Brothers, along with the fabricated story. It was a variation of the story Mom had always told me about her and my real father. She had just twisted it around a little bit.

I felt angry with her then, a palpable anger, for caring more about appearances than family, and angry with Aunt Peggy, too, for conspiring to help her keep the secret. And I was angry with myself for trying to please both of them by buying that stupid dress and trying so hard to make my hair look decent, with that lame flip.

Worried that some reporter might find me, Aunt Peggy forbade me to answer the phone for several days. She went to every magazine stand in Atlantic City, buying all the copies she could so that no one else in town would see the story. One of my classmates bought a copy before she did and was floored to realize that the tale I had told at school about my stepfather's being in *F Troop* was true.

I swore her to secrecy and told Regina she couldn't tell anybody either. She agreed.

Aunt Peggy fretted that I might not repeat the story Mom had so carefully crafted for the fan magazine.

"June, people are still prejudiced down South. If southern stations get wind of this, they could refuse to run *F Troop*! This whole thing could damage Larry's career! He wouldn't be able to work. There would be no more trips to California, no more nice clothes. It would affect him, Norma, you, all of us—economically, financially. This whole house of cards could come tumbling down. We would lose everything!"

Peggy wanted me to understand a larger truth: the economic cost of darker skin. The 1960 census had determined that Negro per capita income was three-fifths that of whites. In the early sixties, the journalist Louis Lomax counted twenty-five black millionaires and cited only four hundred black Americans who earned over fifty thousand dollars a year. Aunt Peggy herself earned nine thousand dollars a year, after two decades of teaching, and Paul made less. Larry earned four times that every week. The money he contributed to our household counted. A lot.

Finally, I realized that this was no game—everyone's survival depended on my keeping my mouth shut and on convincing my friends to keep theirs shut, too.

Maybe Uncle Paul felt sorry for me, or maybe I was just at that age when developing girls draw closer to their fathers. In any event, Paul and I grew closer after that summer.

Our relationship had always been difficult: I had always felt that I didn't measure up to Uncle Paul's expectations. My table manners never suited him. He had wanted to raise me as a Catholic; he had wanted me to accompany him fishing. His tone signaled annoyance, even though I knew that he had emphysema, and that therefore the very act of breathing made his gravelly voice sound commanding or annoyed, even when he didn't intend it.

Uncle Paul had been a cook in the army, and he brought his KP training to the house at 407 Indiana Avenue. The kitchen was Paul's kingdom. Everything had to be just so: plates arranged according to size, cups set up in a line inside the cupboard, dishes dried with a towel after they were washed. He taught me how to clean pots by scrubbing with a Brillo pad in little circular motions.

"You've got to put some elbow grease into it," he pointed out, irritated, when I left a spot. He would inspect my work when he came home after his shift of cab driving. If he found a speck of food on a dish or a glass left in the sink, I had to get out of bed to do it all over.

Peggy called Paul "punctilious," and in the family dynamic I could usually count on her to take my side against him.

But after my kitchen debut with steak au poivre, Paul and I seemed to find common ground at the stove. He taught me how to cook in the New Orleans fashion, starting with breakfast: scrambled eggs with hamburger or sausage, onion, and green pepper.

"You need to start cooking with some bacon grease or Crisco," he explained. "Then you cut up your onion fine and sauté it with your green pepper and add your salt and pepper, see? Out of this you can make anything. Then add your hamburg."

While the hamburger was cooking, he stirred the eggs, added some milk, and then turned the meat into the eggs (this allowed a little egg to congeal around the hot meat) before putting the whole mixture back into the pan.

Gradually, he taught me how to make other things: pan-fried catfish with grits, fried tomatoes, and greens; and lamb chops smothered with gravy and onions. One night when Paul started fussing about the dishes being left to air-dry instead of being towel-dried, Aunt Peggy asked whether I agreed Uncle Paul was acting like an army sergeant.

"No," I said. "I'll dry them," and to her amazement I did.

Following that incident, Aunt Peggy would sit at the kitchen table after dinner working on her lesson plans, and Paul and I would sit in the living room, drinking root beer floats and watching *Combat!* or *Bonanza* on the large color-TV console Mom and Larry had bought us.

Maybe it was *Bonanza* that finally brought us together. Hoss was boss, and on that we could both agree.

While Uncle Paul and I forged our relationship, he and Aunt Peggy seemed to be going through a rough patch. At its root lay Uncle Paul's failing upholstery business, which Aunt Peggy had subsidized for years. They finally sold the property, but then they couldn't agree on what to do with the money. Paul wanted to take a share of it to buy a new business; Peggy wanted to put money down on a house in Margate. After a while, anything—a coat left on a chair, the oil bill, her bridge club meetings, the barking dog—would set off an argument between them.

One day, I tape-recorded one of these heated exchanges and told them that I wanted to play it back so that they could hear how ridiculous they sounded. Before I even reached the "play" knob, Uncle Paul wanted to wring my neck. Aunt Peggy tried to intercede; he hit her by accident, and their arguing started all over again.

Paul's late-night refrain, "Give me my money!" became the sound track for our lives. Once I asked Peggy why she didn't just give him the money to bring peace to the house, but she told me curtly that this was an adult matter and that I had no business in it. I considered it my business, since I had to live with the constant battling between the two of them.

Aunt Peggy developed her own way of dealing with these arguments. She had read a *Reader's Digest* article suggesting that lying on the floor and screaming like a baby might help release pent-up frustrations. So that's what she did. Sometimes she and I practiced "the baby" together, screaming and wailing away while our limbs flailed the air.

That New Year's Eve, when Uncle Paul started fussing, as usual, about money, Peggy walked into the living room and got down on the carpet on her knees, rolled onto her back, and proceeded to kick her legs and arms in the air while she pretended to bawl like a crying baby. Sometimes her antics made Paul stop fussing, sometimes he tried to yell over us, and sometimes he left the house altogether.

That evening, though, when Aunt Peggy got down on the floor and began her routine, Paul's face and shoulders fell. He turned and ambled back into the kitchen, sat down, lit a cigarette, and started reading the *National Enquirer*.

On the carpet in the living room, Aunt Peggy continued her yelling, while I watched her, disheartened. Mom and Larry didn't fight like this.

It was New Year's Eve, and here our house was in disharmony.

One week later, just after my thirteenth birthday, I came home from school and hesitated at the wrought-iron gate. The set of the house against the gloomy winter sky looked foreboding. I shrugged it off. I was supposed to take down the Christmas tree, a task I normally did with Paul, but he was nursing a bad cold, so I'd have to take it down by myself.

I opened the front door and saw, sitting on the piano stool, two members of Aunt Peggy's bridge club. When I greeted them, they put their heads together and whispered. Three more women sat bunched together on the sofa, like birds on a limb.

In the dining room were more women whom I knew from church but had never seen in our house, women Peggy gossiped about on the phone. They sat at the dining room table, still decorated with bayberry candles and holly wreaths and dressed in its red holiday cloth a week after Epiphany. In the kitchen Regina's grandmother, Mrs. McKee, stood at the stove. The familiar smell of her cooking seemed foreign in our house.

Four more friends of Aunt Peggy's sat clustered around the kitchen table. There, in Uncle Paul's chair, sat Aunt Peggy herself: hunched over, diminished, dabbing her eyes with a balled-up napkin.

"What's going on?" I asked.

Aunt Peggy answered in a voice as brittle as she looked. She told me to go upstairs and that she would tell me later.

I went upstairs, schoolbooks in hand, to say hello to Uncle Paul.

But Uncle Paul was not there.

For months Aunt Peggy had carped at him to cut down his smoking, and finally he had—from six packs a day to two or three—not enough, his doctor told him. He should quit entirely.

The previous night he had come downstairs to have a bowl of soup, wheezing between spoonfuls. After he'd finished, he'd hoisted himself up from the table and started upstairs. Aunt Peggy and I had listened as his leather slippers slid against the wood. We heard a hacking, wet cough, a pause, his labored breath. Two more steps. Four wheezing breaths. One step. One step. Another spell of coughing.

At the top stairs, he had thumped down heavily, struggling to breathe before shuffling up the hall to the bedroom.

"Poor guy," Aunt Peggy had said, concern on her face. She had given up trying to get him to quit smoking—all she could do was try to alleviate his symptoms with a steaming pot of mentholated water. She had come home from school that day at lunchtime to see how he was doing. He'd had his soup, then begun his painstaking journey up the stairs. She heard him reach the top step and thought he was resting, so she called the oil company to schedule a delivery. They had kept her on hold for some time.

By the time she had found him, slumped against the banister at the top of the stairs, he was already cold.

After she told me this story, Aunt Peggy fell into the pillow, sobbing. I sat beside her, fiddling with the folds of my new plaid skirt. Aunt Peggy had taught me what to say on occasions like this—to express sympathy, kindness, and offer to do what little I could for the bereaved—but my mother had trained me not to cry. Crying, especially, would change nothing.

Now, although I longed to find the appropriate response, I couldn't. I had spent too long learning to mask my emotions. The obvious words felt shallow. The obvious emotions wouldn't come.

Aunt Peggy wept beside me for several minutes, then suddenly sat up, wiped her tears, and left me alone.

After a while I went up into the attic and sat at the window where the cat slept. As the sky darkened, two tears fell from my eyes.

From Detroit, where Larry was working, my mother sent a sympathy card and flowers for the funeral. They were addressed only to Peggy. My mother probably called, although I don't remember, but in any event, with the house so full of strangers, we could not have had a real conversation.

I had known little of Paul's life. From his obituary I discovered that he had gone to school to train as a dental technician; that he had served in a Negro-only maintenance unit in the army; that he had been born in Washington, D.C., the youngest of five children.

The obituary listed Aunt Peggy, his two surviving brothers, and his nieces from Ohio—but not me.

I asked one of the mourners why I wasn't listed, and she said, "Well, obituaries only list blood relatives. You're more like his play niece, not a blood relative."

Her words seared my soul. A "play" niece? Didn't I live in the same house with him? Hadn't I been calling him "Uncle Paul" since I was four? Hadn't he taught me how to wash and brush my teeth, how to brown hamburger with onions, green peppers, and garlic—the New Orleans way? Hadn't he nitpicked my eating habits from the first day I came to Atlantic City? Hadn't we put up the Christmas tree together every year and taken it down every year the day after Epiphany?

What did being a blood relative have to do with any of this?

Aunt Peggy was sympathetic. "The person who took the information didn't know," she said. "We'll fix it."

But the damage was done. First I had become my own mother's niece, then her adopted daughter, and now I wasn't even part of Paul's family because we weren't *blood*.

His *blood* nieces arrived from Ohio. I resented their high-pitched expressions of sorrow, however genuine. If Paul had meant so much to them, why had they so rarely come to visit?

When the limos lined up three days later to go to the cemetery, the usher ordered family first. Aunt Peggy and the nieces climbed in. There was no room for me, so I traveled in a second limo reserved for friends of the family. Among them were Aunt Sylvia and Uncle Hugh Gregory. Aunt Syl reached out and smoothed my hair—the only touch of solace I would receive during the whole ordeal. I felt grateful to her beyond words.

The processional rolled slowly, headlights on in midmorning, heedless of traffic lights.

Uncle Paul's funeral service gave me the grace of faith. The ritual of the Catholic church comforted me. I would cling to the rituals of faith as I made my way through adolescence.

After the funeral I ended up sitting next to Aunt Peggy in the car. Weeping, she reached out and grasped my hand tightly—until she realized whose hand it was she'd grasped. Then she asked me to switch seats with Aunt Syl, and I felt slighted anew—my hand not good enough to grasp because my grief wasn't weighty enough. I got up and folded myself into the opposite corner of the limousine. Staring out the window, I affected a distant and mournful look so that no one would bother me, but at the same time I prayed that someone would just touch my arm, lightly, so that I might bury my head in a warm and understanding shoulder and cry.

Aunt Peggy and I avoided Thanksgiving and Christmas in the house at 407 North Indiana Avenue for several years after Uncle Paul died. Instead we visited the Gregorys at their homes in New York and Washington. We were like lost geese, traveling south, then north, seeking a familiar flock.

The drives in either direction took three hours, and as we drove, I found out more about Aunt Peggy's life.

She had been thirty years old when she married Paul, and he was thirty-one, in May 1937. She was considered an old maid; she'd had two failed engagements. The first time, she said, the man turned out to be a heel. The second time she discovered that her fiancé was homosexual.

That second engagement weighed on her. She and the man involved—his name was Albert—had enjoyed a meeting of the minds. They liked the same music, the ballet, art museums, talking till late in the evening, but she couldn't get over the feeling, she told me, that something was wrong. He rarely kissed her. Then one day when she saw him on the street with another man, she knew.

She confronted him with the question—do you like men?—and he hung his head in shame and admitted that yes, he did. But it would make no difference, he said. He would still love her and marry her, and he would never bring it up to her face, never "rub her nose in it," as he put it.

"But I couldn't do that," she said sadly. It was the first hint I ever got that the physical union of marriage was as important to her as the sanctity of the vows.

A second hint came when she explained why she had married Paul. "I liked the way he looked in his pants," she said with a little laugh.

In Washington we visited Aunt Hugh and Uncle T. M. Gregory. They had left Atlantic City after Uncle Gum retired from the schools and moved to be closer to their two youngest daughters, Mignon and Sheila. Aunt Mignon lived with her husband, Uncle Ernie, and their three children, Chico, Wendy, and Greg. I spent time with them while Aunt Peggy stayed with Aunt Hugh and Uncle Gum. She spent slow Sunday mornings swinging in Aunt Hugh's hammock, reading the *Washington Post*, and helping Aunt Hugh build her Japanese rock garden.

Aunt Mignon, the second-youngest Gregory daughter, and her husband, Ernie Wilson, a dean at Howard University, ran what amounted to a salon in Washington in those days, much as Mignon's parents had when they lived in Atlantic City. They were a chain-smoking, hard-drinking couple. On any given evening, people like the poet Sterling Brown and Councilwoman Charlene Drew Jarvis (a distant Gregory cousin herself) dropped by to discuss politics, poetry, or Nancy Wilson's latest album.

Uncle Ernie and Aunt Mignon cherished individuality and self-expression. They also encouraged intellectual achievement—an intellect they showed off at the dinner table and at parties, not one that hid in the corner reading books, as I was inclined to do. If they found me writing a poem in a quiet moment, they begged me to read it out loud after dinner, and it was always well received.

Of all the Gregorys, Aunt Mignon reminded me most of Mom: pretty, young at heart, smart, and witty. She forever surprised me. One night the entire family stayed up until 3:00 A.M. discussing the lyrics of the Beatles' *White Album*. Uncle Ernie kept jumping up from the table to put on Miles Davis, John Coltrane, or Leadbelly to emphasize his point that John, Paul, George, and Ringo had really ripped off black musicians.

Mignon and Ernie encouraged creativity from all their children; they delighted in spur-of-the-moment artistic displays—a song, a reading, or some new licks on the drum set that their youngest son, Greg, was learning, and anything from their daughter, Wendy, one year my senior.

Wendy was an irrepressible fountain of talent: a painter blessed with a singing voice like Diana Ross's and a personality like Sammy Davis's, she had enough chutzpah to stand toe to toe with either of them, even at fourteen. She refused to let me be withdrawn, cajoling me into becoming Mary Wilson or Cindy Birdsong or the supporting cast—the entire supporting cast—of her latest play.

Wendy and I commiserated over the square clothes Aunt Peggy made me wear in a vain effort to hide my figure. At thirteen, I had already reached my full height—five foot seven—and weighed 130 pounds. Wendy showed me how to put on makeup, revealing the mysteries of the eye-shadow palette and demonstrating how eyeliner could bring my eyes out from behind my glasses. She helped me roll up and pin my dowager skirts at a more fashionable length, taught me how to dance the bop, and took me out to parties, where I clung against the wall, trying to avoid boys while hoping desperately that they would notice me. I found boys to be simultaneously dangerous and exciting. Aunt Peggy wanted me to stay away from them, so I naturally wanted to learn more about them. "Plenty of time for that," she would pooh-pooh. I was too afraid to experiment in Atlantic City, where everyone knew who I was, but in Washington, in those dark basement parties, I shared my first kisses.

My visits to D.C. weren't all play, though. Chico, Wendy's older brother, was in his first year at Harvard, the third generation of Gregory men to matriculate there. The Gregorys all brought such a sense of entitlement to the idea of higher education that I began to think seriously about college for the first time.

I asked my mother where she had gone to college. She had never graduated, she said—she had dropped out during her first semester at Long Beach Junior College in California. My brother, Lary, for his part, had graduated Phi Beta Kappa from George Washington University, and Mom said she expected the same from me.

But I had no such expectations of myself. I didn't think I was particularly smart, and as for following my brother, I'd never even heard of most of the books he'd read, so I didn't see how I could possibly follow in his footsteps, despite my mother's dreams.

On one of our trips north to New York in that first year after Paul died, Aunt Peggy took me back to Brooklyn's Park Slope area, where she spent her adolescence. She had lived there with her god-mother, Daisy, while her father worked near the Flatiron Building in downtown Manhattan.

"My father was a construction foreman," she told me during one visit. "They didn't allow colored to be foremen in those days, but he passed for white and got the job. The other colored laborers knew he was colored, but they didn't say anything."

Aunt Peggy had skin the color of a walnut. Her father's skin was the color of curdled cream. I wondered what her mother had looked like. She didn't have any pictures of her mother. She said she couldn't remember her at all.

"Did you ever come down here and visit your father?" I asked.

"Sometimes I would stand across the street and watch. And oh, my heart was full to bursting with pride! But I couldn't cross the street and talk to him. I would have given it all away."

I would have given it all away.

Sometime after Aunt Peggy died, I remembered that conversation, and only then did the full impact of what she'd said strike me. It made me think of our relationship as a kind of karmic continuum: a daughter whose mother was white, raised by a daughter whose father had passed for white and couldn't claim her as his own.

Then I saw how similar circumstance had made us and how that history made us family in a way that genes and bloodlines never would.

ABC canceled *F Troop* after two seasons, in the spring of 1967.

The show had been an anachronism from the first, but in the wake of the civil-rights movement and the escalating war in Vietnam, a TV comedy about soldiers sent to win the Wild West in cahoots with the Indians just wasn't appropriate. Before he died, President Kennedy had declared a race to the moon, and executives in Hollywood were looking toward the future—that year *Star Trek* had been the breakout hit.

"Something else will come along," Mom said brightly, and she had reason to believe so. Alone among the cast, Larry had been nominated for a prime-time Emmy for his work in *F Troop*, and, although he would lose to Don Adams of *Get Smart*, Larry had already demonstrated a talent for reinventing himself—from vaudeville mimic to stand-up comic to actor.

The entire country was undergoing a sea change, although what it would become, no one could say. The black-Jewish-progressive alliance that had spearheaded passage of the Civil Rights Act of 1963 and the Voting Rights Act of 1965 had splintered, the dream of a Great Society that would eliminate poverty had shattered; instead the country seemed to be descending into a nightmarish war.

The summer of 1967 would become known as the "Summer of Love," a milestone for Baby Boomers like myself, a generation that questioned authority and embraced idealism. Aretha Franklin's hit "Respect" became a national anthem, while Jimi Hendrix reinterpreted the old "Star-Spangled Banner" at Monterey that summer. During my annual August visit to California, my brother Lary turned me on to the Jimi Hendrix Experience and Jim Morrison and the Doors. We smoked pot. We played guitar and sang Bob Dylan songs. I tagged along when he went to a party of graduate students, wearing a long fake ponytail and my mother's false eyelashes.

I was thirteen. Aunt Peggy would have had a heart attack had she known what I was doing, but I didn't care. I felt very hip.

For me, 1967 became the summer when I began to embrace paradox. Lary introduced me to friends of his who had divorced and remained friends, to sons of rich men who lived like paupers. I began to consider the idea that I could be black and proud and still love my white relatives. Such slogans sound facile, but the lessons helped me see beyond the sometimes simplistic absolutes imposed upon me by Aunt Peggy and the isolation of Atlantic City's Northside, and by my mother's convenient notions of kinship.

Sometimes idealism meant embracing ambiguity. But it would take me a long time to learn that lesson.

My white half brother introduced me to the new black literary style. It started when he asked what books I was reading.

I pulled out my reading diary and showed him my list. I had just finished *Moby-Dick* and was starting *Wuthering Heights*, which I liked much better.

"Have you read Baldwin?" he asked.

"Baldwin who?" I responded.

"*James* Baldwin," he said, astonished that I seemed unfamiliar with the name.

I didn't remember the name ever being raised in our house, and since black authors weren't taught at Friends School, it didn't appear on my summer reading lists either.

Back at his apartment near UCLA, Lary went to the bookshelf and handed me a copy of *Blues for Mister Charlie*. The next day he bought me *Go Tell It on the Mountain* and E. Franklin Frazier's *Black Bourgeoisie*. Frazier's book I knew. Uncle Hugh and Aunt Peggy had discussed it for a long time. Aunt Peggy found its depiction of a self-absorbed, self-hating black middle class inaccurate and unfair. Uncle Hugh, though, thought its analysis was dead-on. There were some educated black folks who didn't have their heads stuck up their asses, he maintained, but they were the exception. Furthermore, he predicted that as integration proceeded, the masses of black people would not benefit. The way he saw it, there was no way the economy could generate enough well-paying jobs to accommodate us all. The door would be open for a while, he said, and then it would slam shut.

Aunt Peggy called him a cynic, but I had a feeling he might be right.

While visiting Mom and Larry during the summer of 1968, I was careful about swimming in the pool. Although I had a slight perm, I was afraid of the chlorine's effects on my hair.

One day while I was swimming toward the far end, trying to keep my head above the water, I thought I heard my mother say, "Why do blacks try so hard to be like white people?"

I paused, turned, and treaded water while I asked her to repeat herself.

"Why do blacks try so hard to be like white people? In other words, with the hair and everything. Why don't they just accept themselves as they are and be what they are instead of trying to remake themselves?"

Mom had been reading Eldridge Cleaver's *Soul on Ice*. Cleaver's book of essays, written in prison, detailed his political awakening—a quest that had included robbery and the rape of white women as he acted out his anger against being "colonized" by white America. The book had become a bestseller, but Eldridge Cleaver had written nothing about black women and their hair—and Mom didn't understand the implication of her question. In the 'hood, asking someone an indirect but pointed question like that is called "signifyin'." Her question was tantamount to asking, "Who do you think you are, trying to be white?" In the 'hood, such a question would probably lead to a fight.

But my mother knew nothing about signifyin', so I squelched the impulse to challenge her.

"I think most of us believe that if we look more like whites, they will accept us." This was how it was now between her and me—she was "they" and I was "us."

"But straight hair doesn't change skin color," Mom pointed out.

No, but it allows us to pretend, Eldridge Cleaver would have written.

On second thought, I decided Mom had said it about as well as Cleaver could have, so I dunked my head.

I returned to Atlantic City late that summer with an Afro.

By 1968 my generation appeared poised to transform the social order—if we weren't killed off first. That spring the country's icons of hope had been picked off one by one—in February, students in Orangeburg, South Carolina; in April, Martin Luther King; in June, Bobby Kennedy.

Aunt Peggy and I watched the Democratic convention that August on TV. The demonstrators had no single agenda—civil rights, antiwar, pro-labor, libertarianism, anticapitalism. There were hippies, Yippies, Black Panthers, and Weathermen. Unshaven and audacious, they looked nothing like the clean-cut civil-rights demonstrators who, just four years earlier, had stood up to the police in Birmingham and Selma. Aunt Peggy and I were dumbfounded at the culmination of the horror and social chaos that seemed to have gripped the country since Dr. King's assassination.

The Chicago police cracked heads, jailed nonviolent demonstrators, and threw tear gas, treating white antiwar demonstrators outside the Democratic convention the same way Alabama cops had treated blacks in Selma.

Mom and Larry were in London, visiting with Tony Curtis and his third wife, Lesley Allen. Mom wrote breathless postcards about their life, about driving around London in Curtis's plum red Rolls-Royce, complete with a chauffeur—"Rolls are like Mustangs in the states," she wrote.

I don't know that I could have identified it this way then, but for the first time her preoccupations seemed frivolous. The right of free expression, the struggle for economic justice, the need to consult with Congress before declaring war—these principles were at stake in Chicago; I could have cared less about the number of Rolls-Royces in London.

Three days after the Democrats nominated Hubert Humphrey, I received a long letter from my brother.

We both seem to be imprisoned by the same ferocious animal that thwarts our communication: our own fears. Fear freezes. Fear pervaded in Chicago, fear stops relationships, fear divides black and white. Our goal should be to batter this blinding fog and emit sunshine.

Perhaps writing can initiate the process, I don't know. I remember your stay out here with nostalgia. It is something remembered because it brought pleasure, a desire to relive, and it's also a feeling of loss. I feel the vacancy that you are there and I am here. That situation cannot be avoided. To rescind it would be a mistake, and I wholeheartedly believe that Peggy has been very good for you. In fact, I can remember how much I desired to stay with

her as a child, so I know that your condition has numer-
ous advantages. Yet I experience the distance in miles and
years with a deep sense of something lost.

My friends ask me how you are, and, since all of my in-
formation is indirect, I answer, "she's fine." This begs the
question, "are you fine?"

I don't know that I answered that letter. I don't believe I would
have known how.

"Hey, J.B.!" Larry called me from the living room. "They're talking about your father on TV!"

It was the summer of 1969. There was Dizzy Gillespie on *The
Joan Rivers Show*, describing how his horn had been bent into its
legendary shape by a comedian who fell on it during a set break.

"You bent Dizzy Gillespie's horn?" I asked.

"No, not me. Your father, James. James Cross."

It had happened on January 6, 1953, at a birthday party for
Dizzy's wife, Lorraine. The date struck me, because that was nearly
a year to the day before I was born. My mother, who was there that
night, told me that she gave Dizzy—notorious for his bad temper—
the rent money to keep him from beating Jimmy up.

My father had been absent when I was born, as he would be for
every one of my birthdays. Now here he was, a mention on *The Joan
Rivers Show*.

His name popped up at the oddest times.

The summer of my fifteenth year, my brother and his fiancée,
Lany, the daughter of a prominent research gynecologist, came to
visit Aunt Peggy and me in Atlantic City. I had not been invited to
Lary's first wedding, at my mother's request. His bride had been from
North Carolina, and while *she* liked me, Mom feared that her parents might "react" upon learning that their daughter's sister-in-law
was black.

Aunt Peggy and I had taken turns, upon hearing this news, making up scenarios that could be best called "Guess Who's Coming to the Wedding?": The new mother-in-law would faint at the altar. The father-in-law would grab his daughter's hand and drag her back up the aisle, away from this mongrel family. The congregation would run away in horror. We laughed ourselves silly, using humor to deflect hurt and anger. Humor—poking fun at the unjustifiable—allowed me to endure.

Although they had traveled across the country together, Aunt Peggy wouldn't let Lary and Lany sleep in the same bedroom. Lany got Papa's old room, while Lary had to sleep on the sofa downstairs. We connived a way to get Aunt Peggy out of the house, but she came back early and walked in on them fooling around. She turned, closed the door, and never mentioned the incident.

Together, Lary, Lany, and I roamed the boardwalk. My brother and I got into water fights while he washed his car. We stayed up all night talking.

It was a glorious visit. Maybe Aunt Peggy became a little jealous of our closeness. Maybe that's why, a day or two after they left, she felt compelled to point out that I might not always be able to count on Lary.

I asked her what she meant.

"Well, he's getting ready to start his own family. He may find it more convenient to say you're not his sister in the long run."

I didn't believe that my brother would do such a thing, no matter how much Aunt Peggy insisted.

"You can't trust white people," she told me. "They put their self-interest first. Like Norma. She loves you, but sometimes she finds it more expedient to say she's not your mother. Lary may do the same thing. You don't know what will happen as he moves forward in his career."

I walked away and flopped into the chair by the telephone. I didn't want to believe it. My brother wasn't my mother, I argued. He had nothing to gain by disowning me.

Aunt Peggy persisted. Most black families could recount a variant of my family tale. Aunt Peggy knew this. She had seen more and knew more about the lengths people would go to to keep their backgrounds secret. "Now he says you're his sister, but after he's married and has a family, he may find it easier at some point in the future to deny it," she said.

Devastated, I screamed at her to leave me alone and stomped upstairs to the shelter of my room and the sanctuary of my record collection.

Aunt Peggy would prove to be wrong about Lary—he would never deny our relationship. He and Lany did invite me to their wedding, which took place on the beach in Santa Monica. But I scheduled my college-board exams for that day, and missed the nuptials.

Better to be safe than sorry.

That was my way of protecting my heart.

10. UNDER THE BOARDWALK

At sixteen and a senior in high school, I was round-shouldered and bookish with gold, rectangular wire-frame glasses on my nose. I wore my hair cut in a large, oval-shaped Afro. I daydreamed about having a lover in every port, and harbored darker fantasies in which being physically beaten was the price I had to pay to be loved. My Gregory aunts said I seemed withdrawn. They wondered whether I was unhappy.

I thought I kept up a good front—and Aunt Peggy told me that my moodiness was normal for a teenager. After two years at Friends, I had convinced her and Mom to let me attend the local public high school. I started ninth grade at integrated Atlantic City High. There I was a part of many social circles but a real member of none. Regina and her family had moved to New Rochelle, New York, and we saw each other infrequently. The most popular black girls, calling me a bookworm, rejected me from their social club. I had white friends but couldn't really call myself part of their clique either. I did have a cadre of black friends with whom I had bonded in elementary school, and a few white friends who transferred with me from Friends School.

Atlantic City, like the rest of the United States, was caught in the racial tenor that consumed the country after Reverend King's assassination: black anger, white guilt. But the realities were more complex than the popular conception. The all-black NAACP Youth League met at St. Augustine's Episcopal Church—home to the black upper class (and mainly lighter-skinned) elite of Atlantic City. Yet many of us also worked with the Black Panther Party (not least because the brother who headed the Panthers in Atlantic City was considered fine, fine, fine). I even sold Black Panther newspapers on Atlantic Avenue, but when Aunt Peggy found out, she absolutely forbade it. No daughter of hers was going to be "common," as she put it, selling papers on the street corners—especially papers that advocated the violent overthrow of the United States government.

"Power to the people" was the Panthers' slogan. We were committed to the elimination of social classes, to the glorification of the lumpenproletariat. I worked with the Panthers' breakfast program soliciting food from grocers and helping to prepare eggs and bacon for children of "the lumpen" in neighborhood church basements while we taught them about black history—the Panthers referred to the latter as "knowledge of self."

"Community service and knowledge of self for revolutionary action"—that's what attracted me to the Black Panthers; even more than their slick leather jackets and black berets, I liked the idea of raising awareness.

Besides, political activity hid my essential loneliness. I had too many secrets—too much to expose through intimacy. I had many friends, no one best friend. I concentrated on doing well in school and studying piano. I also became a good tap dancer.

If some of my classmates thought I was different—peculiar, even—it was not because my mother was white and my stepfather rumored to be in show business. It was because I tended to show up in September wearing the latest styles from Los Angeles: Nehru jackets, love beads, bell-bottom jeans, and fringed cowboy jackets. I also listened to what was considered "white folks' music": the Beatles, Laura Nyro, Blood, Sweat & Tears. I listened to these white artists, secretly, behind the closed doors of my bedroom. The fact that I preferred them to the Temptations, the Four Tops, or Kool & the Gang was a source of shame and guilt. Somehow I had become like Regina. But unlike Regina, I wanted to work for the cause of black people the way Aunt Yvonne Gregory had when, back in 1950, she had researched lynchings and helped Paul Robeson write "We Charge Genocide: the Crime of the U.S. Government Against the Negro People," a petition the great actor presented to the United Nations in 1951. We rarely saw Yvonne anymore—she was consumed by alcoholism. Still, I believed, as Yvonne had, as Aunt Peggy did, that racism was the result of ignorance, and I thought that by becoming a reporter I could help educate the masses.

As a high-school senior, I was elected class secretary; I worked as front-page editor for the high-school paper. Saturdays I worked as a copygirl for the *Press of Atlantic City*. I also taught Sunday school. I had read the Bible while I was at Friends, and its stories—about the blind faith of Noah; the odd triangle of Abraham, Sarah, and Hagar; and, of course, the exodus of the slaves from Egypt—fascinated me. My Sunday-school classes were more like literature courses than theology—and probably way over the heads of my fourth-grade students, with whom I explored the dilemmas and compromises made by Old Testament characters in the name of faith.

I had become adept at compromise myself. That was why I made friends with everybody. It was a defense mechanism. Measuring my words and actions, I gave no one an excuse to peer beneath my veneer, and my achievements became my shield.

By December 1970, the fall of my senior year in high school, college applications had gone out. Aunt Peggy and my guidance counselor had pushed me, so I participated in the application ritual without any desire beyond the affirmation of acceptance. I waited for responses from Swarthmore, Douglass, Bennington, and Syracuse. I thought that if I were really lucky, Bennington or Swarthmore might take me; more likely I'd end up at Rutgers's women's college, Douglass.

One day someone knocked at the door. Peeking through the window, I saw it was Jim Henderson, a boy I knew vaguely as "Ripper," the grandson of a neighbor around the corner. He lived in Trenton but came to Atlantic City every summer. He was mannerly, of average height, the color of stained oak, with a slightly diffident bearing. He introduced himself as a Harvard sophomore. Harvard and its sister college, Radcliffe, he explained, were recruiting talented black students to apply, and I had been identified by my high school as someone who might be interested.

My response caught him off guard: I laughed for about ten minutes at the absurdity of the idea. I remained an erratic student, moved to study fiercely when the subject interested me but also capable of disappearing into flights of fancy and extracurricular activities that took me miles away from my studies—not exactly the stereotypical Radcliffe student. My guidance counselor had had to push me to apply to Swarthmore and Bennington. As far as I was concerned, the Ivy League was Gregory territory.

It took a lot of convincing from Ripper, Aunt Peggy, and my teachers at school, but finally I filled out the application.

Whatever school I went to, I'd need scholarship money. Larry hadn't had steady work in two years. In order to maximize my financial-aid package, Aunt Peggy and Mom planned to say that Peggy was raising me with minimum help from Norma and Larry. At night after the dishes were put away, I listened to the scratch of her fountain pen as she sat at the gray linoleum kitchen table, creating yet another version of my life.

That table was littered with sheets of the plain, coarse yellow school paper she used for arithmetic tests, and they in turn were covered with fragmented paragraphs and crossed-out sentences. The nib of her pen had split and stained her fingertips indigo blue: a tattoo of fibbing.

She had begun each version the same way: "June is the product of an interracial marriage."

"Why do you have to put it that way, like I'm a can of soup?" I asked.

She said that was the way such a thing was usually expressed.

Aunt Peggy liked to remind me how lucky I was to have so many loving adults in my life. But I didn't feel lucky. I felt like a foundling.

I looked at the draft she was writing.

"Her father is not in the picture. We have acted as June's guardians, and her mother contributes when she can, but this has not been a consistent pattern."

She made me sound like a bear performing at the circus. Peggy was the ringmaster. In the front row sat my mother, the financier.

During the second semester of my senior year, while most of my classmates slacked off on their studies, learning once again became interesting to me. Maybe my coursework had caught up to my experiences: I had traveled alone to Europe during the previous summer, spending two weeks in Rome with Mom and Larry before proceeding to Paris to join Lary and Lany on their postponed honeymoon. Together we toured Normandy, Austria, Amsterdam, and Germany. As a student, I needed grounding to make academics relevant. Seeing the Louvre and visiting Mont Saint-Michel made me curious about the history of those who had lived while those shrines were being built. Now that I was in advanced-placement French and AP English, Baudelaire and Chaucer seemed more real to me. I read Baudelaire in French and struggled through Chaucer in Middle English. I wrote parodies of *The Canterbury Tales* about my teachers and friends. I found courses in the humanities stimulating and fun but struggled with the sciences and math. One quarter, to challenge myself, I decided to see if I could get an A in chemistry. I did, but I received a C grade in every other course.

I became editor of the high-school literary magazine. Most of the literary magazine staff took advanced-placement English class with the English department chair, Robert Linblad, but a few were in regular college prep. None of the magazine's staff was enrolled in business or vocational education, because by tradition the literary magazine was open only to "college track." Their exclusion offended our egalitarian sensibilities.

We argued with our advisers till they agreed to open the literary magazine to all high-school students. Then we decided to judge each poem anonymously, so that we couldn't play favorites among our friends. In order to do that, we retyped all the poems and assigned each one a number.

Since this had been my bright idea, I offered to do the retyping. A fellow member of the editorial staff, whom I will call John, volunteered to share that chore with me.

He was about five feet six or seven, a little shorter than I. He had thick brown hair, slight shoulders, and a cocky demeanor. He wore brown corduroy pants, Earth Shoes, and a dark plaid shirt. He had acne, and his fingernails were chewed to the quick. His narrow eyes peered through me like a ferret's as he questioned me during our breaks in typing.

"What do you think of the war?" he asked one day.

I had given lip service to opposition, but hadn't thought deeply about Vietnam.

I told John that I couldn't get very excited about what a bunch of politicians decided to do in a country on the other side of the world. He found my position indefensible. "Don't you see that the reason people in this country are starving is because they're spending all the money in Vietnam?" he insisted.

"The War on Poverty hasn't been won because this asshole President Nixon is waging his own war that he doesn't have the balls to ask Congress to declare! It's illegal! It's against the Constitution of the United States," he argued. "They're killing North Vietnamese who only want the right of self-determination. *That's* immoral!"

He made me feel guilty for being so apathetic.

John told me that he planned to join a national protest in Washington at the Pentagon. The bus would leave that Saturday morning and return Saturday night. Did I want to come?

I thought about it for maybe twenty seconds. A bus ride to D.C.? A national protest with young people from all over the country? On my own? Sure, I wanted to go, I said.

First, however, I had to get permission. Aunt Peggy questioned me skeptically when I asked her. She folded her arms and wrinkled her brows in unison. This was a bad sign.

Aunt Peggy still supported Nixon in opposition to almost all of the Gregorys—and my brother. She agreed with the domino-theory scenario: that if Vietnam fell to Communism, then the next country would, then another, and finally all the way across the Pacific Ocean to Hawaii and the mainland United States. She didn't cotton to the idea of a bunch of young demonstrators taking on the military establishment and the president. And she saw straight through my improvised list of fellow protesters. She wanted to know who this John was and how I knew him.

I said he was a kid from school with whom I was coediting the literary magazine.

As a teacher herself, Aunt Peggy had a network she consulted about the background and parentage of any friend whose house I wanted to visit. While her network didn't extend to the white teachers, she could easily get the records from the board of education. She probably already knew the home situations and IQ of everyone in my English class.

"No, he's not in Mr. Linblad's class," I said about John. "He's in Mrs. Johnston's."

Mrs. Johnston taught regular college-prep English, not advanced placement. When Aunt Peggy learned that John wasn't in Mr. Linblad's class, she pursed her lips so they came forward at the same angle as her eyebrows.

I decided to let the matter drop.

I didn't know who John's parents were or what they did. I called one of my girlfriends from school. She said that John's dad owned the clothing store across the street from her parents' place on Atlantic Avenue. His mother worked there.

I reported back to Aunt Peggy. She was unimpressed.

"Humph," she said, tossing her head back and sticking out her lower lip in disdain. "I've seen that woman behind the counter. She's a low-class-looking so-and-so." She stared at me sharply. "When did you start being so buddy-buddy with this John?"

What did John's parents' jobs have to do with Nixon's undeclared war and the threat to the Constitution? The bus was leaving Saturday, arriving for the protest at 2:00 P.M., and departing to return that same night. Could I go or not?

"No," she said. "You're too young to go on an unsupervised trip."

What a specious argument. I'd been traveling by myself to see my mother in New York City since I was seven. Six months earlier I'd gone to Europe by myself. Maybe she was simply afraid for me to go and demonstrate against the government, or else she feared that I would come under the influence of forces outside her experience. At Harvard, Uncle Ernie's son Chico had become one of the leaders of the student movement. Uncle Ernie kept saying that he had sent Chico up there to get an education, not to become a radical and get his head busted open by the police.

Hearing no room for negotiation in Aunt Peggy's voice, I let the matter drop.

That weekend Aunt Peggy and I watched footage of the demonstration in Washington on NBC's *Huntley-Brinkley Report*. Thousands of demonstrators had shown up, chanting and singing antiwar songs around the Pentagon.

Monday, John was energized by the possibility that popular opposition—opposition from those, like him, who could be called on to fight—might change the direction of the war. He described the singing, the marching, how he stood in the faces of the National Guardsmen and yelled, "Fuck you!"

I was impressed—not with his story but at the fact that his parents had allowed him to go.

"I didn't ask permission," he said. "I just told my mother I was going—and I went."

"What about your dad?" I asked.

"Dad goes along with whatever my mother says."

I said that having parents who went along with whatever you wanted to do must be nice, and he said no, it was pretty terrible, that sometimes he felt invisible, like it didn't make any difference whether he lived there or not.

I was surprised at his reaction, but I knew that feeling of invisibility all too well.

One day we sat in Mr. Linblad's office with our feet up on the old oak table that was littered with books and papers. Some of them were Mr. Linblad's, but most of them were from the literary magazine, which used his office for its headquarters.

I showed John the foreword I'd written for the magazine.

> *with words*
> *to capture the entire universe*
> *to recognize ourselves through inexhaustible discovery*
> *to admit*
> *that Life is a Story of Our Own Telling.*

He thought it was bullshit. "We have no control over acts of God, over hurricanes or earthquakes. We don't even have control over whether the president conducts this fucking war."

I said that those were big things, but that in our personal lives I thought we could write the script. We got into an argument over whether historical events determine the course of one's life or not, until I finally I said it was just the foreword to a poetry magazine, not a religious statement.

"But it *is* a statement. It's a philosophical statement about life! Why are you backing off from it? You wrote it, defend it!"

But I hadn't been raised to consider my feelings worth defending.

We finally agreed to table the discussion. Then, to clear our heads, we went for a walk.

The boardwalk lay a half block from the high school. It was still early March, and there were no hotels and few restaurants by the high school, so we had the place to ourselves. John produced a joint, which we went under the boardwalk to share on the beach. The sand was chilly. We watched the sea foam blow about like tumbleweed in the sharp wind.

Halfway through the joint, John said, "You're beautiful when you're angry."

It was like a line out of a bad movie. But back then no male had ever called me beautiful straight out like that.

At that same moment, I decided I could use the poem in the class yearbook instead of the literary magazine and thereby avoid further argument.

I laughed at the sneakiness of my idea.

John must have thought I was laughing at his calling me beautiful, because suddenly he kissed me.

I kissed him back, and my carefully balanced world began to tremble.

The meaning of the Drifters song hit my marijuana-addled brain like the apple hit Newton's head.

"Hey, we're 'Under the Boardwalk'!" I pointed out.

"So we are," he said, more calmly than I was used to hearing him talk. He couldn't remember the lyrics to the song, so I sang it while he sang a doo-do-doo-do-doo-doo part.

We continued singing as we walked down the boardwalk one mile to Indiana Avenue, where I lived on the north side of Atlantic Avenue.

There would be days to come when John walked me home and we made out and fondled each other on the hunter green carpet in the living room, but that first day there were still boundaries a white boy and a black girl dared not cross. Instead, at the south side of Pacific Avenue, John kissed me good-bye, and turned to walk back, past the high school, into Ventnor, the white suburb of Atlantic City where he lived.

That year some black and white students at Atlantic City High had had a cafeteria fight. It was the first outbreak of racial tension in the city, which had been spared even on the night that Martin Luther King was assassinated. No one was seriously hurt in what the local paper called "a racial melee"; nevertheless, the local chamber of commerce, with an eye toward the summer tourist season, wanted to forestall further trouble. Working with the board of education, they instituted a six-week "can't we all get along?" workshop called "Project WILL" which took fifty black, white, and Hispanic student leaders and put them in rooms together inside one of the larger hotels. Meanwhile the city imposed a curfew on youths under age seventeen.

The fight had polarized the student body, so John and I avoided holding hands in school. The beach became our haven, and it was there that, after two weeks of sneaking off together, John and I declared our love.

Soon after, I wanted to go meet his parents and was stunned when he refused. He said he wouldn't even tell his mother about me. He was afraid to risk her anger.

"My mother would kill me!" he said, staring at the sand. "It's bad enough that you're a goy, but a *shvartzeh* on top of that! I'd be skinned alive! Besides," he added, "every time I've opened up and shared something I've got with someone, I've lost it. I don't want to lose you."

Accepting a shadow existence seemed part of the tax I paid for being black in this life. So, reluctantly, I agreed to keep my relationship with John a secret.

Besides, I finally felt accepted by my black classmates. I had worked hard at it. I had an Afro worthy of Angela Davis. I wrote Afrocentric, political poetry in the pages of the student newspaper. I went out of my way to be friendly with my classmates in the vocational-education and business tracks. I wasn't putting on an act—many of them I had known since elementary school. Besides, the position my mother had put me in made me feel a kinship with those society labeled as "not good enough."

My acceptance among my peers seemed personified by the class treasurer, Tony, a tall, lithe brother on the track team, who had "expressed interest," as Aunt Peggy used to put it. I didn't know whether I liked him or not, but I felt flattered by his attentions. After working so hard to appear "regular," I wasn't about to become known as the sister in the AP classes who dated a white boy. That would have been totally politically incorrect; I would be labeled a traitor to the race, and lose my hard-fought-for popularity.

With so much at stake, I feared that my classmates could see the truth about John written all over my face: in the gleam in my eyes when I talked about him, in my smile when I smiled at him. After exhausting days of smuggling notes and hiding our affection for one another in school, we released the tension through long, aggressive tickling matches in the sanctuary provided by Mr. Linblad's cluttered office.

John had me on the ground one day, screaming for mercy, when I looked up to see Tony with Jim, one of his track teammates, standing in the open doorway. Tony had come to pick me up and walk me home.

Startled, John and I jumped up and composed ourselves as best we could. Tony and his friend said nothing, but I sensed their disapproval.

On the way home, Jim said to Tony, as though I weren't there, "Man, I don't think that's right. He was tickling her a little too high."

I caught my breath.

Tony tossed it off. "Oh, that's all right. John's safe. He just gets his kicks tickling girls." I exhaled, relieved that he had interpreted our misdemeanor as innocent play.

For the first time, I considered how hard it must have been for my mother to have hidden her relationship with my father. The next time I talked to her on the phone I told her so.

She told me it had been very difficult, indeed. "We were stared at and remarked upon everywhere we went," she said. It was the first time she'd ever commented on the emotional toll of her relationship with my father—the first time I'd ever asked. "His own mother refused to meet me. She would come visit him and brush right by me as if I weren't there."

Mom said she had finally reached the point where she refused to go out with my father at all.

Twenty years later, I found myself in a similar situation. It seemed hard to imagine what would be worse for me and John: the silence of saying nothing, or the silence to be endured if our secret became known.

Aunt Peggy hated the idea that I was seeing a "low-class" white boy. Mom convinced her that open opposition would only drive me further into the relationship. So Peggy tried a more subtle approach. I was setting the kitchen table one night when she asked whether I had met John's parents.

When I said no, I hadn't met them, she said she wanted to meet them if I was going to spend all this time with John. She already knew Tony's mother and respected her as a "hardworking woman raising that boy by herself," but she didn't think Tony was good enough for me either. She wanted me to meet a boy from a good family at college, get married, and have kids. I wanted to go to college and begin a career as a reporter. It was a constant back-and-forth: Aunt Peggy said reporters were hard and cynical and no man would want to marry one; I said I wouldn't marry anyone who couldn't accept me as I was.

That night, knowing that I was in a relationship with a boy who in fact *couldn't* accept me as I was—whose "low-class" parents wouldn't deign to meet my aunt—I plopped down the silverware, both to escape and to drown out Peggy's words.

"Did you hear me?" she persisted. She stopped preparing dinner to focus her full attention on me.

I took a very deep breath and stared into the rabbit hole. "He hasn't told his mother he's seeing me. She doesn't want him dating non-Jewish girls," I said matter-of-factly.

This time Aunt Peggy was the one who took in a sharp breath. "You mean you're seeing a boy who's ashamed of you?"

I went to the sink and turned the faucet on full force but couldn't drown out her words.

"You've got looks, you've got intelligence, you've got talent— baby, you've got it all. And why you want to go waste it on some poor white trash . . ." She was just getting started. Next came the sermon on needing to meet a boy from a good family, remaining pure, having kids, and living happily ever after.

I went to the cupboard and got the dishes, trying to set the table faster.

"If you're not careful, you'll end up like Yvonne!" she said, referring to Uncle Hugh's older sister. "Yvonne went and married that German fella—he seemed all right till they got to Germany. Then she wasn't accepted and had to start passing. That's what started her problems." She told me what I already knew—Yvonne had had several breakdowns in the past ten years. "Don't put yourself through that. Before I would put myself through that, baby, I would say, 'Good-bye, baby, bye-bye!' "

I finished setting the table and stomped off to my room, angrier because I agreed with everything she'd said. Maybe my feelings for John had allowed me to concede too much.

I put Laura Nyro's *New York Tendaberry* on the turntable. That spring her song "Captain for Dark Mornings" formed the sound track for my imagination. Glass wind chimes blew in the ocean breeze. I dreamed of meeting a soul mate whose words would melt my heart. I didn't know whether he would be black or white, from a good family or not, rich or poor, but I knew what the feeling would feel like.

I imagined surrendering my body to such a man. I would look for him the way a heroin addict looks for drugs. I would search New York's Lower East Side. He was there now, living in an apartment overlooking a black wrought-iron fire escape just east of Orchard Street. Every day, he walked through Chinatown, where street merchants pushed their carts along the narrow streets. He was looking for me but he didn't know it. One day our eyes would meet. I would be looking down at him as I sat on the fire escape, wearing a long silky nightgown of navy blue or black, brushing my long black hair and waiting for this bearded captain of the streets to claim me.

I daydreamed about all this, seventeen-year-old virgin that I was, lying on the twin bed of my little room in Atlantic City, listening to Laura Nyro. Mom had given me the record player the year after Paul died. I cherished it because it took me to places that the color television—which she had also given us—could not, took me inside of my imagination, to places where Aunt Peggy feared for me to go.

We seemed endlessly on the edge of argument.

"You've raised me all these years," I would say, insulted by her lack of faith in me. "Don't you believe I'll make the right decisions?"

"You're young and impressionable. You don't know the world," she retorted.

I thought I knew more about life than she realized.

Frustrated by the seeming impasse of my romantic dilemma, I decided to have sex with Tony. I had been fooling around with both Tony and John, but I couldn't see myself having sex with John, and Tony had been pressing the issue. I thought that by having sex with Tony, I might be able to get rid of them both: John would get angry with me for "cheating," and Tony . . . well, if he acted the way Aunt Peggy said men did when they only wanted one thing, that would be the end of him, too.

There was one obstacle: I didn't want to risk getting pregnant, but I knew nothing about birth control.

I called my mother. Although we often talked about handsome men and my crushes on this or that rock star, we had never discussed my sexuality outright.

She was unprepared.

"You're not having sex already, are you?" she asked hesitantly.

I had just turned seventeen. Old enough, I thought. She had gotten pregnant with my brother when she was my age.

I told her no, I just wanted to be ready. When I described my plan to get rid of both of my suitors, she said my logic seemed dubious. Awkwardly, she tried to advise me about my birth control options.

"Well, there's condoms—but they don't work," she began. "Birth-control pills are better."

I told her that pills wouldn't work for me. I would have to go to the doctor for a prescription, and Aunt Peggy and I shared the same one.

"There's the diaphragm," Mom suggested.

When I asked her what a diaphragm was, she stammered and said she'd ask my sister-in-law Lany to give me a call.

Tony had been hanging around, catching me after school whenever I didn't leave with John, having lunch with me in the cafeteria. One day he sidled up to me in the hallway as the spring days were getting longer and said, "I got them."

"Got what?" I asked.

"The rubbers," he said.

I caught my breath. The moment of truth, and he was not a "Captain for Dark Mornings," although he was a tall captain—of the track team.

Tony and I went to my house and put on a Delfonics record. We kissed, my enjoyment of the moment hampered by fear. I had been hoping for the feeling I felt when I listened to Laura Nyro, but Tony's lips on mine felt like those candy wax lips, his hands like the latex hands of a Halloween costume.

I wanted to get it over with. We undressed on the same hunter green living room rug where John and I had fooled around many days, catching stolen moments before Aunt Peggy came home. He pulled out a rubber, which I examined like a specimen in a petri dish before he took it from me to put on. The rubber was already lubricated.

I barely felt him inside me. Almost immediately he stiffened and finished, and I thought, Is that all it is?

Afterward, I asked him to leave. He looked at me strangely. Then he went into the bathroom for a few minutes and left.

I was astonished when, later, he said he wanted to see me again. Although we had spent a lot of time together, I had no feelings for him at all and no desire to have sex with him again. I told him that I would call him later. But I never did.

I felt badly for using Tony as a cover—it made me feel like one of those men Aunt Peggy had always warned would use me.

———

In the public library one day soon afterward, I looked up from my book and saw John. He pointed to the gele I had wrapped around my head, African-style.

"I don't like that," he said. "It makes you look like Aunt Jemima."

I recoiled at his presumption to tell me how to look.

"So—you only love the part of me you can accept on your terms?" I said evenly.

Suddenly we were talking about something far more fundamental than a gele. I conveniently ignored the fact that I'd had sex with Tony, without John's knowledge, to avoid being seen as a white boy's girlfriend, and accused John of being a hypocrite, hiding me from his parents out of shame.

"I can do this! I can! *You're* the one who's breaking under the pressure!" he cried in a fierce whisper. There were tears in his eyes.

I didn't argue with him. "Maybe you're right," I replied. "Maybe this is more than I can do."

The first letter was a wait-list notice, from Swarthmore. That came on Friday.

The following Wednesday, Aunt Peggy called me out of Mr. Linblad's class at school to say that I had large envelopes from Syracuse, Douglass, Bennington—and Radcliffe! Bennington had accepted me without scholarship aid, while Radcliffe sweetened the offer by including a complete scholarship/financial-aid package.

I was ambivalent about going to Cambridge. I wanted to attend a small college, where I could read, write, and grow slowly into erudition, but only one of my high-school teachers supported me. Everyone else wanted me to go to Harvard. My mother saw the status of the Harvard degree, my brother the four-year financial aid package. Aunt Peggy, dazzled by the Gregory legend, dreamed that at Harvard I would at last "find a boy from a good family and settle down."

"Don't men from good families go to Swarthmore?" I asked her, reduced to sophistry after Swarthmore came through with an acceptance and some money. When my brother Lary called and told me I was out of my mind for even thinking about declining Harvard's offer, I buckled under the pressure. Conceding to the will of the majority, I put away my dreams of small classes and personal tutorials.

And so, in late September 1971, Aunt Peggy and Uncle Float, the retired postal worker and caterer whom she had begun dating, packed my trunk and suitcases in the car to drive me up to Cambridge. I sat with my pet schnauzer, Gigi, in the backseat of Peggy's newly acquired 1969 pastel-yellow Cadillac. As we drove away, a melancholia settled over me. Heading north on the New Jersey Turnpike, I relived every bus ride between Atlantic City and New York. I had always thought of those trips as a *going to:* to my mother, to Aunt Peggy, to Europe.

This journey, I felt keenly, would be a leave-taking.

11. IN PHARAOH'S LAND

When I entered college in September 1971, I was one of fifty-six black women admitted to Radcliffe, the women's college; 165 black men had been admitted to Harvard. Women had been allowed in the same classrooms as men since 1943, but they were only allotted seats during the sixties—before that they either had to stand in the back or sit on the floor.

Aunt Hugh had written a letter of recommendation to Radcliffe on my behalf. "June may not be a Gregory by blood," she wrote, "but she is one by nurture. In every way, she has grown up a part of this family."

But I didn't feel a part of a family that had produced three generations of Harvard graduates—or if I did, it was only because they had adopted me. I was more like the family's pet stray, not one of its heirs apparent. In the political atmosphere of 1971, Harvard's admissions policies did little to convince me otherwise: blacks constituted exactly 10 percent of the incoming class. That number joined the others I'd lived by: half black, half white, three-quarters of the year in Atlantic City, one-quarter in Los Angeles.

Members of the Gregory family had walked Harvard Yard in the days when black students were counted in single digits, not even by percentages. During my first weeks at school, I walked the mile from the Radcliffe Quad toward the Charles River and searched out stately Lowell House. Uncle Gum had lived there during his undergraduate days at the turn of the century, exactly seventy years before me. Aunt Peggy had told me that one of Uncle Gum's roommates had been southern, to the antebellum manor born. When this roommate's parents visited, Uncle Gum had had to pretend he was his roommate's servant, for if the parents had discovered that Harvard allowed blacks and whites to room together, there would have been an uproar.

I felt a mixture of anger and tears that he ever had to undergo such humiliation.

Among the black freshmen matriculated into Harvard in September 1971, I fell within the mean: a high-school grade-point average of 3.8; SAT scores of 1200. Assistant Dean of Admissions David Evans, who had forsaken an engineering career at IBM to help Harvard find qualified black candidates, greeted us individually at the first black freshman mixer. As we introduced ourselves, Evans, Harvard's first black admissions officer, quoted, from memory, each freshman's hometown high school, SAT score, and place in our graduating class. His welcoming ritual was meant to reassure each one of us that we were not "affirmative action" babies, but as I listened to my classmates' scores, I felt dubious about my own case. I'd achieved that 1200 SAT with a perfect score on the verbal portion of the test, but a dismal 400 in math. I had many black classmates with perfect 1600s.

But we soon discovered the common experiences we'd all had in high school, which bound us. We had echoed the "power to the people!" slogans and supported black liberation while secretly admiring the language of Shakespeare, Donne, and Shelley (or Galileo, Pythagoras, and Einstein). It wasn't that we disagreed with the supposition that black people were oppressed in the United States, but we had found things to appreciate in the culture of our oppressors. Like Kabuki players, we had learned to change masks. Finally we formed our own tribe: the young, gifted, and black, and we celebrated with libation and dance.

For me, becoming free of Aunt Peggy's sheltering rules during the dawn of women's liberation and the sexual revolution felt like being dropped in the middle of a turbulent ocean in a daysailer.

As a first-semester freshman, I applied for an upper-class poetry workshop. I was admitted but soon discovered that I knew little about the modern poets whose work formed the foundation of the class. In high school we had studied the usual suspects: Robert Frost, Walt Whitman, Emily Dickinson, and T. S. Eliot—early Eliot, not "The Wasteland." I was unfamiliar with John Berryman or even Anne Sexton, although I had heard their names. Aunt Peggy did not want me to read them—particularly Sexton, because she didn't want me "getting ideas." Now I read them and became infatuated with the idea of writing from the depths of despair.

During class I experienced the sensation of being perched like a seagull at the window, observing myself while my professor and the upperclassmen discussed poems I didn't understand. Rather than assume that the material itself didn't speak to me or to my experience, I assumed that the fault was mine; what's worse, I assumed that nothing I could say, write, or bring to the class would speak to my classmates' experiences either.

Sensing that I was floundering, my professor suggested that I bring my "black perspective" to the class. I did not know what he meant, having only the perspective I had been raised with in Atlantic City. There was no academic canon of Afro-American literature taught in schools in 1971. I knew only what I had been taught, and I had no perspective on that at all.

My freshman roommate, Monique, and I shared a deep insecurity and chronic shyness, along with a penchant for fantasizing about Harvard men who scarcely knew we existed. We often stayed up all night listening to Gladys Knight and the Pips sing "If I Was Your Woman," or Aretha Franklin's "Young, Gifted and Black," or Carly Simon, turning off the lights at sunrise, watching as men from Harvard Yard crept from our Radcliffe dorm. We knew they hadn't been at dinner the night before. They were seeing somebody on the QT. Some white girl, more than likely, we surmised. Putting the clues together, we developed a clandestine social register for our class.

It was the season of Angela Davis's trial, so prisons were hip. It was also the time when the Black Panther Party transformed itself from an organization advocating armed struggle against the government to one advocating community service, so community service was hip. Intellectuals were absorbed in debates about the relevance of art to "the movement." I thought of myself as a poet, but I wanted to be a socially relevant poet. So when one of my classmates recruited me to come teach at a local prison, I agreed.

Bridgewater's Drug Treatment Center was an institution for nonviolent offenders. I wasn't at all sure I could play teacher to a bunch of drug addicts and drug dealers. Frankly, I was terrified of setting foot inside Bridgewater. But the prison looked less like a fortress than a compound of cement bungalows, populated mostly by convicts serving time for marijuana possession or for selling small amounts. All of them had been mandated to undergo treatment as part of their sentence.

They wore blue-and-gray pinstriped denim trousers and blue denim workshirts. I was surprised at how young and bright they were and, as time went by and I heard their reading skills, how ill-served they had been by Boston's public-school system.

Our group grew slowly. The first week there were about five or six, then twelve, the next week about fifteen. I thought this growth reflected my teaching skills until an inmate named Charles set me straight. He told me that the word had spread about this pretty young sister from Radcliffe teaching literature.

I wanted to go through a series of books—*Manchild in the Promised Land* by Claude Brown, Cleaver's *Soul on Ice*, Sam Greenlee's *The Spook Who Sat by the Door*—but the prison library had only one copy of *Soul on Ice*.

"What do you know about any of this stuff?" one convict asked me. "You're a get-over!" they said, referring to someone who had figured out how to work the white man's system.

I could see how they would say that, but I told them that the fact that I was "gettin' over" didn't mean I hadn't known hard times.

"Like what?" they demanded to know.

"Well, my mother is white and my father is black. He was an alcoholic, and he beat my mother up. She finally ran off, but she couldn't afford to raise us. My brother grew up in foster homes. I was raised by my father's sister. I hid in books instead of looking to drugs, like you all did. That's how I got to Radcliffe."

It was a version of my life that drew on the iconic myths popularized by the Temptations song "Poppa Was a Rollin' Stone"—and it wasn't far at all from what my mother and Aunt Peggy had come up with for that fan magazine. My ability to recognize the emotional void that people often sought helped me connect with my imprisoned students. Some of them shared versions of their life stories.

After four or five weeks, I proposed that we read James Baldwin.

"Isn't he a homo?" Bubba asked. He came to the classes, I suspected, less for the books and more for the eye candy.

"Naw, I ain't reading anything by no faggots," Charles insisted.

"Faggots," I said, picking up their vocabulary, "can speak to the condition of black people as well as anyone else."

"I ain't reading no faggot," they spoke in unison.

"You got to understand," Charles said, breaking it down to me as if I were a four-year-old, "when you're inside here, your sexuality is constantly being questioned. Anybody catches any one of us reading a book by a faggot, we might as well be a faggot."

My teenage verve would not be denied. "What's who a person sleeps with got to do with whether they write well or not?" I demanded. But as a concession to their predicament, the next week I brought in several copies of Baldwin's short stories that I had found in a used-book store. I tore the covers off so that no one would know what they were reading and handed them out.

"So if you don't tell anyone you're reading a faggot, no one will know. But we're going to discuss the work of this faggot, 'cause he's got something to say."

The work was "Sonny's Blues," Baldwin's story of a heroin-addicted musician. Only three of them admitted that they read it, but they identified with what they read, and they persuaded the group to get past Baldwin's sexuality and read *Go Tell It on the Mountain* and *Blues for Mister Charlie*.

I was very proud of this small victory and told my family about it. Mom cheered me on. Aunt Peggy was mortified that I had developed relationships with a group of *prisoners*. Even Uncle Hugh, who normally took my side when it came to social issues, tried to talk me out of it. He said one of my students might find out where I lived, stalk me, and attack me in my bed.

I protested that these guys were human beings who just happened to be down on their luck, that they treated me with respect.

"You can't trust drug addicts!" Uncle Hugh said.

I ridiculed his fears as baseless, the bourgeois stereotype of prisoners. But after that conversation I was careful not to reveal where I lived on campus.

One week just after the winter break, we were reading poetry—Etheridge Knight, Nikki Giovanni, Sonia Sanchez. One inmate asked if I wrote poems or just read them. I could hear titters around the room. So the following week I brought in my poetry journals and read several of my more militant ones.

Someone asked to see the rest of the book. I carelessly handed it over. As we took turns reading, it passed throughout the room.

Suddenly Bubba burst out, "You're reading all the militant poems, but you ain't reading these love poems!"

Stung, I halted.

"Yeah," Charles said, "you got one in here you sound like Angela Davis, the next you're writing about roses."

"All right, I'll read one of those," I said softly, trying to think which one might not leave me too vulnerable to questions about my personal life.

"Here's one," Bubba said, stumbling through the words,

> *It's a still life watercolor*
> *In a now-late afternoon*
> *As the sun shines through the curtains*
> *And shadows wash the room*

"I didn't write that!" I exclaimed. "That's the words to a Simon & Garfunkel song!"

"You listen to Simon & Garfunkel?" Bubba asked incredulously.

"Not only does she listen, she writes the words down in her poetry book!" Charles pointed out, laughing.

I felt incriminated by my own listening tastes.

"Yeah," Larry piped in. "You got one white side and one black side, and you don't know what you are."

"Do all poems have to be militant?" I asked plaintively, trying to rescue myself.

"I'm just pointing out how you misrepresenting yourself," Charles said. "You acting like you some down sister, but inside your head it's white."

"Why do I have to have only side? Don't all of us have different sides to our personalities?" I asked, vainly trying to defend my right to multiple voices. I left that night feeling deflated. It was like being back in high school, this idea that there was a "black" way and a "white" way of thinking. Going back to my dorm at Radcliffe, to the company of my friends who saw the similarities between Baldwin and Baudelaire, felt like a refuge.

Later that week I got a letter from one of my students at Bridgewater. He revealed a story similar to mine—his mother was white, and he'd been raised by his father's mother after his mom's family rejected him. He thought that rejection by his white relatives had something to do with his drug addiction.

"Don't let them see you crack," he wrote, referring to the other prisoners. "They find an opening, they'll break you down. It's a game they play. You got to play the game without letting them see you hurt. That's the way it works out here."

That seemed to be the way it worked everywhere.

Inside the sheltered gates of Harvard Yard, at the Freshman Union, a daily celebration of black pride took place. We formed a bas-relief, sitting against the wall, our Afros towering over our heads. Over lunch we adapted "the dozens"—the street game of jiving and taunting one another with jokes about each other's relatives—and played it like star poker players. On the street our gibes would surely have led to a fight, but safe in Cambridge we fired away, developing friendships—and even love affairs—in the midst of our rivalries.

I discovered I had a peculiar talent for these ripostes, even though I would never have dared play the dozens on the streets of Atlantic City.

"Yo' mama's so ugly her face looks like it caught on fire and somebody stamped it out with a football shoe."

"Yeah, well, *your* mama's so ugly she sleeps with a dog."

"Yo' mama so ugly she grateful for whoever will fuck her."

"Yo' mama so ugly she hasn't been fucked since your pet greyhound died ten years ago."

"Yeah, well, yo' mama so ugly she's grateful for whatever she can get. She told me so before I left her last night."

Of course, we weren't all down with the game. Monique avoided these exchanges altogether. Another classmate told me, with a distinguished swagger, that he knew nothing about the dozens, since he had gone to Choate.

"Choke who?" I asked.

"Choate. Choate. It's a boarding school."

"Oh," I said, a note of pity in my voice. I thought boarding schools were for kids whose parents didn't want them.

Monique laughed at my ignorance and told me that Choate was a very exclusive place, along with Exeter and Andover—parents sent their kids to these schools because attendance there practically guaranteed entry into Harvard.

I felt sorry for those who had spent their entire school career scheming to get admitted to Harvard.

Several of my classmates provoked our collective opprobrium: those who chose to socialize exclusively with whites even though their skin, noses, and hair dictated that they join us in the west side of the dining room. There was, for instance, Sara, isolated in South House, a thin, honey-colored woman who wore her hair straightened while the rest of us vied to see who had the biggest Afro. At first we felt sorry for her, over there where *no* black folks lived. She refused to join us at the table, and although she sometimes acknowledged us individually, she would never speak if more than two of us were together.

Who does she think she is? we wondered, our suspicions rising. Maybe, we guessed, falling into the vernacular, heads wagging side to side, she just don't want to *be* black.

One morning, arriving at breakfast early, I found her already in the dining hall. We sat together.

It turned out she had lived on Convent Avenue, not three blocks from Uncle Hugh and Aunt Sylvia.

"We all thought you didn't want to have anything to do with us," I said.

"Why should I be judged on whether or not I'm black by whether or not I speak, or whom I sit with?" she responded. She had a high-pitched, though raspy, voice, with perfect diction.

"Because it's what we do," I said. "It's what makes us black. We acknowledge each other's existence."

"I just refuse to be judged as black by whether or not I speak to strangers," she said.

"But other black people aren't 'strangers,' " I argued. "We're all in the same boat. We help each other out. We're all brothers and sisters."

"I don't have any brothers, and my sister grew up in the same house as me," she said sharply. "My mother taught me not to speak to strangers."

I was so taken aback that it didn't occur to me to ask why she was speaking to me then, at breakfast, when she wouldn't acknowledge my presence if I sat with three or four other black students at the table. I realized, just then, that in terms of defining what was black and what wasn't, I was taking the same point of view that my prisoner-students in Bridgewater had taken with me. So I backed down and asked about her classes.

She wanted to be a creative-writing major. So did I. We promised to read each other's work.

Some of my dormmates, having seen us together, asked me what was the score on Sara. I recounted the conversation.

"Who ever heard of a sistah from Convent Avenue and 141st Street not wanting to talk to black people?" Monique exclaimed, echoing the consensus. "She sounds strange to me."

I wondered how Monique could possibly know, as she herself had grown up on Long Island.

Another classmate, Thomas Washington, presented a different challenge to the black orthodoxy. He came from Virginia, a state we knew to be full of racial miscreants dating back to the seventeenth century. Thomas had that wavy hair and broad nose that might confuse some white folks, but for those of us who "knew," these physical characteristics, combined with that olive tint of his skin, fairly cried out his true ancestry.

Washington avoided not only the black table but all eye contact with anyone black. He refused to acknowledge us even when we spoke to him first. He had an athletic build and walked with a patrician air and a grace that to some of us signaled arrogance—or maybe just that he had been the star quarterback in high school. We scoured the freshman register to learn whether he lived on the black side of Richmond and searched out upperclassmen from his hometown who could provide clues to his pedigree. No one knew his family. Still, we thought we had peeped his secret. After all, who but a black man would name his son *Thomas Washington*?

I went home at Christmas break, eager to tell Aunt Peggy about my joy at finding a community of smart black folks, about our black table and the social shenanigans and judgments that transpired there, but she wasn't happy to hear about any of it.

"It distresses me to hear you talking black, black, black!" she said. "I hope you take advantage of all the opportunities. Don't set yourself apart. You weren't like that in high school—why are you like that now?"

I told her that in high school there had been few black people with whom I could discuss Shakespeare *and* Césaire, George Clinton or the Last Poets *and* Nietzsche. If there had been, I might have sat at such a table there.

I had expected Aunt Peggy to applaud the notion of black students coming together, a sort of permanent Niagara Movement, the group of black Talented Tenth overachievers that W. E. B. DuBois had assembled in 1918 to develop the future of the race. Out of that group, the National Association for the Advancement of Colored People, the NAACP, had emerged. Just the previous summer, I had heard her tell my brother, Lary, that the black-power movement had had a point when they criticized her generation for moving too slow.

"They called us 'accommodationists,' " she'd told him ruefully. "Maybe we were, a little. Maybe we shouldn't have been so gentle about demanding our rights before."

But I had forgotten what an integrationist she really was. Aunt Peggy wanted civil rights so that she could move to a nice house with a wraparound porch in Margate, while I wanted to build a house like the one in Margate right there on Indiana Avenue. I called that "black nationalism."

She warned me not to confuse nationalism with advancing the race. Her warning was prescient. Afrocentricity would raise our self-esteem in the short run, but in the years since, the packaging and commercialization of black street culture as the only "authentic" African-American experience, combined with the way some black teenagers equate educational achievement with "white" behavior, has made a mockery of what the NAACP meant by "equality."

But at seventeen that concept was more than I could foresee.

During the first semester, I saw a notice for a meeting of "mixed-race" students.

The phrase "mixed-race" always bothered me. Who defined

"mixed-race"? I knew students with two black parents, others with two Arab parents or two Latino parents or, in some cases, two white parents, who looked just like some of these "mixed-race" classmates.

The meeting was held on a Tuesday night at a dorm tucked away on the south side of the Radcliffe Quad. I walked in late and stood in the shadows. I saw one of my classmates, a girl with delicate, fine-boned features, the mocha-colored skin of a Southeast Asian, and smooth, wispy hair that drifted down in loose curls to her shoulders. At the black table, we often snidely referred to her as "the white girl with a tan."

I had not known that this girl's mother was white, but I wasn't surprised to hear her say that she felt forced to choose between being black and being white, but she didn't want to make that choice, she said, since it would mean denying either her mother or her father.

Hearing her reminded me of a quote that I had copied in my journal and attributed to Aimé Césaire: "We do not choose our cultures—we belong to them." I had discovered which culture I belonged to many years before, at the 1964 Democratic convention, as the Mississippi Freedom Democratic Party demonstrated for the right to be heard.

A second speaker, an Asian-Afro-American, spoke of his close relationship with his mother, an Asian immigrant, and described how she had raised him and his brother to love both their cultures. His Asian features were set off by a large Afro—his hair was the envy of all the sisters, because it stayed perfectly in place, curly without being nappy, the kind of hair we secretly coveted. He studied Swahili and Japanese, he said, to honor both his mother's teachings and his father's ancestors.

His words convinced me to emerge from the back of the room and take a seat. But as I moved stealthily forward, a third young man raised his hand and asked plaintively, "Why should we have to choose? Why is it so important to be black or white?"

Sucking my teeth, I turned and left. I was nothing like these "mixed-race" students. There was no choice for me to make. I was black by law, laws written during slavery, which decreed that one drop of black blood made me black; and if those laws negated my beloved mother's genetic contribution . . . well, I had a construct for that, too: Mom, white though she was, fit the archetype of the self-sacrificing mother abandoned by the stereotypical no-good Negro. Mom had been a single mother, deserted by a black man and left alone to raise two children. That black man had been denied his livelihood by the tenets of racism, and he had beat his blues out on the woman he loved. Left alone and without a way to feed her family, she had been forced to make the ultimate sacrifice—by leaving her children for others to raise.

Aunt Yvonne, who had been the golden girl of the Gregory family when I was a small child, died of liver cancer during that first semester I was at college.

Once, Aunt Peggy had sat me down and told me that while all of the Gregory girls were beautiful, Yvonne had been the most beautiful of them all, and that while all six children were smart, Yvonne was the most brilliant. Ever since she told me that fairy tale when I was a little girl, Yvonne had been a mythical being in my eyes—part Ava Gardner, part Zora Neale Hurston, a published poet who had worked with Paul Robeson and reported for the *Amsterdam News*. I both wanted to be her—and feared ending up like her.

Aunt Peggy said it was Yvonne's insistence on changing America's racialism that drove her crazy. "You keep up all this thinking about race," she warned me, "black this and black that—and you'll end up the same way."

Yvonne's deterioration had been long and slow. Her marriage to the German dissolved after her multiple nervous breakdowns. She spent long spells homeless in New York City, keeping company with her gin bottle. Uncle Hugh invited her up to his place for the holidays with his kids. Aunt Peggy couldn't understand it, but that was Uncle Hugh. Family was family, crazy or not.

She died an alcoholic bag lady, living in Grand Central Station.

I had last seen her the summer before I left for college. She appeared at the front door, hair matted but arranged, face puffy, wearing a winter coat in the middle of July. She looked like a ghost of Christmas past. Startled, Aunt Peggy could do nothing but invite her in. She entered and sat in Papa's chair.

"Do you have any gin?" Yvonne asked.

Peggy paused. "I don't . . . think I have any in the house," she said evasively.

I knew where the liquor bottles were stored: in Aunt Peggy's darkroom, in rows alternating with her bottles of photographic developing solutions—a method she had devised to keep herself from coming down and getting a sip in the middle of a sleepless night.

"You mean I've come all this way and you can't offer me a drink?" Yvonne said belligerently.

"Well, I'll see what I can find," Aunt Peggy said. She disappeared into the kitchen, and I heard the clanking of bottles. Yvonne and I made small talk. Soon Aunt Peggy emerged with a bottle of gin about a quarter full.

"This is all I have," she said, with a glance to me for emphasis. I figured she had poured the rest into one of her empty bottles of developing solution.

"Thank you," Yvonne said, smiling her once pretty smile. A side tooth was missing. She took the bottle and a glass of ice.

Then Peggy left—to run an errand, she said—and left me sitting across from the bloated, sad-looking, café con leche–colored woman.

"So you once worked with Paul Robeson?" I asked brightly. "What was he like?"

"Oh, I didn't really work *with* him," she said, contemplating her glass. "There was a team of us, assembling clips and things, trying to argue that the United States should be tried before the UN for human-rights violations, because of the way they treated Negroes. We thought that because of the Cold War, we could shame the U.S. into making changes."

She took a long sip.

"What an effort in futility that was. This country's never going to change."

"Why do you say that?" I asked.

She took a longer sip. "Look around you—you see anything changing?" she said.

"Well, they've passed all these laws," I began. "They're not supposed to discriminate anymore. They're letting people into schools—"

"Yeah, they're *letting* people in," she burst out, more forcefully than I thought the conversation warranted. "You watch. They've already decided how many they're going to *let* in, and after that, that door's gonna slam shut and every other muthafucka can fend for himself. This country's never gonna change."

She fiddled with a ring on her finger. "Pursuit of happiness for them that's already got," she mumbled to herself.

She poured herself another glass of gin and sighed.

"Anyway, all that was long ago," she said, lifting the glass to her lips. She held it in her hand, her elbow crooked, as she looked at me, and her dark eyes seemed to flash and shift. "You really want to know about Robeson? He was a *hateful* man. Ego-driven. A drunk. He never did any of that work. We did it for him. He used us to get the publicity!"

I was taken aback, as much by the sudden fire in her voice as by this calumny against an icon of black achievement and resistance.

"What a useless enterprise," she reiterated, setting her glass down hard on the table, "thinking that a bunch of words could change the way things are done in this country. Supplicants, that's all we are. Supplicants at the mercy of these capitalists who exploit the poor to put furs on their own backs."

She leaned forward, as though to confide in me. "At night," she said, "I feel them crawling all over me." She moved her clenched hands across her body.

"The capitalists?" I asked.

"No, termites," she said. "Termites and vermin. They're eating away at the foundations."

"How do you stop them?" I asked.

"With this," she said, raising her glass and finishing it.

I inhaled and held my breath in the shallows of my chest. I knew that Yvonne "wasn't right." My goal was to keep her in a logical conversation till Aunt Peggy came home.

"Let's dispense with these niceties," Yvonne said. "I don't need a fucking glass." She picked up the bottle of gin and took a swig. "Peggy's just like my mother. Trying to maintain all these cultured pretenses."

"What's so pretentious about drinking out of a glass?" I asked, then immediately regretted it.

"She's doing it to you, too. Got you thinking if you act nice enough, sweet enough, the world will be yours on a silver platter." She took another swig. "Peggy and my mother. In love with white people and the beneficence of their corrupt, twisted hearts." Her voice dripped with sarcasm.

I examined her face. All traces of the beauty it once held, a beauty still apparent when she'd walked in the door, had now disappeared. The circles under her dark eyes cast a shadow over her face.

"So," I said, exhaling, trying to find a safe subject, "what brings you to Atlantic City?"

"Why? You don't think I belong here?"

"Oh, of course you do. It's just . . . I haven't seen you in so long. I remember when I was small, once you came and told me fairy tales when I had measles."

"You remember that?"

"Yes. And I went out after that and read every fairy-tale book at the Atlantic City Public Library."

"Well, bully for you."

I stared at the green carpet, feeling ridiculous. My eyes caught her curled black toenails, dirt covering her toes like dried mud, poking out from worn, dirty sandals. I wondered if there was anything I could say that wouldn't draw one of her sarcastic asides. She belched, and from across the room I smelled stale gin and cigarettes.

"I remember when your mother brought you down here," she said.

"You do?" I brightened. I remembered so little from that period of my life then. It would take me years to recover those memories.

"Yeah, I remember. It was summertime. Your mother brought you down, and we were in the backyard. My mother's magnolia trees were blooming, and everyone was making a to-do over you, like you were some kind of flower. 'Oh, isn't she cute! Isn't she cute!' "

I smiled at the thought.

"You *were* cute, for a half-breed."

My smile froze in place. "Do . . . you remember meeting my mother?"

"Oh, yeah. She was a pretty white woman. But I guess she got rid of you fast enough." Her face twisted into a sneer, and my stomach twisted with it. "You could tell she didn't know what to do with you. She had your hair all chopped off, and it was all matted"—she gnarled her fingers for effect—"matted like you'd been sleeping on it for days and nobody ever combed it. It looked like things were crawling around inside it, all kinds of vermin."

I had begun to believe her, but her repetition of that word—"vermin"—signaled that her words sprang from that termite-infested place in her mind, not from her memory.

"So . . . where do these vermin come from?" I asked her.

"What vermin?"

"The vermin you see—the vermin that crawl on you at night."

"They live in hell. They think I can't find them there, but I can." She went on to give a vivid description of the place. It was nearly word for word a description of purgatory from Dante's *Inferno*.

I followed her as she rambled on. Her mother's roses, which had dotted the backyard along with the magnolias, became rotted branches of thorns, her wedding in her mother's house a charade of manners in which her husband had been paid to take her off the family's hands—even the lace on her wedding dress a manifestation of the bugs crawling up her arms. Listening to her, I could see that everything had two sides: beauty and truth, ugliness and falsehoods.

Her vision frightened me, because the perception depended entirely on where you stood.

I refused to attend Yvonne's funeral, although Aunt Peggy begged me. Instead, on the day and appointed hour of her memorial service, I sat alone for an hour in the chapel near Radcliffe Yard. Yvonne had been too smart, too beautiful—and born too early. Today her illness—classic schizophrenia and bipolar disorder—would have been treatable. But then mental illness was considered shameful. Everyone thought she literally had driven herself crazy with her fixation on race.

Sitting alone in the chapel, remembering the conversation from that gin-filled afternoon, I determined that I would honor Yvonne's memory by succeeding as a writer. I would question the racial assumptions.

And I would not go crazy.

In April, Mom asked me to come out to Las Vegas for her fiftieth birthday. I hemmed and hawed. How counterrevolutionary was it to be teaching the brothers in prison during the week and then go jetting off to Las Vegas for the weekend?

My alternatives were to remain alone at school during spring break or visit Atlantic City. I'd never been to Vegas, and my dalliance with a Harvard classmate who liked to spin Black English versions of Shakespearean monologues had sputtered to an end; I needed to get away. Besides, playing Vegas was a triumph for Larry, and I wanted to support him.

After *F Troop*, Larry's television career had alternately stalled and soared. After losing the Emmy for Best Actor to Don Adams, he had done several guest appearances on *Get Smart*; he'd also appeared on *I Dream of Jeannie*. He got a script for another military comedy but decided he didn't want to be pigeonholed and turned down a role in the series that became *M*A*S*H*.

Larry had moments of brilliance, but he needed a straight man like Forrest Tucker. Unfortunately, "Tuck," as everyone called him, was sick—his heavy drinking had finally caught up with him.

Larry revived his nightclub act and landed Vegas. He had seventy-five weeks, guaranteed, opening for Bobbie Gentry, whose hits "Ode to Billie Joe," "Son of a Preacher Man," and "Fancy" had given her headliner status. Mom and Larry hoped that his turn before the Vegas crowd might expose him to a new audience and jump-start his Hollywood career.

They were staying at the Desert Inn, Howard Hughes's old hotel, considered by Las Vegas standards to be a modest casino. To me it seemed anything but: three massive chandeliers hung in a gold-and-red brocaded lobby, mirrored walls reflecting light into infinity. A dissonant symphony assaulted my ears: the shouts of winners, jangling coins, percussive slot machines, hawking dealers, and the groans of losers. I found it overwhelmingly noisy and bewildering, flashy and fascinating. Men strutted through the lobby dressed in turquoise or red satin cowboy shirts with white velvet trim, wearing tight jeans with belt buckles as big as their fists and snakeskin boots in shiny black, red, and emerald green. They reminded me of the Philadelphia pimps on Kentucky Avenue in Atlantic City who bought "fly" suits to match their pink or emerald green Cadillacs.

The Las Vegas women, though, were beyond anything I'd ever seen in Atlantic City. Big hair, layered makeup, inch-long lashes and nails: their sequined dresses fit snugly over skin tanned and dried by the sun, set off by outrageous costume jewelry; or they wore gold jeans and oversized turquoise Indian jewelry, their perfume carrying the scent of flowers and nutmeg through the air-conditioned atmosphere. They outdid the Philadelphia prostitutes, and most of them weren't even working.

Aunt Peggy would have found them cheap, gaudy, and overdone, and that they were, but how they reveled in their fake beauty! In comparison, I felt dowdy and plump: the width of my hips, the fullness of my lips, the kink of my hair, the roundness of my eyeglasses. Mom wanted me to get contact lenses and spruce myself up. "Show off your small waist and that wide ass!" she urged. "Men love it!" I was mortified by her crassness. She wanted to buy me a hip-hugger jean skirt with a wide turquoise buckle belt, red leather cowboy boots, and a suede halter top with beads, but I refused. In Cambridge, women wore sensible low-heeled shoes and long full skirts. I was enough of a church girl to feel uncomfortable in clothes that made me an object of desire. I had no wish to be mistaken for a prostitute if I happened to be walking around alone.

"It must be Peggy's upbringing. No daughter of mine would walk around looking like an old fuddy-duddy," Mom said, her voice on edge.

We had already had one disagreement during this visit. The NAACP had criticized Hollywood for not hiring more black screenwriters, but Mom had thought it ridiculous to insinuate that white writers couldn't write authentic roles for black actors.

"So does that mean black screenwriters can write for white actors?" I had asked her. She had gotten flustered. "That's not the point!" she said. "It's this bigotry that says only blacks can write for blacks, only Chinese for Chinese—it's ridiculous! It destroys the whole idea of the universality of the theater!"

"So why can't black screenwriters be universal?" I asked. She sighed in exasperation, and we let it drop. I had asserted my opinion with my heart in my throat. Then, fearing she'd stay angry, I became deferential. Still, I drew the line at dressing up like a Las Vegas version of Annie Oakley. That was going too far.

Valerie Simpson, the Motown songwriter who'd penned hits for Marvin Gaye and Tammi Terrell, the Temptations, and the Supremes, was headlining nearby at the Mirage. Her first solo album, *Exposed*, had been on my turntable for the past six weeks, and I really wanted to go to the show. I couldn't go alone, since I was underage, but I couldn't work the thought of asking Mom to go with me into my mouth. Mom didn't appreciate black rhythm and blues, not even Aretha Franklin. In any case, I would have been uncomfortable in a black milieu with her, and too self-conscious to engage in the call and response energy generated by the music.

Instead I met the white headliners she and Larry wanted me to meet: Anthony Newley, Johnny Cash, Wayne Newton. I found Tony Newley to be the best showman. "If you've got it, flaunt it," he told me. I wrote it in my journal. I thought Wayne Newton had more kitsch than talent, but I wanted to get his autograph for Aunt Peggy. She liked the way he looked in his pants, so we got him to inscribe the picture "Sorry I'm still wearing pants!" (When I gave it to her, she was mortified. "How can I display such a thing?" she complained. Instead she kept it in the front of her scrapbook.)

I met Muhammad Ali at Johnny Cash's show at Caesars Palace. Ali was the largest man I had ever seen. He wore a gray silk suit with a pastel pink tie. My hand disappeared into his like a six-year-old's.

What was he doing at a Johnny Cash show? I asked. He was from Louisville, he replied. He had grown up on country music.

Country music had never appealed to me, but I liked Johnny Cash's deep, wounded voice and acoustic guitar. He made country sound like white folks' blues. I felt particularly drawn to one refrain:

> *I keep a close watch on this heart of mine,*
> *I keep my eyes wide open all the time. . . .*
> *Because you're mine, I walk the line.*

Cash was a fan of Larry's, and he invited us to visit his suite. As the headliner at the most prestigious club on the strip, he got to stay in the penthouse at Caesars Palace. The suite, done in pale beige and mirrors, was as close to classy as Las Vegas got. It sprawled larger than most houses—almost twice as large as the two-story house where I had grown up in Atlantic City. Its wraparound balcony looked out onto the Sierra Nevada Mountains. It had a fully stocked bar, a telephone, and a color television set in every room—including the two bathrooms.

Cash said he wasn't supposed to be drinking but wouldn't mind smelling some alcohol, so he offered to make a gin and tonic for Mom and got me a Coke. Larry drank his usual—red zinfandel. Mom had started joking that Larry wouldn't drink any juice that wasn't fermented, but his drinking hadn't yet become debilitating. He could still function, even on the half a gallon of wine consumed before he went onstage. The half gallon he drank afterward, however, had begun to be problematic.

While Cash prepared our drinks, we wandered around the suite's spacious living room, admiring the curved couch; the bathroom bigger than most kitchens; the fully-stocked kitchen—a catering staff of ten or more could easily prepare a party without tripping over each other. Larry's voice boomed out, "Oh, this is George! This is George!" at each new turn.

We were most impressed with the master bedroom. A huge canopy bed, larger than king-size, formed its centerpiece. "Oh, what a great bed!" Mom exclaimed.

"You haven't seen the half of it," Cash said, walking in with our drinks. "Look up."

There—where the fabric of the canopy should have been—was a gold-framed mirror. Larry cracked a joke about being able to watch your own movies while you were doing the old bang-ga-bang. Mom and I laughed, but Cash looked down at the floor, seemingly discomfited.

Later Mom told me that Cash was alone because his wife, June Carter, wouldn't put up with his drinking. He had been battling alcohol for years. It was a daily struggle, she said, and it had almost cost him his wife and family.

Something in Mom's voice made me think that she wished she had the strength of June Carter. It would be some time before my mother confided that Larry's drinking was bothering her, and it would be longer before I understood the toll that covering for him exacted from her: choosing his clothes and getting him dressed when he was too sauced to make decisions before curtain call, making excuses for him when he conked out at parties, driving him everywhere because she didn't want him driving home drunk, finding and emptying the bottles of wine he hid everywhere. At the time I was touched by Johnny Cash's story and the determination of Cash himself to stop drinking, for the love of a woman.

All that money and fame, I thought, and still he was all alone.

On the night of her fiftieth birthday, my mother wore a simple blue chiffon sheath by Bill Blass with a white ostrich-feather boa. A matching blue satin skullcap sat on her head at a jaunty angle, and faux-gem hoops dangled from her ears. To me she seemed the centerpiece in a display room full of beautiful women, and I felt as plain as a naked lightbulb.

We ate bloodred steak, french fries, and drank plenty of red wine. As the wine mixed with the vintage years, my mother became maudlin and wistful.

"I want another child," she said, her eyes dry, her voice cracking with tears. I couldn't tell whether she was acting or not.

"What would we do with a kid?" Larry said, tossing back another glass of wine. "We're fifty years old. Diapers, getting up all hours of the night. Who needs it?"

"We'd have one now if you hadn't been such an ass when Candie was born," Mom said caustically.

The hair on my arms rose at the mention of the name. Candie was the love child Mom had given birth to four years before she met my father, the one Larry had denied and who had been put up for adoption. In the intervening years, they had spent thousands of dollars paying private investigators to try and find her, but to no avail: the records had been sealed. Candie had vanished into another life.

That night in Vegas, Larry remained silent, pursed his lips, and poured himself another drink.

"I wasn't ready to have a child then, and I'm not ready now," Larry said testily. "We're happy enough as we are, aren't we?"

"But I want a child!" my mother pouted. "Our child!"

I sat in the corner, listening, thinking, What am I, chopped liver?

12. PAPER CUTS

The *Harvard Crimson* is located in a narrow, three-story, cement-and-brick building on tiny Plympton Street, just south of Harvard Square. The first time I opened its red door and walked in, during the fall of my sophomore year, the sight of newsprint and the smell of ink overwhelmed my senses. The building had a sensibility all its own: piles of newspapers, the string for wrapping them, the editorial books that critiqued them; giant spools of textured paper stacked in a corner; a scent of mineral oil mixed with alcohol so subtle it left an imprint on the tongue; the musty smell of old editions.

I had been working steadily toward my goal of becoming a reporter. During the summer of 1972, I had worked again as a copygirl at the *Press*, maintaining the photo library, called the morgue, and running copy from the editor's desk back to the pressroom. My first feature, about a pastor on my block who recited the Bible in Latin to himself while he built his congregation a new church, was published. I loved the deadline pressure, the freedom to ask questions of total strangers about things that were none of my business. The *Crimson* had been the proving ground for some of the country's finest reporters—and I was determined to become one of them.

But first I had to be admitted. The paper held competitions over the course of the academic year—you wrote stories as a reporter, and if you were considered good enough, they admitted you as a "Crime-ed," or *Crimson* editor, which gave you all the perks of membership, including judging other poor sods like yourself who were trying to prove themselves for posterity.

I never felt comfortable within the *Crimson* hierarchy, a club of smart-assed white boys and prefeminist women, more butch than liberated, who had opinions about everything, especially the things they knew nothing about. They seemed less interested in covering issues than in impressing each other with their witty sarcasms. It was, in fact, the same dynamic in play as at the black dining room table, but one from which I felt culturally alienated.

The big story on campus in 1972 was the battle to develop a Department of Afro-American Studies. It was a story I felt eager to cover. The department was perceived by many professors as an academic ghetto, a hideout for marginal black students seeking refuge within Harvard's walls. Professor Ewart Guinier advocated an Afrocentric department, while those like Professor Martin Kilson, the university's first black tenured professor, pushed for an interdisciplinary approach. Kilson, an expert in the development of African democracies, wrote almost daily missives to the paper detailing the inadequate preparation of the students concentrating in Afro-American studies and the flimsy credibility of its lecturers. To many he seemed a willing shill for those who believed that African-Americans had made absolutely no contribution to the academic canon.

I began covering the debate in tandem with Doug Schoen and Dan Swanson. Nationwide, the development of Afro-American studies programs was front-page news. Every institution except Harvard had, by 1971, a functioning department. Harvard's failure to develop one was seen by many as antagonism toward an overall diversity plan, and certainly proof of its retrograde politics.

I wanted to carve out a niche outside the coverage that Schoen and Swanson were doing on the administration. After all, they were both white guys and I was a black female—I should be able to get some exclusive access, I reasoned. Kilson in particular was known to be vulnerable to a little flirtation. I had picked a public fight with him in the letters-to-the-editor pages of the *Crimson* before I began competing, or "comping," accusing him, in effect, of being an Uncle Tom who was ashamed of his own heritage. Professor Kilson, who had been a mentor to my cousin Chico, fired back a terse reply: "You're too smart to be writing such stupid shit."

Swanson and Schoen referred to Kilson as "Killer" during editorial meetings. I thought the nickname smacked of disrespect—no other professor was referred to so colloquially among the editors.

I was interested in reporting the debate among black students over how to proceed with the new department. There were several student factions, and their discussions were fierce: over whether the program should be interdisciplinary; over how many tenured professors it should hold; over whether there should be an institute named after the university's most prominent black graduate, W. E. B. DuBois, and if so, how it should be funded. I found these arguments fascinating, but the page editor often cut my stories short, and other editors gave me harsh critiques. I told myself that this was their problem, not mine, and rarely argued for my stories.

The truth is that I was seized by an unbearable shyness each time I passed through those red doors on Plympton Street. I wanted to belong so badly, and so feared making a misstep, that I was incapable of making any steps at all.

After six weeks I was "cut."

Undeterred, I went back. This time I sat in on editorial meetings, trying to get a better feel for how the place worked. What struck me most was that, while a good third of the reportorial editors were women, they said little or nothing during these meetings. The men, some of whom I called the "elitist white snots" in my journal, ran the show, determining what went into the paper and what the editorial page wrote about. Those smart, brainy, forceful 'Cliffies were as silent as statuary.

Someone suggested that I get books on reporting from Widener Library. Another suggested that I sleep with the president as a way of facilitating my election. I decided not to follow up on that lead.

The "elitist white snots" faction of the paper was headed by the managing editor, Peter Shapiro, reputedly the son of an oil executive. Shapiro, having no middle name, had taken the initial *i* so he could initial his memos *pis*.

He marked my stories "fair" and "pretty good," but not "very good."

I felt frustrated. Editors kept telling me my work wasn't good enough, but they didn't tell me how to make it better. They seemed

Lary and me in Los Angeles—his motorcycle.

Me and Gigi with the Gregorys—Hugh Jr., Sylvia, Gina, and Hugh Sr.—the summer after Uncle Paul died.

The infamous *F Troop* family photo, 1966.

During the summer of my freshman year in high school I enrolled in a music program at Glassboro State College. I got caught smoking marijuana and was invited to leave.

Sweet sixteen—no more ironed hair.

In Rome with Mom and Larry, the summer before my senior year of high school.

The high school graduate, 1971.

The Harvard sophomore, 1973.

Mom and I take Las Vegas, 1976.

My father, James A. Cross, about five years before he died.

My first meeting with Candie, my mother and Larry's daughter, 1996.

Mom and Larry, the same day.

Big winners at the Emmy Awards, 1997.

July 27, 2000: I was forty-five when I got married, and for the first time, my biological and extended families met each other. We played a game of softball on the beach on Martha's Vineyard.

Lary, Mom, and me at my wedding reception.

Actress Lynda Gravatt, my father's oldest daughter, and me.

With my husband, Waldron Ricks, on Columbia University's campus, 2006.

to think I should pick it up by osmosis. I was a black woman—and I think they feared that I would take anything they said the wrong way. They were probably right.

When the cuts were announced, I had been dropped again.

My brother visited Cambridge during the spring of my sophomore year, and we had lunch at my favorite burger joint around the corner from the *Crimson*. Passersby, seeing the longhaired mustached man with horn-rimmed glasses sitting in conversation with a pudgy, toffee-colored young woman with a round Afro, must have thought we were a tutor and student, not brother and sister.

It began, as most of our conversations did, with him asking me what I was reading.

Ellison's *Invisible Man*, I answered—for the fifth or sixth time by then. My classes at Bridgewater, along with the way I was learning to think about writing at Harvard, had led me to rediscover James Baldwin and his elaborately crafted sentences, which could fit a novel into a paragraph. Ellison and Baldwin explored the emotional ambivalence inside those who lived as the other.

It led Lary and me to a discussion of our own upbringing.

"It's like we lived in a cult," he said thoughtfully. "We have rules and code signals that we know but nobody else does. There's all of these conditions. But Mother has always been very ambivalent when it comes to children, me included."

"What do you mean?" I asked. I knew nothing about my brother's early childhood.

"Well, she wanted to be an actress. She left me mostly with Granny when I was very young. I remember we were so poor we had to steal food. Then she moved to Los Angeles to go to acting school and left me in a boarding school of some kind. I liked that school. We learned about chickens and goats. But then her money ran out, and she left me with Granny again. I remember I got so mad I set fire to a vacant lot."

"Wow," I said. Lary seemed so even-tempered most of the time that I couldn't imagine him acting out like that.

"Wow is right," he said ruefully. "I wish I hadn't done it, because the Child Protective Services came and took me away. I spent the next five years in foster homes."

I felt sorry for him then, sorrier than I'd ever felt for myself. He had eventually gone back to live with Granny, and then, around the time he turned thirteen, Mom had sent for him to live with her and my father, Jimmy.

For the first time in his life, he had a father, and he had a home. In Atlantic City, when he and Jimmy walked down the street, people would point and say, "Look, there's Stump and Little Stump!"

He smiled at the memory, and I wondered how it was that my father had been more of a father to my white brother than he ever had to me.

"We're probably lucky, in a way," Lary said, referring to our mother, "that we were only around when she felt it was convenient. That way we only experienced the side of her that wanted us."

I had always envied Lary's relationship with my mom—they seemed more like best friends than mother and son.

"You had a different mother than I did," I asserted. I was thinking of how she used to cradle me in her arms as she swam laps, thinking of all the times she had been waiting for me as the bus pulled in to Port Authority. She had never been late, not once.

"I mean, she was, what, eighteen when you were born? And she was thirty-two when she had me. That's the difference between a teenage mother and a grown woman."

"Yeah, well, she didn't handle it much differently in the end, did she?" he pointed out.

I had no answer for that one.

Changing the subject, Lary asked whether I had ever seen *This Is the Army*, the movie that my dad had done with Ronald Reagan. I hadn't, and I wasn't interested in watching any movie starring Ronald Reagan. I told Lary I thought Reagan, then governor of California, was one step short of a fascist. He had banned Eldridge Cleaver from teaching at Berkeley, defended the assassination of George and Jonathan Jackson in prison, and abetted the persecution of Angela Davis.

"This is not about Reagan," Lary said, interrupting my tirade. "You don't need to watch the whole movie. But you should see Jimmy's number. It's really great. It's called 'What the Well-Dressed Man from Harlem Will Wear.' Joe Louis was in it with him."

I stopped, a french fry in my fingers. My father, in a movie with Joe Louis?

"I always thought Jimmy was a jazz pianist," I said, thinking of the time he came to visit, during the second week of my piano studies. Peggy always said she thought I inherited my musicality from my father.

"A jazz pianist?" Lary repeated, bewildered. "Whatever gave you that idea? He was a comedian and a dancer. A really funny guy. He was part of this team called Stump and Stumpy."

"Stump and Stumpy?" I repeated dubiously. That sounded like Amos 'n Andy stuff. Stepin Fetchit. Aunt Jemima.

"No, he wasn't like that, that blackface comedy, really," Lary insisted. "He wasn't vaudeville. He was kinda postvaudeville, postminstrelsy, but pre–Redd Foxx." I didn't understand the distinction but nodded anyway. "He was very funny. You should watch for the movie. They air it on late nights."

I didn't want to commit myself, so I changed the subject. "When did they get divorced?" I asked.

Dumbfounded, he looked at me. "Divorced?" he repeated. "They were never married!"

I stopped chewing. "They weren't?"

"Jesus, didn't they tell you anything?" he muttered, half to himself.

I struggled to digest this latest amendment to my life story. "You mean, they . . . just . . . lived together?"

"Yeah." Now he looked disgusted—maybe at Aunt Peggy and her high moralizing, which sheltered me from my own life story, maybe at my mother's refusal to disclose it on her own. Maybe he was just grappling with what would happen when Mom and Peggy found out he had told me the truth. "You really never knew this?"

"No."

The burger and fries lay forgotten on my plate.

"We've really been fortunate in a way," Lary mused.

"Fortunate?" I repeated from within my daze.

"Well, yes. There's all this hand-wringing going on now about divorce and the effects of breaking up families—children bouncing back and forth between parents and how that will affect them. And, shit, we never had that, so we're ahead of the curve."

"I guess so." I was revising my entire life story through the prism of the new information: how Aunt Peggy had fretted when Jack and Jill, a social club for the children of the black bourgeosie, refused to admit me. She had said it was because I didn't live with my parents. But now I understood.

I was illegitimate.

My mother was an unwed mother.

"Did I ever tell you I almost ended up living with you and Peggy and Paul, too?" Lary was full of revelations today.

"Really?" I asked.

"Yeah, but Peggy thought it would be too hard, raise too many questions, a white boy living with a black family."

He looked off into the distance a moment, then looked back at me and said with finality, "So that's how we got separated. I went off with Granny. You stayed with Peggy."

Back in my room, I reconsidered the arc of my life. Somehow, being a love child seemed even harder to accept than being called Larry Storch's adopted daughter. My father—he'd been like one of those brothers in our dorm who slept with white girls but didn't want to deal with the consequences. And Mom had tried to get away with "tipping over the fence" of the color line, but she'd gotten caught—with me.

After some deliberation I competed for a spot on the *Crimson* a third time during the early fall of my sophomore year, more as a formality than with any real hope that I would make it.

In the "open book" that editors used to critique the previous day's edition, my work drew better comments: "good" and "pretty good"—up from the "fair" judgments which had characterized my work the first time around.

One day, however, I snuck into the editors' lounge and looked into the "closed book" they used to discuss internal matters among themselves.

"June needs a lot of guidance," the managing editor, Peter Shapiro, had written, "or she'll be guided out of the door come first cuts. Her last story was an abortion." Since no one had said anything like that to my face, I was taken aback. When I asked Doug about it, he shrugged it off. "What do you expect from a guy who signs his name 'pis'?" he asked.

I managed to get a run of stories concerning the student committee that was shadowing the administration's Afro-American Studies efforts. The students had drafted their own manifesto arguing the case for a permanent chair, an institute that would be named after W. E. B. DuBois, at least two tenured faculty, and at least seven lecturers. Schoen thought my coverage added something to the paper's overall coverage. The night that elections were held to choose the next set of *Crimson* editors, he called me at around nine-thirty and reported, "The executive board is behind you—it looks like you've made it." I was ecstatic.

But when I walked into Shapiro's cubicle the next day, he looked at me with a serious face.

"Well, June, I'm sorry but you didn't make it again."

This couldn't be happening, I thought.

"What do you mean I didn't make it?" I said. "I got a phone call last night saying the executive board was behind me!"

"Well, whoever called you shouldn't have—who called you anyway?" Peter asked. I remained silent. "Probably Doug," he guessed. "He shouldn't have done that."

I felt emotion welling in my chest, which I refused, absolutely refused, to allow anywhere near my eyes. I concentrated on pushing the tip of my tongue along the gum line at the back of my front teeth as he spoke.

"The meeting went on for quite a while after he left, and some things got reversed."

I knew there was a power struggle going on between Shapiro and the new president, but couldn't imagine how—or why—I had gotten caught up in it.

"You're just not assertive enough," he said. "You're not aggressive either, in the newsroom or out in the field." As a result of not having enough information, my stories ran shorter than the average length of a *Crimson* story.

I felt like I'd entered a penis-measuring contest. "You must be kidding," I said. Even through the haze of my disappointment, this seemed like a spurious measure of potential.

"No, I'm not," he said, and to prove it, he took out a ruler and copies of the previous week's paper. He measured my stories, which came in at between four and a half and five inches, then measured the rest of the stories on the front page, which ran between five and six inches.

"You just don't have what it takes," he advised. "Go find yourself another discipline. You'll never be a reporter."

I inhaled, turned, and walked out into the bitter November day, then into the warmth of Brigham's ice cream shop. There I ordered a cheeseburger, fries, and a black-and-white shake. I thought back to the good old days with Mommie when we were living in New York city, when eating a grilled cheese sandwich with a Schrafft's vanilla shake constituted perfection in my world.

That dreary day, sitting in Brigham's, I also remembered going to Schrafft's with my mother when I was three or four. She had brought me to meet Dixon, an army colonel she was dating. I'd been warned to be on my best behavior so that Dixon would think well of me.

When he arrived, he took one look at me and exploded at my mother. "A nigger? You've got a nigger child?!"

Mom had grabbed my arm, yanked me from my chair, and dragged me out of there so fast my feet barely touched ground, tears running down her cheeks, tears of incomprehension running down mine—what had I done? Why couldn't I finish my lunch? Why had the man yelled at her?

It had been afterward, I think, that she started leaving me in Atlantic City. Fifteen years later, feeling that same sense of incomprehension, that something was wrong with me but I didn't know what, I put my head down on the table and cried.

Depressed and covered with a rash that refused to respond to creams or pills, I sought psychological counseling. I thought my failure to adequately grasp the rules at the *Crimson* was the problem. The counselor, Mac, asked me when else I had felt like a failure. In response, I described Uncle Paul's funeral and how I felt unable to summon the grief necessary to be a proper member of the funeral party. As I talked about how I hadn't been considered immediate family, he dug further, inquiring about my background.

I took a deep breath. Where to begin? The truth was, I couldn't remember much about my life at all, then.

I recalled the incident, back when I was four or five, when I had fought with Uncle Paul over eating Aunt Peggy's overcooked string beans, but after that, my memory was sketchy and fragmented. As I tried to tell the story, it became apparent that I was as disconnected from my own history as I had been from the *Crimson* hierarchy.

Mac told me he thought it was more important for me to come to terms with that half-forgotten past than my failure at the *Crimson*. He wanted me to schedule weekly appointments.

Aunt Peggy thought that was the worst thing I could do. "I don't see why you want to go digging around in all that," she told me during one of our phone conversations. "It's not wise. You risk greater confusion. You need some source of stability. When was the last time you went to church?" she asked.

I felt exasperated. Church services in Cambridge weren't as stirring as those in Atlantic City, and I had drifted away from communion. Besides, whatever was wrong with me, I was convinced it was beyond God's power to cure. I wasn't trying to stir up the past, just *remember* it.

Unmentioned, the memory of Aunt Yvonne hovered between us.

Aunt Hugh called me one day as I sat nursing the blues in my dorm room. She wasn't well; she had been on a downward slide since Yvonne had died.

"You've got a lot of talent, June. Don't fiddle it away," she said, in what was to be one of our last conversations. "I don't want you idling your time away, dancing to jazz music and playing cards. Soak up all the beauty you can now and absorb it so that it can come out of you later."

I appreciated her advice, even if I disagreed with her about jazz and cards. Jotting down notes of our talk, I thought that maybe if I read her words often enough, I could bring myself to believe them.

"Why don't you take some time and come home for a few days?" Aunt Peggy suggested. She thought that taking a break from school would be better than seeing a psychologist.

I refused.

"What's there to come home for?" I retorted, my words thorn sharp. "There's nothing in Atlantic City."

"Oh!" she cried, like a wounded bird.

I had meant there was nothing to *do* in Atlantic City, but that's not how it came out.

During the spring of my junior year, I was assigned an East Indian graduate student for English tutorial.

I no longer remember her name or what she looked like. I have an image of her forearms, lovely dark brown skin the color of mahogany, and straight black shoulder-length hair. It crossed my mind that the administration of Harvard's English department, in its naiveté, had paired us because we shared darker skin.

Uncle Hugh warned me that dark-skinned Indians could be even more racist than American whites. I shrugged it off—India was India, this was Harvard.

She wore her brusque Oxford accent like a starched white shirt. When she asked about my secondary schooling and I said "public high school," she wrinkled her nose the way strangers had when I was a toddler with my mother in the supermarket.

Her English reserve made it difficult for us to establish a rapport.

One day I asked whether dark-skinned Indians faced discrimination within India's Anglophile culture. She refused to answer the question and seemed to feel offended that I had even asked it.

I wondered whether Uncle Hugh might be right.

She asked very sharp questions, to which I often did not have sharp enough answers. I had never been one to read a book for the author's mastery of metaphor or language. I read for plot, for the twists of a strong narrative, the nuances of complicated character. Hungry for the good scene, the showdown, I often raced ahead, trying to find the denouement, where the characters are brought into focus. What the author intended to say, the significance of the circumstances—these things crossed my mind days after I put the book down. Those nuances, however, were exactly what a Harvard English major was expected to master.

We were discussing T. S. Eliot and James Joyce one day when my tutor asked about the author's moment of epiphany.

I gave her a blank look. "Epiphany," I said, drawing out the word slowly. Uncle Paul had died near Epiphany. Now, as my tutor sucked her teeth waiting for my answer, I considered the three magi and the last holiday I spent with Uncle Paul, wondering what they could possibly have to do with the matter at hand.

She interrupted my rumination. "Don't tell me you don't know what an epiphany is!"

I told her I knew that it's the celebration of the day the three magi found the infant Jesus and that it is celebrated as the twelfth day of Christmas. In Spain they exchange gifts on that day.

That didn't strike me as an ignorant answer, as answers go. In fact, I thought it was a fine answer.

What does the giving of gifts have to do with writing? I asked her, and even as I framed the question, the answer formed on the horizon of my consciousness.

She sighed impatiently, then rose, huffing and puffing with resolute footsteps down the hall into someone's office—I believe it was the director of the tutorial program. I heard her voice rising, and I rose myself, tiptoeing across the short-napped rug to the hallway door so I could eavesdrop on her conversation.

Her words echoed down the hall. They reverberate across the years. ". . . inadequately prepared!" she says. "Knows nothing of the basic concepts of literature! These quota students should not be let in!" I hear the murmur of the tutorial director or whoever it is she is venting to, and I tiptoe back to my seat, racking my brain. Epiphany. Epiphany. I must have been playing hooky on the day that Mr. Linblad taught Epiphany as a literary concept.

She returned, and the wall between us was erected.

"An epiphany," she began as if I were in kindergarten, "is a moment when the main character has a sudden realization about his life, an insight."

"Oh," I said, wondering how that meaning derived from the three magi, but not daring to ask. I had evidently confirmed her notion that black students were inadequately prepared.

After that I went and bought every book I could about the concept of epiphany and read every author whose work was associated with the term. While taking my self-constructed minitutorial in epiphany, I lost myself in marijuana and the lyrics of Leonard Cohen. My other grades fell. My brother, Lary, summoned by my mother and Aunt Peggy, was unsympathetic. He accused me of trying to flunk out of school, calling it my revenge on Mom and Aunt Peggy for pressuring me to go to Harvard.

His arguments had no effect. I had found my version of Yvonne's inferno, and it suited me to stay there awhile.

Uncle Hugh seemed to understand my cynicism and torpor as no one else did. He had left Lever Brothers for a vice presidency at Procter & Gamble, then left that job, too. Now he was working double shifts as a New York City taxi driver.

"It's all pretense," he agreed when I complained about my tutor and about the rules at the *Crimson*. "But what are you going to do? You either learn to play their game or you spend your life homeless. At least you're learning that it's a pretense now, instead of discovering it in middle age like I did. Just choose the pretense that's least objectionable."

Omaha Hilton

August 10, 1973

Dear Peggy,
Don't worry about June—I think everything is getting
better. Lary was there a few weekends ago and he intro-
duced her to a lot of people, so I think she feels more at
home. . . .

That year I went to Los Angeles in August, as I had every August. As I walked into the airport pickup area and spotted Mom, I was amazed to see that we wore the same pink, red, and green tie-dyed shorts. We had bought them separately—she in Los Angeles, I in Boston.

Larry was no longer a big star on the cover of *TV Guide*. He had been doing cartoon voices—his latest was the movie version of *Treasure Island*—and before that he had been doing *Sabrina, the Teenage Witch*.

He and Mom now introduced me as "our daughter, June," and let their friends think whatever they thought. I found out much later that many thought I was *Larry's* biological daughter, from an affair he'd once had with Pearl Bailey!

We went to a series of dinner parties where the guest list counted for more than the conversation, and the conversation was as substantial as air kisses. I began to believe that East Coast snobbism that one loses five points of IQ for every year spent in L.A.

Mom wanted me to impress everyone with my brilliance and the sparkle of my Harvard education. I couldn't perform on cue any more than could Larry, who had to get drunk in order to do it. He was a funny drunk; the more he drank the more adventurous he became, trying out new ideas, new characters, new lines. Occasionally he got falling-down drunk, but then that wasn't unusual for their circle in those days.

Everyone at these parties was in the business: Ann-Margret's manager, Tony Curtis, Sally Field, Barbara Eden of *I Dream of Jeannie*. In the magazines these stars seemed awe-inspiring, all primped and blow-dried and made up to perfection. But in person they seemed insecure, scared, and vulnerable; maybe that was why some of them drank and smoked more grass in one evening than my buddies and I did in an average week.

When I got back to Cambridge, I had dinner with two friends who'd spent their summer working for a freelance filmmaker. The filmmaker, Topper Carew, had just been picked to be the producer/host of the local black community-affairs program *Say Brother*, on WGBH, the PBS affiliate in Boston.

Topper reminded me of Wild Bill Hickok, except instead of flowing red locks he had a huge black Afro with a beard and mustache. His wardrobe of cowboy boots required a closet all its own.

Topper was looking for a work-study intern. Over dinner he asked whether I'd be interested in coming to work for him at WGBH.

"Sure," I said. "Do you need a résumé?"

"Naw," he said. "If you're as smart as these two are, you'll work out fine."

Mom was delighted that I'd found work in the family profession. Aunt Peggy worried that it would take me out of the orbit of school. That was the point, I told her. I wanted to leave school and had begged her to let me take a leave of absence, but Aunt Peggy wouldn't hear of it. She was afraid that if I left, I might never return, and, against my mother in this matter, she prevailed.

WGBH offered the closest thing to a year off I could get. It would also offer me a future I had never dreamed of. Immediately I fell in love with television: with the research and writing, which was like newspapering; with its fast pace, which left no room for error; with the intense concentration and attention to detail in editing. Most of all I liked the collaboration involved in producing a show. During my last two years at Harvard, I spent three or four days a week at the station. Topper Carew and his staff believed in my abilities and nurtured me, even when I screwed up. The show had little money, but it did a solid job of providing Boston's black community with an outlet during the city's school-desegregation case. I began to learn the difference between writing for print and writing for broadcast as I helped write host introductions. Slowly, I began to rebuild confidence in myself. Some weeks I spent more time at *Say Brother* than I did at school.

I also fell in love late that fall with a math major who read Ralph Ellison and Herman Melville and played classical guitar. I nicknamed him Michaelmas, because loving him felt like Christmas.

We had gotten to know one another in San Diego the previous summer, while I was visiting Mom and Larry. Larry had picked up a weekend gig there at the Hotel del Coronado. Trying to find someone my own age, I had looked through Harvard's "facebook" of incoming freshmen, known as the Freshman Register, and Michael's name was the first one I saw listed in San Diego.

Michael had met Mom and Larry that weekend, and when we were alone, I explained that Mom was my biological mother and Larry my stepdad. Mom wasn't as hypervigilant about hiding the truth as she once had been, and I wasn't in the frame of mind to care even if she was.

I didn't, however, explain all the ins and outs of the story to Michael. I rarely explained the whole story to anyone. I just said that Mom was my mother, Larry was my stepfather, and that I had been raised by my father's people in Atlantic City after my real dad disappeared drunk somewhere. It was an entirely plausible scenario.

Besides, Michael and I had plenty of other things to talk about. We liked the same music. He read my poems and understood them. He was fascinated by fractal geometry. As he explained abstract mathematics, it began to seem that there might be a place in the natural order for me after all.

There was beauty in chaos, I decided.

As part of a class called Biology and Social Sciences, I made more of an impact than I ever did as a reporter at the *Harvard Crimson*, as I helped write a report that led to the closing of a state-run truancy home for boys.

I remember their faces, not their names, which were protected by the juvenile laws in any case. They were aged seven to sixteen and predominantly white; considered pests in the school system, they had been sent to the Essex County Training School for Truant Boys in Lawrence, Massachusetts. They were younger versions of the men I'd met at Bridgewater.

They all looked similar: blond hair, limp; brown eyes, downcast. Dirty fingernails. Faces slightly smudged. They were poster kids for poverty of the mill-town variety. They had lived lives that made mine seem like a fairy tale in comparison. They were ill-educated, even considering the amount of school they had skipped, and no serious attempt was ever made to get them caught up to grade level.

These children were considered dispensable before they ever finished high school. As I interviewed them, I kept thinking of Fagin's boys from *Oliver!*

"Why didn't you do right in school?" I asked a group of them.

"School was boring."

"The teacher was an idiot."

"My mother never had my clothes ready."

"I was so mad that by the time I got to school, I picked a fight with anybody."

The school itself looked like an old Victorian home with brick extensions. Lawrence had once been home to a textile mill, then to a shoe factory. The textile industry had gone south; the shoe factory had moved to Brazil. The town was an abandoned monument to the glory days of manufacturing.

Inside, the school was grimy, dark, and weathered, its maintenance perpetually postponed. The gym was a poured-concrete floor filled with cracks, the pool green with algae, the steam heat leaking hot water from asbestos-covered pipes. The boys lived, ate, and bathed communally.

The report our nineteen-member group wrote recommended that the place be closed, and ultimately it was. The closing of the Essex County School for Truant Boys marked the beginning of a movement toward juvenile rehabilitation in Massachusetts.

I felt good about that report, which seemed, finally, to vindicate my Harvard career. Something I had done made a difference. In learning about the lives of those boys, I considered how luck, class, and economics trumped race in that mill town. Any one of them could have been my brother Lary. For the first time, I thought I had been fortunate in my own upbringing, however painful it had been; and at last I was shaken from my state of self-pity.

By 1974, Hollywood had decided that racial themes might sell. My mother had an idea for a movie, which she shopped around to the studios.

> This is the story of a black girl who has a white mother. She has been brought up by a black family in Atlantic City. Her mother supported, loved, and visited her all her life but could never acknowledge her. After graduation from Harvard the girl moves to Washington, D.C., and rises rapidly in black politics. Meanwhile, the mother has married a well-to-do lawyer. They, too, live in Washington, D.C., but because of the girl's career, she now has to hide her white parents in the closet. The situation is completely reversed.

Several studio executives were intrigued, Mom reported. "My heart went out to that poor girl," one executive had said, referring to the mother, not the daughter. He loved the story, but he wasn't interested in it as a drama—he asked Mom if she could turn it into a situation comedy.

Mom asked if I wanted to develop it with her, but as I read the treatment, my bile rose.

"But it's not true!" I protested to her.

"Well, of course it's not true! It's TV!" she responded. "But we could sell it and make a million dollars off this!"

Maybe my mother was trying to break the secret then, in the only way she knew how. She certainly was a woman of contradictions. But I wasn't prepared to work with her in constructing yet another version of my life, and soon she let it drop.

All I knew was that, whatever I did with my career, I would never be like the daughter she had constructed in her treatment. I would never want to hide my mother the way she had hidden me. I didn't know when or how, but this secrecy was going to stop with me.

Graduation day began with champagne and strawberries at the dorm. It was a rainy, humid morning, but the weather was of scant consequence.

Aunt Peggy and Aunt Sylvia had come up the night before, but they were merely the opening act. Mom was flying in, in time for graduation.

Mom and Larry rarely took part in typical family celebrations. They had gone to Lary's wedding, but my brother had graduated from college and graduate school alone. I had been crushed when Mom and Larry sent flowers to my high-school graduation. Three months earlier, when my senior project, a stage adaptation of Langston Hughes's Simple tales, had been produced by the campus's black-theater group at the Loeb Experimental Theater, Mom had said she wished she could come but was afraid she might be recognized.

Oh, that again.

Aunt Peggy and Aunt Sylvia had come to see the production, and for a change Aunt Peggy didn't complain that the play was about blacks, written by a black man, adapted by a black woman, produced and acted by an all-black group. Nosiree. Aunt Peggy had been proud as punch.

It was the lure of Harvard, I decided, when I heard that Mom was coming for commencement. And there she was, with Aunt Peggy and Aunt Syl, preening like a peacock. You'd have thought that she raised me, read me stories and sang me songs before bedtime, sent me to dance and piano lessons and made sure I got involved in as many extracurricular activities as my schedule could possibly hold. Sure, she had contributed handsomely to the cost of my Harvard education, and her presence in my life had broadened my horizons immeasurably. But without Aunt Peggy I'm not sure I ever would have been accepted to Harvard or survived the experience once there. Plenty of my black classmates had dropped out before graduation—Michael, my first love, would become one of them.

Nevertheless, I was overjoyed to see Mom. This was her first public acknowledgment of one of my achievements.

"I don't see how your mother can pretend you're not her biological daughter," one of my former roommates, who knew parts of my story, observed. "Anyone who watches you two walk can see that you're built exactly the same way."

Aunt Peggy had long ago reconciled herself to the idea that she came second in my affections. Sometime later, however, Aunt Sylvia made it a point to tell me that it had been Aunt Peggy who, remembering how disappointed I'd been at my high-school graduation, had convinced Mom to fly in.

After commencement I claimed my mother, holding her hand and parading with her through Harvard Yard, showing her the buildings where I'd had classes, while Aunt Peggy and Aunt Sylvia trailed out of earshot.

"You know Peggy tried to get me to cut you off financially," Mom whispered.

"Really? Why?"

"She wanted me to force you to stop living with your boyfriend."

Michael and I had moved in together. Aunt Peggy had been furious about it, but Mom had taken my side. I often complained about Aunt Peggy's Victorian morals to Mom, and to Aunt Peggy I made sarcastic remarks about my mother's constantly shifting allegiances and friendships. We called this tendency of my mother's her "Bridge on the River Kwai" routine—she could make a friendship and burn the bridge as soon as the next opportunity came along.

But that day Mom and I were best friends. We gossiped like schoolgirl chums—about my classmates, the professors, the *Crimson*, and especially about Aunt Peggy. Peggy was so puritanical. She dressed old-fashioned. She hated the fact that I had sought psychological counseling.

Analysis was wonderful, my mother confirmed. Her ten years in analysis had saved her life.

We concluded that Aunt Peggy was just an old fogy.

13. WOMEN

Mom wanted me to come west after I graduated in 1975, and take a job in Hollywood. Larry was filming *The Happy Hooker Goes to Washington*. They needed a script girl. I told Mom no thanks, Hollywood had no allure for me. She was disappointed, but Aunt Peggy was glad. She always worried about me hanging around those bohemians in Hollywood.

I accepted an internship at the *Boston Globe*, covering for vacationing reporters during the summer. By then, Judge Paul Garrity had ordered busing to desegregate Boston's all-black Roxbury section and the poor, all-white section of South Boston. Unbelievably, the scenes associated with southern intransigence during the sixties came north and replayed themselves, as whites in Southie protested the integration of schools ordered by the Supreme Court twenty years earlier.

It was a difficult story for me to cover, and I tried to avoid it. My life experience told me that kids in Roxbury where undoubtedly being shortchanged, but my time listening to the boys in Lawrence at the Essex County school told me that kids in Southie probably weren't getting a much better deal. The Boston bluebloods, the upper crust that controlled papers like the *Globe*, had already arranged things so that, with a few exceptions, only the children of the well-off were guaranteed a decent education in Boston.

I finished my *Globe* internship and continued writing freelance for them. To make the rent, I also began reporting for Boston's black community weekly, the *Bay State Banner*. At the *Banner* I was the sole staff reporter, assigned to write five or six stories a week. Under the repetition I felt myself becoming surer of the questions I needed to ask and developing a quicker instinct about how to frame a story. I began to develop friendships with other black reporters, notably Luix Overbea of the *Christian Science Monitor*. Overbea, a slightly built man with a bean-shaped head and thick rectangular glasses, wore a perpetually wrinkled raincoat and worked at a desk that was impossible to find under a mound of papers and reports. He gave me copies of the background briefings and filings that undergirded the school-desegregation case and helped me sort out the political players in Boston's byzantine school system. He steered me toward leads and gave me feedback on my stories.

Then, in 1977, the NAACP held its annual convention in Boston. Overbea vouched for my talent, and that seemed enough to admit me to the club. I met most of the country's black reportorial elite, all at once. Vernon Jarrett from the *Chicago Tribune*, Acel Moore from the *Philadelphia Inquirer*, Barbara Reynolds, then Washington reporter for the *Chicago Tribune*, Ethel Payne from the *Chicago Defender*— all of them had begun their careers writing for all-black newspapers. They had been culled in the wake of the 1968 riots, when the mainstream newsrooms discovered that their lily-white staffs couldn't get access to ghetto stories.

The NAACP convention gave these reporters a chance to reconnect, share gossip, and regroup from the strain of working in all-white newsrooms. They talked about journalists, black and white, whose work they admired and told war stories about survival on big-city papers. As I listened, I realized that my *Crimson* experience would be just the first time I would find myself the only black face in a seemingly hostile newsroom. But for the rest, I would be prepared.

Overbea introduced me to Tom Johnson of the *New York Times*. Tom had just finished a tour as the *Times'* Africa bureau chief. He invited me to tag along as he worked the convention. I was struck by his interviewing technique: he listened more than he asked questions, and he rarely used a notepad.

"Every once in a while, I disappear to my room and write it all down," he said when I asked him how he remembered everything. "People get intimidated when they see a notebook."

Tom later introduced me to his colleague Charlayne Hunter-Gault, the urbane and intelligent reporter who would become pivotal in my career. At the time I knew she had been one of two black students who had integrated the University of Georgia, but I was more impressed with her work for the *Times*. Hunter-Gault found beat news in Harlem at a time when the paper ignored it except to cover riots and sensational crimes. She found stories in the comings and goings of its everyday citizens and elevated their daily struggles to front-page news.

In the fall of 1977, Hunter-Gault and Barbara Reynolds sat on a panel of judges as I applied for a Ford Foundation training grant for minority journalists. Since I already knew the two of them, I thought I would be a shoo-in. Instead I got a rejection letter. "You're going to make it with or without this fellowship," Hunter-Gault told me, saying that she had argued against me. "This grant is for those who need a leg up."

Making less than a hundred dollars a week at the *Banner* and constantly waiting on various freelance checks to arrive, I could have used a leg up right then. So when a full-time job materialized at WGBH's *Say Brother*, the weekly public-affairs program where I had worked as an intern, I grabbed it. Although I missed the chance to get out in the street and report a story, I liked the collegiality of television, and I loved knitting the elements of a story together to make a whole piece. I would stay at WGBH for two more years, until 1979.

As I made these first career moves, I consciously avoided the paths my mother and Aunt Peggy had taken. Mom had always wanted to act on the stage. Peggy had wanted to be a photographer. Instead they had gotten married, then watched their dreams dissipate.

I had broken up with Michael after four years, and I intended to play the field for a while. As far as I could tell, when men and careers mixed in a woman's life, men won.

Dearest June

I wish it were 1957. I miss 41 W. I miss our life together, staring into your eyes for minutes at a time, going to Schrafft's, our daily trips to the park. But here we are, you there in a strange city, me here writing this letter.

This play—how can I begin to tell you the problems it has caused? Last night, for the umpteenth time, I threw all the bottles of wine over the side of the mountain, and for the umpteenth time he promised he would stop, or go to AA, or whatever. I no longer believe him, but I don't know what to do. I can't start over; I'm too old.

Still, I love you always, that will never change.

—Mom

In addition to drinking when he was at home relaxing and when he needed to loosen up to go to a party, Larry had found another reason to drink: he was afraid of forgetting his lines. He dropped out of several plays rather than risk it.

I felt bad for Mom. There was little I could do, but I decided to go out and visit her during that August of 1977.

But Larry's slide into alcohol dependency seemed to have left my mother at a loss. There was nothing she could do to stop him, and nothing she could do to help him either.

To pick herself out of the doldrums, she decided to have a brunch for "The Ladies Who Lunch." Her inspiration was that Stephen Sondheim song, written for the musical *Company*.

Dittendorf filled with the smell of steaming tamales and the fragrance of fresh cilantro, cumin, and chili. I sat in a bamboo rocker while we chatted. Ironing gaily colored linen napkins, Mom told me that this would be the first time she'd ever had a lunch where only women were invited.

"Don't you have girlfriends?" I asked. I'd rarely met any, but what did that mean?

"Well, no," she answered, sounding somewhat flustered by the tone of my question. "My whole life revolves around Larry and his friends. I used to, when I was younger, have one or two here and there. But this will be the first in a long time. I'm so excited!"

One more reason to avoid marriage, I thought.

"I can help dust."

"No, no. I have a certain way I want to do it. I have to do it the way Mother taught me, and you don't know how to do it that way. But here, if you want to do something, iron these napkins."

Silence fell between us at the mention of her mother.

I hadn't seen my grandmother since I was a toddler, although she stayed in touch with my brother and his children. They had relationships with Granny, while I thought of her in the same terms as the witch who hands Snow White the apple, or Sleeping Beauty's jealous stepmother. It was Granny, I sometimes thought, who had erected the barriers between my mother and me.

When I was three or four, she had come to visit us in New York. She smelled of lavender and wore flared skirt dresses that cinched her eighteen-inch waist with a wide belt. Too young to understand their conversation, I had watched them while they talked. Granny didn't seem like Mommie's mommie; she seemed almost to recoil from my mother's neatly manicured hands folded on her lap, which occasionally reached toward her as if in supplication. Granny seemed as though this visit were more ceremonial than heartfelt. She talked plainly and dressed plainly, though stylishly. Mommie ignored me and talked to her. Granny did her best to ignore me, too, a toddler scuttling around her knees.

Then, while I played with the cat in the corner, I realized she was talking about me.

"She's a cute little monkey once you get used to looking at her," I heard her say.

I had seen monkeys in the Central Park Zoo. They were not cute. They lived in smelly cages, and they stank. They were covered with fur. They ate with their hands and feet. Although I was aware at the time that adults used terms of endearment like this, I knew, somehow, that hers was not a term of endearment.

I accidentally spilled coffee on her lap and I was not sorry. Granny spent a weekend with us, and after that I never saw her again.

Now, in California twenty years later, I wondered whether she ever asked about me, whether my mother had told Granny that her granddaughter, "the little monkey," had graduated from Harvard. When my brother first introduced Granny to his future wife's parents and my name came up, she had referred to me as the little colored girl Norma and Larry adopted, the little colored girl who stayed in Atlantic City. I wondered whether Mom was still intimidated by her.

Granny had pressed the quest for perfection into my mother as firmly as the crease in the napkins I was ironing, and my existence was like a wrinkle in the corner.

I observed my mother's cleaning ritual. She had prepared a bowl of milk and, with a clean rag, was brushing each plant leaf with it. When I was a child, I had been amazed that the milk did not turn the plant leaves white. After Mom cleaned the leaves, she took another clean rag and removed each book from the bookcase, running the smooth cloth along the tops of the pages and down the bindings before replacing them. Then, pulling out the vacuum cleaner, the extension rod, and its attachments for curtains, she ran that over all the surfaces. I watched as she balanced on the arm of the sofa, stretching to reach the corners of the ceiling with the vacuum. I had never seen Mom dust underneath a bed or a sofa, the way Mrs. Amos had taught me to do. On the other hand, I had never seen Mrs. Amos stretch to reach the corners of a ceiling with a vacuum.

I wondered whether this was a black or a white thing, or just a cleaning preference.

The women my mother had invited to lunch were the various well-preserved wives of Larry's colleagues. They raved over the tamales and gazpacho and drank bottomless glasses of white California wine. They discussed which plastic surgeons did eyes better than chins, the relative merits of breast enhancement. They raved over the latest interior designer featured in the women's news sheet *W*, and they shared information about the latest chic boutiques (Rodeo Drive was too "gauche").

Then the conversation turned to the latest hot young male star.

"He could put his shoes under my bed anytime," my mother said.

"Mo-oom!" I burst out, my twenty-three-year-old sense of propriety violated.

"I didn't say I was *going* to invite him to put his shoes under my bed. I just said if he did, I wouldn't refuse him. Infidelity doesn't count unless you act on it."

The women laughed knowingly. I blushed.

"Are you a virgin?" one of Mom's friends asked.

"No," I answered, blushing even more, my eyes cast down.

"June's gone through half the class at Harvard," Mom announced, a bit of pride in her voice.

"Mo-ther!" I protested. There was enough of Peggy—and still enough of a teenager—in me to be mortified that my mother was broadcasting news about my personal life.

"What? It's not half the class?" she asked, more as a point of information than a rebuke.

Mom's friends laughed, proud of a fellow woman's sexual conquests.

"And why not?" a former Las Vegas showgirl said. "Why shouldn't a woman have as much fun as a man?"

Why not, indeed—that was the constant argument between Aunt Peggy and me.

"I want to take a poll," my mother announced to the circle. "How many men would you say you've slept with?"

"Hundreds," one of the women said.

Only Aunt Peggy's training kept my mouth from dropping open. These were glamorous, rich women in "good" marriages, boasting about their sexual conquests. I had never met any women like them. In Aunt Peggy's world, where men didn't marry women who had sex with them first, they shouldn't exist.

"How did you all keep from getting pregnant?" I asked.

"We didn't," they uttered in chorus. Around the room there were five women. Twenty-four abortions. At Harvard a form of RU-486, the "morning-after pill," had been available long before the FDA approved it. My mother's friends, on the other hand, had reached sexual maturity when a single woman's pregnancy meant public shame. They described sneaking around like thieves to find a doctor willing to perform an abortion; talked about prodding their own cervixes with coat hangers on the bathroom floor; discussed the underground network that shared the names of doctors in Mexico who, for the right money, would get rid of a pregnancy; reminisced about a doctor on New York's Lower East Side who operated in the backseat of a car, without anesthetic, because he thought it would teach women a lesson about keeping their legs closed; and lamented the often painful aftermath of infections and infertility.

Back in Atlantic City, I told Aunt Peggy about my mother's friends. I left out some details, because she and I never talked about what she referred to as "biological functions," but I did tell her about the abortions.

She wasn't at all surprised. My mother's friends were showbiz women, many of them former chorus girls in Vegas, who lived the fast life, she explained.

Then, after a long pause, she said, "I did that once."

I felt the room zooming away from me. How many secret lives had my two mothers led?

Aunt Peggy explained that it had been when she and Paul had just married and had little money. Someone told her that if she soaked her feet in hot vinegar and took Epsom salts baths, it would get rid of the baby. So she assumed that she had harmed herself in some way with the hot Epsom salts baths and vinegar soaks.

It seemed as though the space that separated us in the room widened. I had learned that hot baths and vinegar didn't work in ninth-grade sex-education class.

"You did," I repeated flatly. My mind phrased it as a question but it came out as an affirmation.

"Yes," she said. "And I never got pregnant again. I think that was God's way of punishing me for being so arrogant as to think I knew best when I should have a baby."

"Do you really believe that?" I asked, referring not to whether her infertility was God's punishment but to whether she really believed that soaking her feet in vinegar and Epsom salts had aborted a fetus.

"A child is the most precious gift," she said wistfully, perhaps mistaking my measured response for a rejection of her dreams. "Don't you want to have children?"

No, I replied. Even as a girl, I had never wanted children. I had been impatient to escape childhood itself, and I wanted no reminders of it as an adult. Deep down, in a place so deep I would scarcely admit it to myself, I feared I would end up treating my own children the way my mother had treated me. No, I repeated. I wanted a career. I didn't want to be tied to a man or a child.

Aunt Peggy got angry with me when I said such things. She said that all I had learned at Harvard was how to be "a hot-time screw," a trait she blamed on my mother's genes. She warned me that I'd end up alone and bitter, that every woman found fulfillment as a wife and mother.

I sighed and walked into the kitchen to make some tea. Once she started on this subject, communication between us stopped.

My eye wandered to a picture on the windowsill of Aunt Peggy and Uncle Paul, early in their marriage, walking arm in arm down the boardwalk. He wore a white suit, she a white dress, and they smiled into each other's eyes, obviously infatuated. It was maybe as close to a fine romance as they had ever gotten.

There was a story behind Uncle Paul's white suit that I would discover after Aunt Peggy died, in the draft of a letter she had written to the priest who married them. In the early days of their marriage, she confided, Uncle Paul had gone to the bank, taken out a loan in both their names for two thousand dollars, and promptly spent the money on the white suit, a pair of fine shoes, and a car.

Aunt Peggy had been left to pay off the loan.

She'd been the breadwinner in their partnership, I would realize, and her desire for me to "marry a boy from a good family" was her way of trying to ensure that I didn't meet the same fate. On that score she and Mom were in agreement.

———

In 1979, I got another call from Charlayne Hunter-Gault. She had left the *Times* to join public television's nightly news program, *The MacNeil/Lehrer Report*. The show's black reporter had just given notice. Was I interested in the job?

She got me in for the interview, and I got the position.

The MacNeil/Lehrer Report didn't air in Atlantic City, but Aunt Peggy had heard of it. "That's a highly respected program," she said, impressed. Still, she didn't want me to stay in journalism.

"It's okay for a couple of years," she said, "but don't become hard and cynical. You won't attract a man that way."

Mom was delighted. Reporters got to travel all over the world, she said. Would I be on air? I said no, I would be an off-air reporter, researching issues, booking guests, and writing the background analyses and preinterviews for Jim Lehrer and Robin MacNeil.

There was no pleasing either one of them, but for once it didn't matter. I finally had the title "reporter" under my name. I could travel on someone else's money and ask questions that were none of my business. I planned to see all those corners of the world that my mother had written me postcards from, and a few she hadn't seen besides.

14. DISCOVERIES

The next year at Thanksgiving, I went to visit my brother and his family for the holiday. Lary and Lany had been begging me to come visit them, and in 1980 I finally conceded.

During my visit Lary showed me Marshall Stearns's book *Jazz Dance*, which described Stump and Stumpy's act.

Although years earlier I had bought the tape of *This Is the Army*, the movie Jimmy had been in, I'd never watched it. My father was a drunk. He had left us. He had beaten my mother. Why should I give a damn about him? I thumbed through Stearns's book and left it on the shelf for the duration of my visit. Then, on the morning of my departure, curiosity conquered pride. I looked up James Cross in the index and found a description of his act:

One more among many first-rate teams, *Stump* (James Cross) and *Stumpy* (Harold Cromer), carried on the tradition of *Stringbeans and Sweetie May*, satirizing a well-known attitude of Southern Negroes. It occurred in a skit at the Apollo Theater in Harlem. Both dark-skinned, they are seated happily in a night club "up North." Behind Stump and out of his sight stands a light-skinned and threatening bouncer-waiter, a napkin over his arm. His glowering presence sobers Stumpy, who is facing him. Stump, unaware of the threat, tries to cheer up his buddy: "Whatsa matter, man? You up No'th, now, let's have a ball!" He is convinced that his troubles are over since he has left the South. Stumpy, watching the bouncer, tries to hush Stump, who is becoming noisier and noisier. "You up No'th, man!" Stump cries.

At last Stumpy catches Stump's eyes and nods fearfully at the bouncer. Stump turns around, puzzled at first by the figure towering above him. For a moment his newly won confidence does not falter. He pulls his buddy's coat, points wildly at the bouncer, and commands: "Straighten that fool *out*, man, straighten that fool *out*!" Whereupon the bouncer picks him up, and, as the audience screams with laughter, thrashes him unmercifully. The act is climaxed by some fine flash dancing.

It sounded vaudevillian, a relic of minstrelsy. Still, the relic was my father. For the first time, I wondered where he was now.

Back in New York, I found Joe Fox's book, *Showtime at the Apollo*, which quoted James Cross at even greater length. I called Fox, introduced myself, and asked if he still knew where Jimmy was.

Fox was cautious. He said he would check with Jimmy's agent and call me back. Within two hours he did, giving me the name and number of my father's agent—Harold Basden, who lived on Ninety-fifth Street off Columbus Avenue.

Harold's wife, Lois, answered the phone in a gregarious tone that intimated we had known each other all our lives. She told me that she had also been Jimmy's wife and that she had also left him because of the drinking. When her former husband met her new one, they liked each other so much that Harold had agreed to act as Jimmy's manager.

"So now whenever Jimmy introduces me," Lois wrapped up, "he says, 'You remember my wife, Lois,' and then he points to Harold and says, 'And this is her husband, Harold,' and everyone just laughs, because they know what he means."

I could almost hear Aunt Peggy's voice wondering what kind of showbiz rat's nest I might be walking into.

Harold and Lois lived on the top floor of a high-rise, at the end of a long hall. Lois opened the door and stepped out as I walked toward her, a griot shouting welcomes as I approached. I felt as if I were about to be inducted into a new tribe or, more accurately, as if I were being welcomed back into a tribe from which I'd been stolen. A part of me disconnected from my emotions. It stood back while I approached a woman who in another life might have been my mother. She could have passed for white or black: a short, round, alabaster-skinned woman with short, curly, red hair. She wore a long muumuu-style housedress made of African-print material.

When I reached the doorway, she gave me a big hug.

"It's so good to meet you, my darling daughter!" she exclaimed, and I felt glad to meet her, too. She introduced me to Harold, who sat as if holding court at a round smoked-glass table in front of the balcony window. Harold was a big grizzly bear of a man with several chins and a salt-and-pepper Afro. A green dashiki covered his barrel chest.

Buffered between Lois in the door and Harold at the table, on a long orange couch against a lavender wall, sat a man whom I recognized from pictures as my father. He did not look particularly distinguished or handsome; he did not look particularly like me. He wore a mud-colored suit and checkered shirt. As we made eye contact, he stood.

He was smaller than I had expected, slightly shorter than I. A circular etched brass Indian table sat between us. We reached across it, grasping hands, not as in a handshake but in the way someone falling off a cliff would grasp the hand of his rescuer. Then my father walked around the table, and hugged me.

Even as we embraced, the slurs ran through my mind. *Wife beater. Drunk. Deserter.* He had been reduced to these three phrases for so long that I had a hard time bringing him into the third dimension. I pulled away and saw his eyes well up with tears.

Jimmy was dying. He had cancer of the throat and chin. The cancer had already destroyed his vocal cords, and on his chin a small fissure had opened, just below his bottom lip. From it a drop of liquid formed, as if his emotions, greater even than the sum of the tears in his eyes, had found some other egress.

He dabbed at the oozing chancre with a handkerchief.

"June . . . how big you've gotten!" he whispered.

The last time he'd seen me, I'd been eight years old, just learning to play the piano. That had been over twenty years earlier.

He repeated my name as he squeezed my hands, bewildering me with the power a parent—even a long-absent parent—had to make me feel small again.

Nervously, I smiled.

My smile smiled back at me.

We sat down. Being a reporter, and not knowing what else to do, I asked questions. Since Jimmy couldn't talk much, he looked to Harold, who answered them. Harold talked enough for three people, providing background and opinions beyond Jimmy's answers.

Had Jimmy been working? Not for several years . . . the cancer.

Last gig? At New Paltz, New York, the state college there.

Really? I had just begun dating a guy who'd gone to New Paltz. So where else had he been?

The world: Africa, Russia, London. Been everywhere. Did everything. Spent most of his time recently, though, here in New York, right here on this orange couch.

Jimmy pulled out a scrap of paper and jotted down answers to those questions for which Harold didn't know the answer:

Where were my people from?

Philadelphia.

What was my grandmother's name?

Rose.

Did he have any brothers or sisters?

A sister, Margaret.

Did I?

A sister, Lynda. Jimmy had named her after the song "Something About Linda." He had named me after "June in January."

A sister. I have a sister.

Younger?

Older.

I have a sister.

Where is she?

Acting, in D.C., or maybe somewhere in Texas or Arizona; they had lost track.

That first meeting was as short as I could politely make it. We promised to stay in touch, and I wondered whether I would.

Once home, I called my mother and told her I had found Jimmy.

"Really?" she said with genuine interest. "Where is he?" I told her. She seemed excited. She called to her husband of twenty-five years. "Larry, June's found Jimmy. He's living in a room in Harlem."

I told her he was dying of cancer.

"Oh, gee," she said, sympathy in her voice. "Well, give him our best," she said.

One day, twenty years later, when we finally sat down and talked about it, my mother would insist that she had never loved my father. She had initially moved in with him because he was making money and she had no place else to go. Yet between the day I met my father and the day he died, she always inquired about his welfare, as if she, too, had been wondering about him all those years.

My father had contributed his coloring to my complexion, his smile to my face, and even a particular sense of pacing to the stories I edited for TV. We smoked the same brand of cigarettes and shared the same sense of humor. I stayed in touch. During his chemotherapy treatments, I would go visit him at the VA hospital. I hated that place: it reeked with the earthy, rancid odor of sick and dying men; its doctors, overworked, seemed pitted against an ancient, cold-hearted, bureaucratic regime. It was no place for anyone to die, but I did not know my father well enough to care for him the way I had watched Aunt Peggy care for Papa when I was a child.

After Jimmy got out of the VA in the fall of 1980, I went to visit him about once or twice a week when my reporting schedule allowed. Our conversations were easy, as though we had once been great friends and, many years later, merely resumed our relationship. He lay on the orange sofa at Lois and Harold's, eating vanilla ice cream while we ate Chinese food. He claimed ice cream and

Kool-Aid were the only substances he could taste, but Lois countered that his sweet tooth predated the cancer; his childhood nickname had been "Sugey."

Once, when he felt well enough to go out, we went to see Betty Carter at the Village Vanguard, and afterward he introduced me.

"I played with you while your father was onstage!" she crowed, and again I recognized the recurring theme in my life: forever left in the care of others while my parents' lives took shape elsewhere.

As he introduced me around, my father's friends recalled how he would bring me to Charlie's Bar on Fifty-second Street, a favorite show-business watering hole, when I could barely talk. He had taught me a version of Judy Garland's "The Man That Got Away." They shared a good laugh, remembering how I would stand on the bar, stomping my foot as I sang

> *The road gets rougher,*
> *It's lonelier and tougher*
> *With hope you burn up*
> *Tomorrow he might turn up*

Listening to their memories of that toddler June, now an undeniably reserved reporter working for a mainstream national news program, I racked my brain and heart trying to recollect that uninhibited child. I bought the Judy Garland album *Live at Carnegie Hall* and played and replayed the song, searching the rhythm of its refrain for the memory of my foot stomping out a common meter on the smooth, hard grain of a bar top. For the first time, I wondered what kind of life I might have led had my father and mother stayed together.

"You know, she was dating Larry when I met her," Jimmy told me one day.

Yes, I responded. Well, I knew she and Larry had been dating and that there'd been a breakup.

But the story turned out thicker than that. Norma and Larry,

Jimmy said, had been an item in Manhattan for some time, even after that fling in San Francisco. Over drinks Larry would sometimes complain about "some broad who had his kid and was trying to stick him for money."

But when my mother introduced herself, wearing a smashing black dress, pearls, and high heels, Jimmy's first thought was, Whoa, this is *some broad*!

They had met backstage at the Paramount. Jimmy was opening for Benny Goodman. Goodman was one of Mom's favorites, and while she had never seen Stump and Stumpy, she knew them by reputation. All the showbiz types knew who invented the most innovative moves, and Stump and Stumpy was one of the acts whose name always came up at Charlie's, where she, too, hung out sometimes, listening for word of upcoming auditions.

At the Paramount she had introduced herself as a friend of Larry Storch's and told Jimmy he was the funniest guy she'd ever seen.

Jimmy said that my mother brought to mind a combination of Katharine Hepburn and Marlene Dietrich. That first night they stayed up talking till dawn. She told him that she had always wanted to be a dramatic actress; as a five-year-old, she had invented a character called "Nadja, Queen of the Night." He told her how he had run away to join the circus when *he* was five. (He had traveled from Philadelphia to Cleveland before being discovered.) Jimmy had collected nickels and dimes as a kid dancing in bars; she had collected nickels and pennies as a kid going door-to-door, doing little skits.

In New York they reinvented themselves as Queen O'Hara of Tara and Sir Hare.

Still, Jimmy had felt as if he were double-crossing Larry. Jimmy had made it a point to ask him about Norma, and Larry indicated it was okay, in a rather stunning fashion.

In 1952, Larry had just finished a week at the Desert Inn; while Stump and Stumpy were en route to Las Vegas to play the Moulin Rouge, Larry told Jimmy he would find a present in the bus-station locker. When Jimmy opened the locker, there was an ounce of marijuana—and a picture of my mother—with a note: "These are for you."

My heart froze as I considered this story. My mother had been passed from man to man—she'd been one of those "loose women" Aunt Peggy always worried I would become.

"She had a look of class about her," my father's partner, Harold Cromer, would recall later. "Nothing low-life, you know? And the first time I remember Jimmy talking about her—we had a saying between us, 'I thought of stickin' witcha.' That meant that you were going to hang out for a while. So she loved Jimmy, and Jimmy loved her."

As I began piecing together the details of my parents' courtship, my mother described a letter she had written to Granny—a letter I would give my eye teeth to see but which is long lost, a letter I can now only imagine. She remembers writing:

> Mother,
> I'm writing because I've met the most wonderful man. I know you think I'm an idiot when it comes to men, but this one is different. His name is Jimmy Cross and he is a rising star; you're going to hear a lot about him. We met at the Paramount. Everyone is talking about him! On-stage he does characters and sings and dances, and Oh, Mother, I just can't wait for you to see him. He's already traveled to Paris and London and Moscow; this spring he is playing a nightclub in Las Vegas. He's booked there for BIIIG money for twelve weeks. Maybe you can come visit us in Vegas!
> Jimmy and I stay up all night talking after his performances. We go club hopping till four, and then stay up talking till the "civilians" head for work. "Civilians," that's what we call the straight people, people who work nine to five. Our schedule is completely backward. Jimmy cooks for me—his specialty is a dish he learned in Paris. He insists that each ingredient, like the green peppers and

*onion, have to be cooked separately so that it doesn't lose
its flavor. He calls them potatoes Lyonnaise, but I just
think of them as fancy hash browns.*

*In any case I can't wait for you to meet him. I know
that if you did, you would change your mind about my
taste in men. Jimmy is so cultured, so witty—and everyone in New York says he is one of the best performers
ever! And he is!*

*I've been working part-time at the millinery depart-
ment at Gimbel's, so I have some regular money. Here's
twenty dollars—don't spend it all at the track. Will send
more later this month when Jimmy gets paid.*

I can imagine my mother sitting at a writing desk in the Warwick
Hotel on Sixth Avenue—the hotel where they lived in a rented room,
a hotel where I stayed while covering stories for *MacNeil/Lehrer*.

A light drizzle falls. She looks back at the paper and bites the tip
of her pen. She remembers what Granny used to say about blacks:
Negroes are okay, but you should never eat with them.

She signs the letter, "Love, Norma," then writes one more line:
"P.S.: Jimmy is a Negro."

She didn't hear from her mother for three or four months after
sending her the letter. When Norma finally called, Granny's fourth
husband said, "She doesn't want to speak with you," and hung up.

My father's partner, Harold, who became Stumpy in 1949 after
my father's first partner, Eddie Hartman, succumbed to a drug addiction, remembers a night when my mother came up to see Stump
and Stumpy where they were working in Boston's North End.
Harold and Jimmy had been appearing for ten days, to enthusiastic
response from both the audience and the club's Italian owners.
Jimmy had learned some Italian during the war; he so charmed his
employers that they paid for all the duo's meals and even gave them
money for gambling in the club's back room. Harold and Jimmy got
new clothes and Italian-made shoes.

Then one weekend my mother appeared, wearing the black dress in which my father had first met her, white pearls on her neck, rhinestones at her ears, black pumps on her shapely legs. She looked like Grace Kelly, Harold said.

When the Italians saw her on the arm of the black comic, the gravy train ended. No more free lunches, no more gambling allowance, no more Italian shoes.

My mother was oblivious to the drama her arrival caused. She remembered that she had saved a picture taken at the club. She took it out and showed it to me when I asked her about this story. In the photo, she is sitting at a table covered with a white linen cloth, carefully posed for the camera. In fact, she had sat between Jimmy and Harold for the shot. She liked the picture so much, she sent it to her mother, but first she carefully excised Jimmy and Harold. The picture that remains is a cutout of her, alone.

I wondered how a woman so neurotic about race ever ended up with my father.

"We just laughed all the time," my father explained, as if laughter itself held the power to dispel racism. "That was what kept us together. We were laughing all the time.

"We had a song," he recalled. "It was 'Our Love Is Here to Stay.' "

When did the laughing stop? When Jimmy's career began to fail? The first time they were turned down for an apartment? The first time my mother was called a slut for walking down a public street with a black man? The first time he hit her?

They stayed together five years. After the first year, she sent for my brother, who had been living with Granny in California.

During that summer of 1953, Stump and Stumpy were working one of the black clubs in Atlantic City. Jimmy, my mother, and my brother were living in the basement apartment of Aunt Peggy and Uncle Paul's house.

Then she discovered she was pregnant with me.

My brother remembers discussions about abortion, but there was no money. Aunt Peggy probably argued against it. This would have been the second year my mother and Jimmy had rented the apartment. By then, Aunt Peggy and Mom had become friends. Mom thirsted after knowledge and culture, and Aunt Peggy represented the sort of genteel womanhood to which she aspired. My mother spent hours reading Peggy's collection of *Life* magazines and discussing current events. She envied the stable life Peggy and Paul seemed to have built in Atlantic City: they owned a house with a yard and enjoyed a middle-class lifestyle.

Nearly thirty years later, in early 1981, seven months after we first met, Jimmy took a turn for the worse. I made a pilgrimage to the room he rented, above a pharmacy on the corner of 125th Street and St. Nicholas Avenue.

He lay propped up in a secondhand hospital bed Lois and Harold had bought for him, dabbing at the fissure in his chin and drinking his Kool-Aid.

I had one question I'd been wanting to ask for a long time, and it needed to be asked when we were alone.

"So, why did you leave us?" I asked.

"I didn't leave," he whispered, a wan smile on his face. "She left me. And with good reason, too."

"She left you? Why?"

"Because I was a drunk." At last, finally, he admitted it.

"I'd always liked a little taste now and then," he continued, "but when my career started going downhill, I started looking for sympathy in the booze."

He told me about the day she left him. They had gone to the movies to see a Marilyn Monroe picture. In the middle of the movie, she left to go to the ladies' room and never came back.

Initially, he had thought she was angry with him for spending the rent money on marijuana. Thinking it would blow over, he went to Charlie's Bar and tied on a couple before going home to face the music.

While he was at the bar, she called him to say she had moved out and wasn't coming back. She had paid the rent for a month, so he'd have time to find a place. Then he realized he had screwed up the best thing he ever had.

"You could have knocked me over with a feather," he said in his raspy voice.

So he went out and drank some more.

She had done the right thing by leaving him, he told me.

He asked for a cigarette. We had been talking for two hours or so, and his voice had been reduced to the ashes of a whisper. I tried to tell him a cigarette wouldn't be good for him.

"What do you think, the cigarette's going to kill me? I've already got cancer!" he proclaimed. I gave him one of my Benson & Hedges.

Next to his bed he kept a plastic bowl, the kind Mazola margarine comes in, filled with ice and Kool-Aid. He had been sipping from the bowl as we talked, like a Japanese person drinking noodle soup, and now it was empty. He asked me to refill it from a pitcher in the refrigerator.

I decided to pour a glass for myself, but when I sipped it, I almost choked. The cherry-flavored Kool-Aid was mixed with pure vodka!

"You old coot!" I laughed as I brought the bowl back to his bedside. "You know you're not supposed to be drinking!"

He pointed out that he wasn't supposed to be smoking either, and flicked the ashes from his cigarette onto his bedroom floor.

We laughed together, and then I was able to ask another question I had been needing to ask all along.

"So where you been my whole life? You knew where I was."

I knew this for a fact because as a child I had heard Uncle Paul say from time to time that he'd seen Jimmy playing the 500 Club or Club Harlem or somewhere on the other side of Missouri Avenue. It had been Uncle Paul, Jimmy had already told me, who invited him to come see me that day long ago when I was eight and just learning how to play the piano.

"I couldn't do nothing for you," he said, "and if I couldn't do nothing for you, what good did it do to muck up your life? I figured you were better off without my bringing my bad luck your way."

"But why didn't you ever visit, at least?" I pressed. "Whether or not you had money, just to say hello?"

"You had Paul there," he countered. "You would just have gotten confused."

I wasn't satisfied with that answer; after all, I had spent my life balancing two mothers, calling uncles and aunts those who weren't really my aunts and uncles, changing my relationship to those closest to me as society commanded—but Jimmy didn't know any of that. He didn't know how, when Uncle Paul died, there was no one who could teach me to pitch a curve ball, play a cool shot at billiards, whistle a decent tune, no one who might have given me the confidence to stand in front of a roomful of strangers and sing a song.

We talked a little while longer, and then I left.

Ten days later I got a call from Lois. Jimmy had died, of pneumonia. I called my mother. She sounded sadder than I'd expected. Mom relayed the message to Larry, and I heard his cry of sorrow. He came to the phone.

"He was one of the great ones, J.B.," he said.

There was in their expressions of sorrow something profound and heartfelt that suggested bonds deeper than I had ever suspected.

By this time I had owned a video of Jimmy's movie, *This Is the Army*, for ten years, but I still had not watched it. After Jimmy's death Lois and Harold cued up the scene and made me sit down on the orange couch to view it.

The number featured an all-black dance ensemble. It had been edited into the movie with a dark backstage scene leading into and out of it, so that projectionists in the South could easily remove it. The scene began with Jimmy reassuring the Ronald Reagan character that he would do a good job, then cut to a wide shot showing the entire stage as it might have looked from the front-row balcony.

It would be twenty years before I learned the whole story about how my father came to await his entrance on that stage. He told me before he died that show business had been in his blood ever since that day when, as a child, he ran away to join the circus. I would learn from his friends how pervasive a form tap dancing was during the 1920s: a renegade's art, looking for mainstream acceptance, much the same as rap music is now. My father was both a dancer and an athlete who perfected a kind of exaggerated virtuosity, his friends told me. It was a style that married comedy, art, and innovation. Before I met him, Jimmy had told Marshall Stearns that his greatest influence had been a dancer with Cab Calloway's band, a man known as "Dynamite"*:

> Wearing white tails, Dynamite hit stage center to a very fast version of . . . "Black Rhythm" . . . and vibrated all over, holding his arms out like a jittery scarecrow, while his hands dangled uselessly—brute speed and energy. One of his pet steps was a straddle-legged stomp, in which he simply jumped up and down on the beat with his legs apart. After four or five minutes they banged a gong as a signal to quit.
>
> Offstage, however, Dynamite was another "Cool cat." He had a voice like a hoarse Louis Armstrong and a habit of bobbing his head to some unheard rhythms. As a youngster, James Cross of the team of Stump and Stumpy remembers being greatly impressed with Dynamite's knowing ways. "Why, he'd just stand in a doorway bobbing his head and looking cool, and everybody would tiptoe around him with the greatest respect. Then when he spoke in that gravelly voice, you *knew* he was something else!"

Jimmy adapted Dynamite's steps, and they became his signature. After his aborted attempt to join the circus, Lois told me, his mother, Rose, realized the depths of his passion and his talent, so by the time he was eight, she had him touring the neighborhood bars, dancing for money. She fed him sugar cubes to keep him awake, and that's how he earned the nickname "Sugey." His father, a shipyard worker named Percy, drank, and he was a mean drunk. Jimmy had told me before he died that he tried his best to stay out of his father's way.

It was my father's imitation of Louis Armstrong that first brought him notice, at age twelve, in the pages of the *Pittsburgh Courier*. The reviewer was describing a Philadelphia radio show called *Colored Kiddies of the Air*. These were the days before television: at that

---

Jazz Dance. Marshall and Jean Stearns. Schirmer Books. From interviews, 1960.

time in America, show business was as segregated as housing. In Philadelphia every Friday, Horn & Hardart, the cafeteria chain, sponsored a live amateur hour for white kids at one of the downtown theaters. Eddie Lieberman, a local promoter, arranged for a black dry cleaners called Parisian Tailors to sponsor a similar show at the Pearl Theater for black kids on Sundays. On the colored side of town, it became a popular hustle to scalp passes to *Colored Kiddies of the Air.*

It was Lieberman who paired another child performer, Eddie Hartman, with Jimmy, thinking their fancy footwork and choreographed caricatures might make a good combination. Several popular acts back then went by names that rhymed: Chuck and Chuckles, Buck and Bubbles; Lieberman named the duo "Stump and Stumpy." Stump, my father, was the taller, at five foot seven. Eddie Hartman was so short he couldn't even get drafted.

In 1937 they got a call from New York.

Jimmy told an interviewer once that leaving Philly's street corners was "a dream he had never dared to dream," yet there he was, barely sixteen, opening not just in New York City, but at the Cotton Club, the hottest club in the hottest city in the world. He would remember forever a particular drizzly night during the second week of his run, watching as a cab drove up with a beautiful woman standing in its opened sunroof; a woman the color of café con leche, her wavy black hair pulled back in a bun, one hand holding a glass of scotch, her full lips drawing sensuously on a black cigarette holder that she held in the other.

"You're Stump Cross!" exclaimed Billie Holiday as she left the cab. She offered him a cigarette and planted a kiss on his cheek, then floated by on a wave of perfume and chiffon.

Sixteen-year-old Jimmy Cross knew then that he had arrived.

By the time the movie version of Irving Berlin's *This Is the Army* was released in 1943, Jimmy was twenty-two. The song was Berlin's, but the dancing in the interlude was adapted from Stump and Stumpy's act. Jimmy had perfected his entrance. A horn flourish signaled the opening, paused, and he emerged, turning, from behind the curtain, as if he'd been caught in the middle of doing something else and would, after consideration, drop it to sing this song, which began with a scat lick:

> Bee Dop a doo radda da zoo!
> There's a change in fashion that shows
> In the Lenox Avenue clothes:
> Mister Dude has disappeared with his flashy tie . . .

I found the song itself a bit corny in that World War II kind of way, but there was no denying Jimmy's energy. After the interlude, he danced a duet with a man dressed up as a woman (the subterfuge carefully revealed by an additional camera angle when the partner left the stage). Then the entire ensemble gathered for some fancy footwork in double time, interrupted by Jimmy entering again in a spectacular series of three round-offs and a somersault to land stage center, where, incredibly, the entire pace of the number picked up again.

I watched the man who would become my father perform the kind of athletic dancing that might have made Gene Kelly himself jealous. In homage to his childhood hero, Dynamite, he bounced up and down in wide second as though he were on a pogo stick; his feet went into double time, then triple time, heedless, it appeared, of the rest of his body. Meanwhile, the company of dancers—all 125 of them—kept up as they sang a rousing chorus.

I struggled to connect the vibrant, energetic dancer in the movie to the small, worn, pathetic man I had met barely eight months earlier.

"He was quite a dancer," I said to Lois and Harold after it was over.

Having studied tap myself, I rewound the tape, trying out some of the steps. Lois and Harold then showed me the *New York Times* review of the original Broadway production of *This Is the Army*. Berlin had written the show as part of the wartime effort and eventually donated over $2 million from the show's proceeds to the military. The reviewer noted that my father's first-act closing number had received the only standing ovation in the show. He ended with a racist trope: "James Cross and his troupe prove that Negro rhythm is an inborn gift that the white man might as well give up trying to acquire right now."

By 1950 Stump and Stumpy had become a headline act at black venues like the Apollo and the Cotton Club, and at white ones like the Paramount. Jimmy had opened on Broadway and toured through Europe, appearing before the queen of England and Joseph Stalin. He was twenty-nine years old and making good money: he had a guaranteed ten weeks in Las Vegas every year, worth forty thousand dollars.

When he met my mother backstage at the Paramount in 1952, he was poised to become the country's first Negro crossover performer.

My father's wake was held at Benta's Funeral Home, at 135th Street on Edgecombe Avenue.

This was a neighborhood I usually passed through on the way to Uncle Hugh and Aunt Sylvia's; they knew the owner of Benta's. I had met him at the parties of their friends, and now I was in his establishment for the wake of my father, who had never known Hugh and Sylvia at all.

The wake was filled with black showbiz types whose names I recognized from a bygone era, men and women who had worked their way into respectability from the mean streets of Philly, New York, Chicago, or some unknown place in the midwest or down South. Their manners were acquired; their clothes had a flashy touch. They spoke loudly and signified broadly. They meant well, but I felt cauterized against their condolences. Impatience filled me. Ever since I first learned of her existence, I had looked forward to meeting my sister. What I knew was that her name was Lynda Gravatt and that she was an actor. She had been working with a repertory company in Houston, Texas, and was flying in for the funeral.

Lynda was six years older than I was; her mother, Marge, was the second or third white woman Jimmy took up with, according to

Harold, who kept a mental list of all my father's conquests, by race. He told me Marge had deposited her daughter with a middle-class black couple—a teacher and a postal clerk—in Harlem, and never bothered to see her again.

During my father's wake, I kept turning toward the door, looking for a woman who might be my sister. As yet another stranger took my hands to impress upon me the depth of my father's talent, I glanced up to see a round rose of a woman, a little shorter than I, with a pleasant face and black hair pulled back into a bun. She had my coloring and, when she smiled, the same teeth and that wide grin, the legacy of Jimmy's thousand-megawatt smile. I disentangled myself and walked toward her.

"You look like me. You must be Lynda," I said as she approached.

"You look like me. You must be my baby sister, June," Lynda said, taunting me with my own smile.

Ignoring my outstretched hand, she put her arm around me and we embraced as if we had been missing one another all our lives.

I wrote Jimmy's obituary for the funeral service and badgered the *New York Times* until they published their own obit. In researching his life, I discovered that he had been in another movie, *Ship Ahoy*, and that he had also appeared on *The Ed Sullivan Show* and Milton Berle's show. He had performed before Stalin and President Franklin Roosevelt. Nevertheless, I still thought of him as a has-been. So did Lynda. Neither of us was prepared for the outpouring of black show-business luminaries who came to the funeral service itself: Honi Coles, the Copasetics, Joe Williams, Ralph Cooper, Jimmy Slyde. They were all ready to set Lynda and me straight.

"If it hadn't been for Jerry Lewis," said one after another, "your father should have been Sammy Davis."

At first Lynda and I were puzzled by the references to Jerry Lewis. Then, as Harold explained that many black show-business insiders thought Lewis had "stolen" his zany character from my father, we were annoyed. Sammy Davis had become Sammy Davis. What had stopped Jimmy but his own drinking and irresponsibility?

"He went as far as they let him go," said his boyhood friend LeRoy Meyers, as if a career were set on train tracks and race determined the end of the line. If you were black in the forties and in show business, LeRoy explained, you were relegated to singing and dancing. Comics, the top of the show-business hierarchy, were quick-witted and smart. Blacks were not allowed in this rarefied stratum, and Jimmy's particular genius was comedy.

That was a condition affecting all black people then, Lynda and I told one another. Why was everyone saying that Jerry Lewis had hampered Jimmy's career? We asked Jimmy's surviving partner, Harold Cromer.

Harold had become Jimmy's partner during the late forties. When Jimmy came off the road from touring with *This Is the Army* he had discovered, sadly, that his old partner, Eddie Hartman, was addicted to heroin. Jimmy had to fire Eddie, and hired Harold Cromer, a New Yorker and a mimic who had perfected the skill of tap-dancing on roller skates. The chemistry of Stump and Stumpy never quite clicked the same way, said most of Jimmy's friends, even though Harold, dark-skinned and plump, was a talented entertainer. By the time Lynda and I met him, Harold seemed embittered by what could have been. Weepy with Budweiser, he told this tale.

It seemed Jimmy and his first partner, Eddie, had played in the Catskills during the early thirties. The Catskills were a popular resort location for Jewish vacationers, and Lewis, then a teenager, worked as a bellhop at one of the hotels. Jimmy himself had told me that he taught Lewis the rudiments of comedic timing after hours in the darkened ballroom, when all the guests were long in bed.

After the war, Lewis joined with Dean Martin and worked gigs in Atlantic City at the 500 Club. Meanwhile Stump and Stumpy played across town at the Club Harlem.

Jimmy's friends swore that Martin and Lewis had literally stolen Stump and Stumpy's act. "You went to see them, they were doing 'Stump and Stumpy,' " said Buster Brown, one of the Copasetics. "Lewis was doing Stump, but he wasn't coordinated enough to do the dancing. Stump wasn't as spastic and disturbing as Lewis is."

Lois recalled a story attributed to the infamous Nat Nazarro.

Nazarro managed Stump and Stumpy (along with Pearl Bailey, Butterbeans and Susie, Moms Mabley, and others). He went to see Martin and Lewis at the Paramount one night and, rising from his seat in anger, tore down the aisle, screaming, "You're stealing my act!"

One day years later, I took advantage of an opportunity to interview Jerry Lewis and asked if he remembered my father. He did. He remembered how, when he and Dean Martin played Atlantic City in the late forties, they would dash over from the white nightclub on Atlantic Avenue to the black nightclub on Kentucky Avenue in order to catch Stump and Stumpy's late show. He said he also studied the black comic Moms Mabley. I asked whether there were specific things he got from watching Stump's manic style. "It's hard to say," he answered. "You see, when a performer's influenced by greatness, you don't know that you are because comics are thieves. They thieve. They steal from only greatness, but they place it in a place back here"—he indicated the back of his head—"that they don't even know they've taken an idea or a speck of a notion and develop it." He had no memory of ever meeting my father when he worked as a busboy in the Catskills.

I had never particularly liked Jerry Lewis as a comic. Still, the argument that he alone had caused Jimmy's downfall seemed specious. Racism kept black acts from prime TV spots, and my mother herself had told me that Jimmy refused to retool his act even when it was evident, in the early fifties, that audience tastes had changed. When I asked him, even Jimmy seemed to downplay the Lewis story.

"Imitation is the sincerest form of flattery," was all he would say.

"That's because Jimmy was such a kind, generous man, with such a big heart," Lois said. "He was just incapable of holding a grudge."

I got home from Jimmy's funeral to find a message from my mother and Larry. They had sent a big heart-shaped flower arrangement made of white roses and wanted to know if it had arrived. When I spoke to her, Mom asked whether there had been a telegram or any flowers from Jerry Lewis. I told her there were none.

"The least he could have done was pay for the funeral," she said.

15. LOSING PEGGY

There had been a time, after my mother married Larry, when Aunt Peggy feared that Jimmy would try to blackmail us by threatening to reveal he was my father. Now she warned me about becoming too friendly with Jimmy's crowd. "You don't know what kind of people these are," she admonished, as if I didn't detect her far greater fear: that my father's crowd might pull me still further away from her.

Our relationship had been strained since college. Aunt Peggy never adjusted to the fact that I lived openly with the men in my life. After graduation, I'd dated a computer-systems analyst who wanted to get married, but I wasn't ready. In New York I had just moved in with a political aide to Governor Hugh Carey. He would leave me within months to marry a woman he had gotten pregnant.

I was twenty-seven, a little younger than Aunt Peggy herself had been when she married Uncle Paul.

"You're used goods. It must be in your genes," Aunt Peggy said with disgust. I just sighed. Every conversation circled back to marriage and motherhood, as if matrimony alone could redeem me.

I focused on my career. I loved reporting for *The MacNeil/Lehrer Report*. I had started as minority-affairs reporter and after three years worked my way up—labor, then urban/regional affairs.

Robin MacNeil, the executive editor, periodically liked to reshuffle the beat reporters as a way of keeping the show fresh. I lobbied him to let me take on a more challenging beat—I wanted economics.

He decided to really challenge me—he assigned me to cover the somewhat unwieldy beat called Defense/Middle East and U.S.-Soviet relations. I moved from New York to Washington during the summer of 1981, then concentrated on learning my new beat.

President Ronald Reagan had just taken office. The country was beginning the biggest defense buildup since World War II; SALT II, the arms-control treaty painstakingly negotiated by outgoing president Jimmy Carter, was now up in the air. Israel was expanding its settlements in the West Bank and suffering almost daily attacks from Palestinians on its northern border; in Lebanon a civil war that would ultimately lead to the first terrorist attacks on American troops was beginning.

Learning the nuances of all these issues was like being paid to attend graduate school. I got to work at seven-thirty in the morning and attended seminars at either Georgetown or Johns Hopkins University every night. Corners of the earth I never even contemplated while growing up in Atlantic City were becoming visible. Lebanon, its factions, its history, and its cultural importance to the Arab world fascinated me; the arcane universe of arms control demanded hours of reading and background interviewing. I also had to develop sources inside the Pentagon where generals faced off against congressmen over weapon systems with astronomical price tags.

Going home to Atlantic City felt like being sent back to elementary school. Casino gambling had begun in 1978, after a long battle. By 1980 the city still had only two casinos, and they were both on the boardwalk.

The city, always a vacation resort, had been in a long, slow decline since the fifties, when the advent of air travel led high-roller tourists to go elsewhere. Throughout the sixties and seventies, it had become a shabby sea town. Sheltered within the city's communal warmth, I had never noticed how ravaged its economy had become.

The shops on Atlantic Avenue had long closed, their awnings tattered. Half of the city was unemployed. The ocean, which once seemed lovelier to me than the Caribbean, looked gray and polluted.

To make me feel even more alienated, Aunt Peggy still couldn't understand what I did for a living. After nearly fifty years of teaching, she had retired.

The changing rules of discipline, which forbade a teacher to touch a child, and the increasing standardization in the classroom had driven her out. She said she didn't need to submit lesson plans— she knew what she wanted to teach. She found this new generation of children, schooled in environments that eschewed corporal punishment, undisciplined and ill-mannered. They frightened her.

Gigi, my pet schnauzer, had finally died after a long, slow deterioration. She had lived twenty-two years, the last four or five by dint of Peggy's sheer determination to keep her alive. Gigi represented the last vestige of Peggy's life with me and Uncle Paul.

Peggy lived by herself and was lonely. "I feel like a blade of grass all alone in the world," she wrote me in one letter. She asked me to move back home.

Full of self-importance, caught in the excitement of Washington politics, I told her that I couldn't; my work was too important.

Then she asked Uncle Hugh to move back from New York. She offered to leave him her house if he would come take care of her.

Uncle Hugh had managed to lose his license as a cabdriver; he could not contain his road rage and had too many accidents on his record. He piddled with get-rich schemes in real estate and Amway. Although he could do that anywhere, still, his life was based in New York. His wife, Aunt Sylvia, loved her job as an administrative assistant for the lawyer and civil-rights advocate Heywood Burns at City College. There was no future for them—for anyone—in Atlantic City, filled as it was with retirees biding their time and school-age children waiting for their moment to leave.

Uncle Hugh said he didn't want her house either. He wanted her to get better, to take control of her life. We both wanted the old Aunt Peggy—playful, opinionated, and full of life—to return.

She threw her remaining passion into the citizens' lobby organizing to pass the gambling initiative. One night as she left a meeting, walking alone, a young man—a man whose face she couldn't place among the rosters of her students' faces, a man whose family she didn't know—came along, knocked her down, and stole her pocketbook.

"At least you're alive," I said, when she called me in tears. "Count your blessings. You could have been hurt."

She was not in a state to count blessings. Such a thing would never have happened in the old days, when she commanded the respect of a teacher, when she knew all the children within a three-mile radius of the house. Shortly thereafter she called to say that she couldn't find her prized Rolleiflex camera; she feared that someone—maybe one of the delivery boys?—had stolen it from the darkroom.

In June 1982, Israel had invaded Lebanon; I was working around the clock, it seemed, to keep up with developments. Distracted, I suggested that she might have misplaced it. She hadn't used it in years, after all.

"Oh, you have no compassion!" she exploded, and I fell silent in the face of her eruption.

Uncle Hugh, equally worried, sent long, inspirational letters designed to shift her focus to more positive things. "Turn hope and despair into hope and faith," he implored. I started driving back home once a month. Despite our efforts, she slipped further into depression. She complained that she could eat only the juice from cooked collard greens or Campbell's chicken noodle soup.

I spent my summer vacation, late that August of 1982, in Atlantic City. My brother, Lary; his wife, Lany; and their kids, Michael, Daniel, and Sarah, also came. By then Aunt Peggy, who had complained of being too heavy at 155 pounds, had dropped to 120. She was an unhealthy image of her younger self, her collarbone peeking out from a robe my mother had sent her, a scent strangely foul and sweet on her breath. Too weak to rise for meals, she slept on the downstairs sofa. The two younger children were toddlers, so Lary and Lany set up their playpen in the living room near her. Watching the babies play encouraged her, and she rebounded a bit. We sat on chairs around the children, while Peggy lay on the sofa, and talked into the night the way we had when I was young.

"I'm so glad to see Lary settled and with a family," she said during a moment when my brother and sister-in-law had carried plates into the kitchen. She looked meaningfully in my direction. "A family is the most important thing. Never mind this career business."

I felt tears spring up, stinging my eyes, and sighed, exhaling and pushing my emotions down my throat. Then I rose silently and joined Lany in the kitchen.

"She really is proud of you," Lany said. "She just wants more for you."

"Then why doesn't she ever say so?" I asked despairingly.

"Because she's a parent," Lany said, laughing with self-recognition. "All she can say is what she doesn't see. It goes with the territory."

For several months Aunt Peggy teetered between health and decline; then she slid beyond rescue.

Our black family doctor of many years had retired. Rather than go to one of the two other black doctors in town, she found a white doctor in Ventnor. His gruff manner reminded me of Uncle Paul. He complained that she never took the medication for high blood pressure he prescribed. She complained that the pills he gave her made her feel bloated, and besides, did nothing to ease her primary ailment—indigestion. The doctor claimed the indigestion was caused by her refusal to eat regularly and finally he refused to treat her at all. He claimed that she was malingering.

His arrogance disturbed me. Even I could see that Aunt Peggy suffered from severe gastrointestinal distress after eating. I resolved to go with her on her next trip to the doctor and took a day off from work. Alas, although she had been my "guardian," "foster mother," or "aunt" ever since I could remember, Aunt Peggy and I had no legal relationship, and she refused to authorize the doctor to discuss her condition with me.

"But what about this lump that she keeps feeling when she swallows?" I asked, pushing the doctor during one of my visits, testing the boundaries.

"Probably heartburn," he said. "If she would eat more regularly, it would go away."

"But heartburn doesn't make you vomit!" I pointed out, exasperated. "Isn't there something you can do?"

He finally conceded and sent her to the hospital for a gastrointestinal test called a GI series. After much procrastination she went, but, once there, she discovered that she had to drink what she called "irradiated orange juice" so that they could take the X-rays. She refused to take the test.

Uncle Hugh and I were stymied. I started driving up to spend weekends with her once a month. He took the bus down during the week.

The doctor called her ailment "cachexia" brought on by heart disease, treatable if she took her pills, which she refused to do. Instead she read *Prevention* magazine and lived on cans of chicken noodle soup. Sometimes I made her applesauce from McIntosh apples, a favorite.

She rarely finished a serving.

"Why won't you eat?" I demanded. "How do you expect to get better if you don't eat?"

She looked at me, sullen as an eight-year-old. "Nobody cares about me," she whined. "I could die right here and nobody would care."

Finally I called her bluff. "Do you want to die?"

Her gaze softened, and she shook her head. "No. No, I don't want to die," she said in a small voice, but with such pathos that I was reminded of the time when I was five and couldn't bring myself to acknowledge her in the Wy-Mo-Mays fashion show. She managed a spoonful of soup then, holding the center of her chest as she swallowed.

"I'd get better if you'd come back here to take care of me," she said, slyly looking up at me with her good eye.

"Aunt Peggy, how can I come back here? I have a life and job in D.C.!"

"I'd leave you the house," she said, trying on me what hadn't worked with Uncle Hugh.

"I don't want the house!" I exclaimed.

She put on her wounded voice. "I didn't know you hated Atlantic City so much," she said. "You seemed happy here."

"I don't hate Atlantic City," I said, forcing myself to speak normally. "But I don't like you trying to manipulate me like this. There's nothing for me now in Atlantic City. My future is in Washington."

"That's what you always say, there's nothing for you here. What's the use?"

I called Uncle Hugh for advice. Someone obviously needed to be with Aunt Peggy on a daily basis, but who? How? As we discussed the logistics, I glanced down at the phone table. There she had prepared a list of those to call in case of emergency. She had crossed out my name.

Uncle Hugh suggested we find a day nurse, but first we needed to know what was wrong with Aunt Peggy. He couldn't break away from work, but Aunt Syl came down one Friday to go with us to the doctor. Aunt Peggy even gave the doctor permission to talk to Sylvia about her case. I dropped them off, then occupied myself driving around Ventnor, looking at the houses where blacks, whites, Hispanics, and Arabs now all lived together. Still, there wasn't a house there where I could imagine living.

Aunt Syl and Aunt Peggy emerged from the doctor's office and got into the car. They were silent. Aunt Syl wouldn't say what the doctor had told her.

Back in D.C. several nights later, a call came from Uncle Hugh.

"I think we need to face the fact that Peggy is failing," he said. "She's not going to get better."

For the next several months, I drove my beat-up BMW three hours every weekend to see her. Traveling east through the South Jersey farmlands, I made a mental list of all the things she had asked me to do that I had never done: the thank-you notes that had gone unwritten, the contacts I'd never kept up, the promising piano talent I'd never realized, that young man from a fine family I'd never met and married, the children I'd never had—my guilt rattled behind the car like the chains of Marley's ghost. Aunt Peggy had raised me as the proper daughter of a black middle-class woman, the kind who would drop everything to look after her during her demise, but I was not her daughter, nor her sister's daughter. My perfidy made me feel like a Judas.

There was a time when I felt I could never love Aunt Peggy the way she loved me, another time when I wondered whether I had ever felt love for her at all. I was never sure whether my love for both my mother and Peggy constituted treason toward each. Yet hadn't my mother betrayed me by leaving me with Aunt Peggy? And hadn't Aunt Peggy, in her sly little ways, tried to convince me that my mother didn't deserve respect?

Arriving at 407 in November 1982, I braced myself for the evidence that her body was surrendering life.

I found her lying as delicately as a piece of tissue paper in her pink polyester nightgown, wrapped in a cotton kimono my mother had given her. She was gripped by digestive pains, immobilized on the same plastic-covered sofa where I had lain as a child, folded over with stomach cramps. I made fresh applesauce, but she couldn't bring herself to swallow it.

On the weekends when I came, I gave the home nurse time off, so we were left alone. Peggy couldn't rise from the sofa, not even to relieve herself, so she wore a diaper. When she soiled herself, I cleaned her.

So dumbfounded was she that she couldn't place my face.

"Yvette?" she asked, calling me by Regina's mother's name as I carried her in my arms from the sofa to the tub.

"No, it's June," I said, placing her in the warm water. I found a bar of Yardley's lavender soap, her favorite, and a soft washcloth to wash her face and limbs. She remained silent as I ran the worn washcloth over her skin.

Once she had done this for me, during my first weeks in Atlantic City. The downstairs bathroom filled with the odor of Jean Naté and Yardley's powder, with old memories and painful confusion. For twenty-four years I had lived with this woman and never seen her naked; now I bathed her. Running the washcloth over her, I studied her anatomy: her skin hung from her bones like elephant hide. Her breasts, desiccated by illness, reminded me of the breasts in photos of despairing women in Ethiopia, yet her hair was still black between her thighs. I parted her legs and found myself surprised at how calmly she allowed me to wash between her legs, in the folds of skin between the labia. I bent her forward and wrung the washcloth over her bedsores to avoid touching them directly.

"Yvette, what are you doing here?"

It meant so much to her to see Yvette, but it meant so much to me that she see me. I stared at her, saying nothing.

"Yvette? Yvette?" she repeated in confusion.

"It's June!" I said in exasperation. I wrapped her in a towel and placed her on the toilet seat. She grabbed my shoulder with one hand as she grunted in disagreement: her Little Juney could not be here, because her little Juney was not grown. She had retreated to a world in which I had never grown up, never left, never betrayed her with my own yearnings and feelings.

About a month later, just before Christmas, I was in Washington's National Airport, waiting to board the shuttle to New York. I was scheduled to meet a French reporter plugged in to the Palestinian movement for a background conversation. It was a Wednesday. The weekend before, I had visited Aunt Peggy—she'd been hospitalized.

I'd stood and watched her, willing myself to absorb these last moments, listening to the oxygen tube softly hissing into her nose, her chest fluttering with the beat of her heart, the ebb and flow of air into her lungs. I watched the pulse vibrate in the sinew of her forearm and at her temples in syncopation with the rhythm of her breath. I stared at the polyrhythms in her chest for a long time, wondering how this woman who had always stood like a titan in my world had now become so frail.

In the airport I heard my name paged and immediately knew why.

I decided to keep the appointment. From Manhattan I could make my way to Port Authority and get the early-afternoon bus to Atlantic City.

It was the way Peggy's little Juney would have returned.

Although my brother, Lary, came to the funeral, my mother did not.

Now I feel indignant that the woman who bore me did not pay her respects to the woman who had raised her child. Yet if I return to the mind of the thirty-year-old woman alone in the house at 407 North Indiana Avenue in 1983, I know that I did not expect my mother to come. Larry was traveling, and he needed my mother to tend to him. I also knew something else, something deeper and so accepted that its truth has never even been spoken: that my mother feared being the subject of nods and whispers the way Aunt Peggy feared living alone, that my mother hated being reminded of the years she lived with my father, the hostile looks she got when she walked into bars with him. *The black women especially hated me. I could almost imagine them saying, "There she is, the slut," practically spitting it out. One of them tried to stab me one time.*

No, my mother did not have the strength to confront knowing eyes and stage whispers, and so I knew not to expect her in Atlantic City. I did not expect her because the unspoken contract between us had always been that Peggy and I could cross into her world, but she did not—could not—would not—cross again into ours. When she called, using her most sympathetic voice to tell me how sorry she felt about Peggy's passing, she said, "I know how much she meant to you"; she did not add, "and how much she meant to me."

Peggy understood this side of Norma. Occasionally, she would laugh a wicked little laugh and say, "Norma cuts those bridges and keeps on walking." I thought I heard admiration in her voice, maybe even envy. But now I suspect it was more likely bitterness. Hadn't Aunt Peggy been Mom's confidante, her best friend, during those years with Jimmy? Mom had trusted Peggy enough to leave me with her, but then, after she married Larry and moved to Los Angeles,

Norma had grown more and more remote, their conversations, like a divorced couple's, limited to discussions about bills and whatever was going on with me in school. Mom had moved into a higher social circle, leaving Peggy there in Atlantic City. Mom had moved on because she was brave and, as Aunt Peggy always pointed out, because she could. She could because as a white woman, she simply had more options available to her.

After Aunt Peggy died, Uncle Ernie, Uncle Hugh, his older brother Uncle Monty, and I went through the dozens of boxes of photos Peggy had stashed away. She'd become notorious for taking the pictures but never developing or delivering them to the participants. There, amid negatives and photographs of unnamed classrooms, couples now divorced, teachers now dead, children who must have by then been grandparents themselves, were copies of photos she hadn't taken. These pictured a striking auburn-haired woman, a bona fide Breck girl, in various poses: wearing a white blouse and gray skirt, legs crossed, elegantly bedecked with costume jewelry, wearing a little black dress that appeared painted on her lean, Rita Hayworth–like figure.

"Who's this?" Uncle Hugh asked.

"That's my mother. It's her modeling portfolio," I explained. "She had those pictures made after I was born."

It was the first time any of them had laid eyes on her. "*That's* your mother!?" Uncle Hugh exclaimed. "Lawd have mercy." He turned away from me to share the picture with his brother-in-law, Uncle Ernie, who passed it back to Uncle Monty. "Would you stop traffic for that?"

The men gathered around, leering at the pinup of the woman from whose loins I had sprung. Watching them, I felt a mixture of guilt and regret. Guilt at the jealousy I felt, regret that no man, at least until then, had ever used that tone of voice to refer to me.

———

My tears refused to come on the day of Peggy's funeral, and my faith, which had sustained me through Uncle Paul's funeral, had faded. The previous summer I'd gone on a research trip to Israel and Lebanon; seeing the wreckage of war had shaken me. I'm not sure I believed in God any longer, or if I did, I wasn't at all convinced that God cared about mankind. Maybe Aunt Peggy was right—I was becoming cynical. For her sake, though, I made the arrangements for the funeral and provided for her to be buried next to Paul. But I was sleepwalking. I remember nothing of the funeral service itself.

One image did stay with me—Aunt Sylvia, standing on the porch, her back to the house, turning when I called her, tears in her eyes.

"It's the passing of an era," she explained. "Just the passing of an era."

Aunt Peggy was the last of the generation older than she—Uncle Gum and Aunt Hugh had passed while I was in college, and her own parents were long gone. Aunt Peggy had nurtured and supported Aunt Syl through years of marriage, through Uncle Hugh's rages and the downward flow of his career, while she raised two children. In two years we would be burying Aunt Sylvia herself after she died from a brain tumor at fifty-four; two years after that we would bury Uncle Hugh's sister Mignon at fifty-seven; the next year her husband, Uncle Ernie, at sixty-one; and then Uncle Hugh at sixty-seven.

By then I would come to understand what a generation means to a family. But as we buried Aunt Peggy, I began to contemplate my mother's funeral, the distance between her family and all those I called mine.

Who would comfort me when the time came to grieve the loss of the woman, still in the world, that I loved most?

Six months after Aunt Peggy died, I went back to the house at 407 North Indiana to clean out my old room.

I had expected memories to come flooding back as I went through my things, but they didn't. It was as if my memories had been buried with Aunt Peggy, or gone with me to college and gotten lost. I packed my papers and decided what I wanted to take: the Beatles records, yes; the *World Book Encyclopedia*, no; Aunt Peggy's boxes of photographs depicting the children and teachers at Indiana Avenue, the unidentified weddings, and portraits of unknown children, definitely; the dresses Mrs. McKee made for me when I started school . . . well, why not?

I had gathered my things and was standing in the hall at the top of the stairs. As I looked out at the Claridge Hotel, sensations hit me so hard that I had to sit down. The stair landing had been the nerve center of the house. The sun rose on that side in the mornings, and I liked to play with my cat as he lay sunning himself there under the window. I'd sat here and listened to the congregation sing in the AME church next door. The linoleum floor had the best surface for playing jacks. I'd eavesdropped on Aunt Peggy's telephone conversations with my mother and listened to Peggy and Paul fuss about money.

Uncle Paul had died on this very spot.

On the day the Harvard recruiter visited, I'd peeped down from the top of the stairs to look through the door window and see who was there before I answered the door.

Looking out the window now, I saw the Claridge Hotel beckoning, but its brightly lit letters had been replaced by a garishly bright yellow neon sign that would have kept me awake at night.

The beige vinyl floor was buckling, and the radiator had long ago come loose from the wall. It stood like a rusted marker.

"Good-bye, house," I whispered, and within a minute I was locking the front door for the last time.

16. KARMA

By mid-1983, Larry Storch's career had stalled. A decade earlier he had commanded $250,000 a week in Vegas; in 1982 he didn't work at all. One of the successes of the civil-rights movement was that Latinos, Asians, and blacks were now able to play themselves, meaning that many white character actors were out of work. Furthermore, Larry's stand-up act had been built on a kind of ethnic humor that walked the line of stereotype. As values changed, he grew more fearful of causing offense. His progressing alcoholism had the same effect on his career as it had had on my father's. But Larry insisted he didn't have a problem. He said he could stop whenever he wanted to. He just didn't want to.

Every weekend my mother and Larry went to visit friends in Palm Springs. Larry drank, told jokes, and passed out. Mom covered for him by joking that the life of the party had just died, but inwardly, she was suffocating. She told me she dreamed of leaving her marriage to open a restaurant somewhere. Cooking and entertaining were the only skills she had, she said.

Finally, a family friend told Larry that the reason he wasn't working was that alcohol had destroyed his reputation. Those words accomplished what years of my mother's nagging had failed to do: that day he emptied the bottles of wine down the toilet. Within a month he had accepted a small role in the touring company of *Porgy and Bess*.

"We'll be traveling all over the United States and Europe! It will be wonderful!" Mom crowed. She didn't tell me that they had accepted the role for a wage at half of scale, to prove that Larry could be depended on to show up and work.

I joined them in Florence that winter. We hadn't been in Italy together since I was sixteen. Larry was the only white character in the touring company, and I was the only black person *not* in the company.

"It's been so long since I've been around so many blacks," Mom told me one morning as we sipped cappuccino. "You know, blacks and whites really do have different attitudes about life. Whites can be so uptight. Blacks, no matter what happens, they can find the joke. They're so much more fun to be around."

My mother would often say things like this, and I never quite knew the appropriate response.

"Maybe it's just black folks in showbiz versus that Palm Springs crowd you hang out with," I quipped. "Rich Republicans tend to be a little uptight."

We changed the subject.

During the day while Larry rehearsed, Mom and I wandered the streets, investigated the flea markets, and drank cappuccino. I had finally grown up enough to appreciate her. When we weren't talking about race, she was tough, funny, smart, articulate, and constantly seeking new experiences. I liked the woman I got to know.

There was something I had long wanted to ask her, so one day while we were sitting in our favorite café, I asked.

"So did you and Larry really have a child?" Even though I already knew about Candie, this seemed the best way to approach the subject.

She froze momentarily as she sipped the foam from her coffee, then set it down.

"Yes, Larry and I did have a child," she said. "Her name was Candie. She was born in 1948. September 3, 1948, so she would be six years older than you." Her voice cracked. "Larry and I had just met, and I knew he wasn't serious about me, and his mother just hated me. She thought I was trying to stick him with this child that wasn't his—'a gold digger,' she called me."

"So that's why his mother disowned him when you got married?" I asked.

"Yes," she said. She began to cry openly, like a child trying to explain a mistake. "I didn't have any money, and I was still trying to take care of Lary; my mother thought I was an idiot. It was one of the worst times of my life."

Handing her a Kleenex, I remembered finding a small black-and-white picture when I was very young. I had shown it to my mother and asked her who it was.

"Oh, this is your sister," she'd said sadly, her voice full of emotion.

"My sister?" I'd asked. "Where is she now?"

"Her name was Candie. She died, of polio," my mother had lied, tears flowing down her cheeks. That had been the only other time I'd ever seen my mother cry until now, thirty years later, in this café in Florence.

"I've always thought that I must have been a bad person in a previous life," she said now, drying her eyes.

"Why?" I asked.

"Because I've not been allowed to raise any of my children," she said, breaking down again. "What terrible thing could I have done to be denied raising all of my children?"

I didn't believe then in karma from past lives. It seemed to me that an explanation rooted in this life might be more on point.

That fall of 1983, *The MacNeil/Lehrer Report* became the *MacNeil/Lehrer NewsHour*. I covered Jesse Jackson, Gary Hart, and Walter Mondale during the presidential campaign in 1984 and later that year applied for a job as a producer/correspondent with the program.

Background reporters didn't easily cross over to on-air work. However, I had read that CBS's Ed Bradley had gotten his first job in radio by going out and covering a story, and so I followed his example. I used outtakes of a story on Senator Paul Simon's reelection bid that I had helped produce with another correspondent. I wrote my own version of the script and convinced a camera crew to shoot my stand-up in a Virginia suburb that could pass for suburban Chicago. Then I waited.

I was sitting in Charlayne Hunter-Gault's office trying to see if she could tell me what was happening. As a senior correspondent, Charlayne was privy to the goings-on of the inner sanctum.

"I'm not supposed to say anything," she said. Then she bit her lip and picked up the phone.

"I'm calling John Atchison's hair salon," she said, referring to the international hairstylist, as she dialed the number. She asked to speak to the owner and was put through immediately.

"John, it's Charlayne," she said, peering at me. "We're about to hire a new correspondent, and she needs help with her hair."

And that's how I found out I had gotten the promotion.

I'd been wearing my hair natural, but Atchison's stylist convinced me that I'd be "more acceptable" if my hair were straightened. Several hours later I emerged looking like an on-air reporter.

Mom loved my new look and my new job. She had always wanted to be a star, and here I was on TV, reporting the news two or three times a week. Mom rarely mentioned the stories themselves, but she always critiqued my delivery, my demeanor, and my look— and usually she liked what she saw.

Christmas 1985

To My darling Daughter—
Every time I tell you I love you it seems so inadequate. I absolutely adore you, everything about you is so very special and precious to me. I see myself in you (I guess that's the parent tree) only better and more true to my early dreams.

Love always and always and always forever

I never felt entirely comfortable, with my straightened hair and classic wardrobe, in the on-air role. I missed developing my own stories from scratch. Worse, people in Washington began to recognize me. What would I say if some reporter, doing a profile of the staff, asked about my background? What story about my mother and father, aunts, uncles, and cousins, could I make up?

After two years I cut off the perm and went back to my natural. The *NewsHour* had been wonderful to me—my reporting had won a number of awards, including an Emmy—but I began to chafe at the limitations of its format. I wanted to explore more creative approaches in my storytelling. A Harvard classmate told me about a position as a producer at CBS's *West 57th*. He got me in the door— and I got the job. In the summer of 1986, I left the *NewsHour*, taking with me Jim Lehrer's motto, "Keep the facts in front of the story and be fair."

Leaving Washington, I also left a four-year relationship with an electrician, a friend of Hugh Jr's. I had always found that moving from one city to another was the easiest way to end a relationship, but the toll seemed greater as I got older. I was beginning to recognize my mother's behavior in my own, burning my bridges as I moved from one chapter to another in my life. I had no words for the feeling then, just a vague unease. And, as always, I buried my feelings in my work.

For broadcast reporters, CBS News had been the gold standard. It was the home of the venerable Walter Cronkite, "the Tiffany Network." Unfortunately, it had just been sold to Larry Tisch, who began eviscerating its news division. Sixty-four staffers were fired my first day on the job. I soon discovered that although my salary had doubled from what I made at PBS, I still earned one-third less than many of the other producers on staff.

I had hoped I could use the resources of the network to do the kind of work PBS couldn't underwrite, but the styles of the two programs were as different as they could be. It was difficult to keep the facts in front of the story when the quest for ratings shadowed the newsgathering. After several weeks of my pitching story ideas without any luck, the show's producers suggested that I redo a piece I had done for the *NewsHour* on navy pilots.

I resisted. Why would I want to do a piece I had already done?

"Well, you could get pilots who are hipper, more like Tom Cruise," they suggested, referring to his latest movie, *Top Gun.*

I had arrived at CBS just as the FCC, under President Ronald Reagan, lifted the requirement for public affairs programming. News divisions began using profit, not public service, as their standard, and ratings began to take precedence over information. Andy Lack, a former ad executive, then the executive producer of *West 57th*, stayed in his office late into the night, brainstorming ways to structure the show so that viewers were "hooked" within the first five minutes. Lack is a barrel-chested, charismatic man with small eyes, a nose rather large for his face, and a booming voice. He instructed his producers to find stories featuring compelling characters in situations that unfolded in front of the camera—the news-as-cinema-verité.

The approach assaulted my reporting values. It presumed that "real" people were boring and that audiences were less interested in facts than in visual tales. News, my refuge from the made-up stories that had governed my entire life, had been infected by show business.

I could see that it would be a tough fit between me and the network.

Reluctantly, I resigned myself and settled for the comforts my higher salary could bring. I bought a two-bedroom apartment in a renovated building on Riverside Drive in Harlem, an uptown version of my mother and Larry's pied à terre on West End Avenue, ten blocks from Uncle Hugh and Aunt Sylvia's place on Convent Avenue. It was airy and sunny, with a bank of windows facing the Hudson River and the George Washington Bridge to the north. As the sun set over New Jersey, I sat on the sofa and wallowed in shots of Sauza Conmemorativo tequila.

My house developed clusters of clothes and unopened mail, piles of unfiled papers and unread magazines. It was as if by filling the space with clutter, I could justify my existence. I entered therapy, and my shrink tried to get me to stop drinking. She told me that alcohol was a depressant.

I told her I'd be even more depressed if I didn't drink.

One night over dinner, I told my mother how alienated from my CBS colleagues I felt, in dress, mannerisms, habits, likes and dislikes. She dissected me with one of her penetrating stares.

"You're living in the wrong neighborhood," she said.

She meant that I was embracing a blackness that set me apart. She thought that I should move from Harlem, move farther downtown, someplace where my colleagues from CBS would feel more comfortable visiting me.

But I felt comfortable in Harlem. My uncle, aunt, and cousins lived there. My *father* had lived there.

Once I asked my mother why she and my father had always lived in a hotel downtown, why they had never looked for an apartment in Harlem and raised me there.

"Whenever I visited someone with Jimmy, the apartments were always so small," she replied, "wallpaper peeling from the ceiling, heat not working, roaches—" She halted, searching for words. "They always made the best of it, but I didn't want to live like that." In her mind "black" and "poverty" were inextricably linked, and physical threat lay just around the corner.

The dichotomy she maintained seemed inexplicable. After all, she had left me in the care of Aunt Peggy and Uncle Paul. Their house was clean and neat. I wondered what kind of friends Jimmy had taken her to see, how the power of the stereotypes she held trumped her memory of the homes she visited.

My mother told me that she had lived an undercover life with my father, like a novella entitled *I Lived Three Lives*.

"What were the three lives?" I asked.

"Well, the one was with relatives," she explained, "the one was with Jimmy, and the one was with my work. With my mother, she never mentioned you, and there had never been a Jimmy. People that I worked with knew nothing about you. I never went to their houses, they never came to mine. With Jimmy, we would only go among the black people."

I wished my mother would recognize the Jimmy in me so that I could feel like more than the dark shadow of her alter ego. I wished that diversity in hiring meant more than hiring people who might have different skin tones but whose minds thought exactly alike. If I lived where my colleagues lived, wore what they wore, and looked the way they looked, what was the point?

So many times, as a plane descended into the Los Angeles night, I had watched the white lights of that city dancing below the clouds, the freeways blazing a trail of red taillights that led to a month's vacation with Mom and Larry.

But in 1989 I came to L.A. as a producer for CBS News. I was coming to produce a segment on the singer Natalie Cole for *West 57th*.

I had pushed to do this profile, against resistance from my executives, because I felt an affinity with Natalie, the youngest daughter of Nat King Cole. As a child she had been shuttled between the black middle-class section of L.A., Baldwin Hills, and a boarding school in New England. When I first learned about Baldwin Hills, shortly after the Watts riots in 1965, it was because I had discovered, in *Ebony* magazine, that Nat King Cole's family lived there. I wanted to meet some black kids, kids like me, in L.A.

I had asked my Mom where Baldwin Hills was. She didn't know. "Somewhere over near Watts," she said vaguely, aligning it with those ominous smoke signals from 1965. I told her that I'd read that middle-class black folks lived there. I wanted to see them, take a drive through. Finally one afternoon I slipped behind the wheel of the Mercedes coupe while Mom and Larry napped, got a map, and found my way.

Baldwin Hills could have been Venice Park in Atlantic City or Hyde Park in Chicago or any Atlanta suburb; it could as easily have been sections of Beverly Hills or Sag Harbor. I found the street where Cole's widow lived.

Nearby, kids my age played. I wanted to meet them, but I didn't know how. I didn't know how to explain who I was. I didn't know how to say I was there because I wanted to meet some black teenagers, teenagers who might be like me, while I was out in L.A. visiting my white parents, so instead I sat parked at the curb, watching them play basketball.

After a while I had turned my mother's wine-colored Mercedes-Benz convertible around and found my way back to Nichols Canyon.

Fifteen years later I could introduce myself as a producer on assignment for CBS News. I was coming to stay with my mother while I shot a story inspired by my adolescent yearning to belong.

A month earlier, in panic, my mother had called me, the tone in her voice the same as Aunt Peggy's the night she was mugged. She had arrived home to find the property defaced, garbage bags floating in the pool. This, she said, combined with two earlier break-ins, had made her paranoid enough to buy a gun—a .45 Magnum, which she hadn't learned how to use because, she said, she was afraid to shoot it. There had even been an item in the *Hollywood Reprter* about her going out to the range for target practice.

Pulling up to the newly installed security gate, I hesitated. Surely Mom and Larry were asleep. I pushed the bell, tentatively. No one answered. Either the bell wasn't working or, more likely, I felt reluctant to ring it repeatedly at 4:00 A.M. I sat in the car a while, watching the digital clock push 4:30, listening to the beats on the radio, watching the lights below and the sky above, searching for the telltale signs of dawn.

I thought to get out of the car and climb over the gate and into the house. I knew a secret way in, through the cat door, but I feared triggering some newly installed alarm. I had a short Afro. I wore jeans and a sweatshirt; to my mother, foggy with sleep, I might look like any other black person. I could imagine her tiptoeing out of her bedroom, asking "Who's there?" and pulling the trigger before I had a chance to answer.

I could imagine the headlines: MOTHER SHOOTS DAUGHTER MISTAKEN FOR INTRUDER.

So I stayed in my rental car, sleeping fitfully, waiting for the gray dawn to reveal my features and bring me to the safety of my mother's arms. Larry found me there in the morning as he walked up the driveway to get the paper.

"What are you doing here, J.B.?" he asked.

I told him the bell hadn't rung, and we walked down to greet my mother.

"I was awake all night waiting for you," she said. "Why didn't you climb the fence?"

"I didn't want to get shot."

"Shot?" she repeated.

"Well, I know you've got that .45 in here," I said, as flippantly as I could.

She paused for three or four beats. "There is no gun," she said, an edge in her voice. "I just said that so the word would be out in case somebody who knows us is defacing the property."

We looked at each other. The unspoken hung between us in the air like a high-voltage wire, the current running from her eyes to mine. I had always measured the distance between us in miles, hours, days. Now we stood in the same room looking across a chasm even our love for one another couldn't bridge.

While in Los Angeles, I planned to catch up with my childhood friend Regina. She had left Yale Drama School for a career as a high-fashion runway model and now lived in Los Angeles. Regina wanted to be an actor; she had gotten good reviews in the Clint Eastwood movie *Tightrope* but had been struggling ever since.

Regina introduced me to the Buddhist chant *Nam-myoho-renge-kyo*, created by the Japanese monk Nichiren Daishonin in the thirteenth century.

"If you chant it long enough" she said, "you will get whatever you want."

Somewhat skeptically, I tried it for ninety days. When a tax mistake unexpectedly led to a hefty refund, I continued.

The practice appealed to me on more than material grounds. Buddhism taught that spirit lived in every sentient being and that all living beings were therefore connected, that chanting could awaken that connection and give individuals the power to draw extraordinary fortune from the everyday muck of their lives.

The repetition of the mantra, sonorous and deep, inspired a kind of meditation, from which it seemed even my unexpressed yearnings were eventually revealed and realized.

I didn't know it at the time, but what I really wanted was to unite the disparate pieces of my life and to feel comfortable in my own skin.

West 57th was canceled after two years, and Andy Lack brought Connie Chung in from NBC to host an hourlong magazine show called *Saturday Night with Connie Chung*. It was the triumph of show business over news: Connie had the highest likability rating of any newscaster in TV news at the time—and the highest salary. We producers figured out that our time with her was worth a quarter for each second—her reported salary was nearly $8 million a year.

The ratings for *Saturday Night* proved to be even lower than those for *West 57th*, lower even than *West 57th* reruns. Connie and Andy spent long hours huddled in his office. They worked late into the night and expected the rest of us to do the same.

While I thought Connie was overpaid, I empathized with her as a woman of color. She had been "the first Asian woman"—and often the only Asian or the only woman—during her entire career; I understood the tradeoffs she must have made to get to where she was. I promised her that I'd make her look good, and I did my best. The skills I'd honed at the *NewsHour*, developing lines of questioning for Jim and Robin, helped me work with her.

One night in Los Angeles, we found ourselves working into the wee hours of the morning doing a profile of talk-show host Arsenio Hall. We were in the ladies' room as she prepped to do a follow-up interview with the comedian in a club where he tried out routines.

"You have a smudge by your nose," I said to her.

"Oh, that *is* my nose," she said. "Being Chinese, I don't have a defined nose, so I use a defining pencil to create the illusion of a nose. I do the same thing for my eyes, so that fold above my eyelids doesn't look so Asian."

"Really?" I said. "And here the rest of us are trying to make up our eyes so that we look Chinese."

We marveled over the fact that no matter how mainstream you get, if you're not a white male, you're made to never feel *enough,* and then we went out and finished the interview. It emerged that Arsenio had a few words to say about being an outsider among the insiders, too. He was tired of critics who disparagingly compared him to Johnny Carson or Jay Leno. He protested that his show was designed to showcase "urban" talent. The critics could accept this difference or, as he put it, "kiss my ass."

The profile we did of him would turn out to be one of our more memorable pieces.

One day Andy Lack called me into his office to ask whether I'd be interested in doing a profile of Altovise Davis, Sammy Davis Jr.'s third wife and now his widow. Sammy Davis had died the previous May, and owed the IRS $7.5 million. Government agents had come to Davis's house, seizing anything of value to auction.

I was ambivalent about taking the assignment. I was trying to arrange a transfer onto the staff of CBS's *Evening News* and didn't want to be caught in the middle of a complicated story if the transfer happened.

Still, I had a personal relationship to Sammy Davis that I had never explored. He had been my godfather when I was christened. With Davis's passing, one more piece of my father was out of reach.

It so happened, moreover, that I had an "in" to Altovise: my mother, who knew her through Buddy Rogers and his second wife, Beverly. I had never met Buddy and Beverly—they were prejudiced, Mom said, and would never accept me. They had introduced her to a new socialite set—the kind I could only read about in *Town & Country.* I called Mom to see if she could find out anything about Altovise from her socialite friends.

She called me back after talking to Beverly Rogers.

"Altovise is doing fine," Mom reported. "The IRS didn't seize the house, and she was able to hide her jewels, so she's feeling okay."

She gave me Altovise's home number. "Tell her who you are, if you think it will help," she said. "But be careful. Make sure she knows not to tell Buddy and Beverly. They're all part of that Palm Springs crowd. They wouldn't understand."

I went numb and felt a stinging behind my eyeballs. Hanging up the phone, I threw the drumsticks that I kept on my desk against the door of my office. The tears forced their way out, but there was not enough time, and this was too public a place. I covered my eyes with my fingertips, pressing the emotion away, until the flow of tears slowed and stopped.

Mom had a new friend. Her name was Marguerite, and she had a headful of saucy red hair.

Mom had been talking about her new best friend for a while—how pretty she was, how much personality she had, how lovely she was. Mom's friends, I'd learned, came in two sorts: those she found likable reflections of herself and older women who often reminded her of her own mother. The latest, besides Marguerite, was named Marajen Chinigo. Mom had met her at a party in Palm Springs. Buddy Rogers had introduced them.

Larry was once again working. He was appearing in *Breaking Legs* at the independent Promenade Theater, the kind of role in which he specializes, taking on an eccentric character and, over time, turning it into someone wacky, bizarre, and wonderful.

I had been introduced at the cast party, two nights earlier, as "our daughter, June."

So as I entered the apartment to meet the new best friend and saw the mane of glorious red hair set off by gold hoop earrings and almond eyes with perfectly articulated eyelashes, I was unprepared for what my mother said:

"This is my friend June."

In the unwritten code between me and my mother, this meant I was to call her "Norma." But I was too shocked to play along. I was, after all, thirty-five, working for CBS News, producing pieces for Connie Chung. I wasn't Mike Wallace, but I wasn't anyone to be ashamed of either.

My friend June.

I smiled numbly, dumbly, and shook her hand. Looking over her head, my eye caught the wall where my mother kept her collection of masks: Mayan, Senegalese, Thai, Indonesian, and Beninese representations seemed to stare down at me.

At home I had begun my own mask collection.

Excusing myself, I went into the bathroom. There I stared into the mirror like a detective, searching my face for signs of culpability. Lately I had felt guilty for everything. I felt guilty for my hostility toward my mother's upper-class lifestyle and guilty for the apparent threat I posed to it. I felt guilty for having been born when she could least afford me, emotionally and financially. I felt guilty for having brought my mother so much grief and guilty because my father had beaten her. I felt guilty because my skin had turned dark after she thought I would be light enough to pass. I felt guilty because after she left him, my skin almost got us kicked out of our apartment.

During my entire career as a news producer, I had thought that if I became perfectly accomplished, perfectly situated, I might atone for these transgressions. Yet here I was, a producer for CBS News, still not good enough to be introduced as my mother's daughter.

I had maintained a relationship with Lois Basden, my father's ex-wife. Harold Basden had died in 1987, and every so often we would get together and go out for drinks and to listen to some music.

For my thirty-fifth birthday, Lois and I went to a nightclub we both liked to frequent in West Harlem. We stayed until the club closed, at 4:00 A.M. The next day, she called me to say she had forgotten to pay the bill. She wanted me to go back with her to explain and take care of the check. I was so hung over that I never wanted to smell alcohol again, let alone go back inside a club that served it.

Soon, however, Lois pulled up in front of my apartment in her burgundy Buick LeSabre with one of her big hats, fully made up, dressed
for another night on the town.

I had prepared by wearing a green-and-black checkered shirt
dress with a hip-slung black belt, black tights, and boots. We paid
the bill, and I said I just wanted to sit and listen to some live music.
Lois knew just the place—a dive across town on 132nd and Madison called the Lickety-Split.

The club sat on the corner, announcing its presence via a tattered
yellow sign with faded red lettering. It had a door covered with pine
veneer and grilles on its windows. Inside, artifacts from the New
Year's celebration just past—pieces of torn tissue paper in red, yellow, and green—were tacked to the ceiling. Lois knew the barmaid,
an aspiring singer named Wanda. The band had just finished a set,
and a Diana Ross song was playing on the jukebox. Lois ordered a
gin and tonic, and despite my intentions, I ordered a Heineken. I
took a swig and set the bottle down. Looking toward the wall, I saw
a dark-skinned young man, slightly taller than I, holding a trumpet.
He winked at me. I smiled indulgently and took a second swig.

The next thing I knew, he was sitting next to me, staring into my
eyes with a look both tender and questioning, a look I have never
tired of responding to. On our first date, Waldron took me to see the
movie *Glory*. Afterward, over dinner at a Jamaican restaurant, he
told me about his family. He was from Detroit, the middle of seven
children, parents divorced. One day when he was fifteen, his mother,
weary of raising three teenaged boys in the inner city and fearful for
their safety, put them on a bus and sent them to live with their father
in New York. They did not even have a chance to say good-bye to
their friends, and they did not see their mother again for three years.

Somehow that wound of being torn from one place and grafted
to another bound us together. It would take me ten years to adjust
myself to the idea of marrying a musician, but eventually, I did.

In early 1991 I joined the staff of *The CBS Evening News with
Dan Rather*. I would stay there less than a year. One of my assign-

ments was to find some young men in the inner city who would talk about their fascination with guns. I located a group of teenagers in Brooklyn, but it took me three months to convince them to go on camera. By then I had done enough research for a documentary. CBS had already produced *48 Hours on Crack Street*—a revealing and terrifying look at the world of drugs and gun violence, but I wanted to go deeper and explore the lives of the young men who perished every day on those street corners. How had they ended up there? There was no interest in such a story at CBS, even though my senior producers conceded it was worth doing.

I pitched the story to David Fanning at *Frontline*, in a fortuitous bit of timing. Jennifer Lawson, then a PBS executive, had told Fanning that if he couldn't find one qualified black producer, she would have difficulty finding more money for the series. He was looking for someone like me at the same time I was looking to be freed from CBS's relentless emphasis on ratings.

Buddhists like to say such coincidences are no coincidence. By the end of 1991, I had left CBS and joined *Frontline*, television's longest-running documentary journalism program.

17. PALI

My first hour for *Frontline*, "A Kid Kills," followed the rippling effect of a gang shooting on one community. Some twenty-five years earlier, when my college class had written the report advocating the closure of the Essex County Training School for Truant Boys, the pendulum was swinging toward leniency for juvenile delinquents. "A Kid Kills" charted the swing of that pendulum back toward punishment. Three teenagers had shot and killed two boys in a turf dispute; the indicted youths faced trial as adults unless they could prove themselves "rehabilitatable" to the juvenile court.

David Fanning and Mike Sullivan, the program's senior executives, persuaded me to use the first person—to insert myself into the narrative—in that documentary. Initially, I fought against it. I had put a tremendous amount of effort into developing these relationships with the teenagers in the Orchard Park Peer Leader Program, and I wanted them to speak for themselves.

"All stories take a point of view," Sullivan argued with me. "This one needs a translator."

I had left CBS, but the tyranny of demographics—who the audience is—still dictated my storytelling. *Frontline*'s demographic is largely white, male, and middle class. Sullivan convinced me that that audience would see the kids as outlaws unless I explained their plight in terms they could understand.

"It's easy for me to sit in judgment of these kids," I wrote in my narration. "I can go home to suburban Boston. I don't have to live here, don't have to live with the consequences of saying I know a murderer or that I feel sympathy for his family. I don't ride the school bus every day with kids from the neighborhood where his victim lived."

The voice worked. In the years following, I made the unobtrusive first-person narrator something of a personal trademark as I did stories on the peace dividend in the wake of the end of the Cold War; the effort to restore Haitian president Jean-Bertrand Aristide; and the generational intractability of poverty, poor education, and drug abuse. I felt I had finally found my creative voice.

In 1994 one of my colleagues returned from a monthlong honeymoon raving about his visit to the Italian villa of an American publishing heiress. He'd been to the home of Contessa Marajen Chinigo, a woman my mother had begun to worship as if she were her own mother.

They had met during one of the Palm Springs weekends through Buddy and Beverly Rogers. The contessa ran an Old World–style salon out of her villa in Ravello, Italy. From the postcards Mom sent, it looked like the manifestation of a Hollywood set, perched above Gore Vidal's villa overlooking the Gulf of Salerno. The contessa printed her own postcards—THE ROMAN TERRACE, THE GREEK TERRACE, THE FRENCH MEDIEVAL ROOM. My mother delighted in sending me weekly updates on their social scene. She described the nightly dinner parties, organized by each guest in turn; the texture of the hand-rolled linen napkins; the outcome of her races across the pool with the contessa.

Marajen was, like Mom, a midwestern girl—a publishing heiress from Indiana—who had married an Italian count. When the count died, he left her his title and his villa.

The contessa, my mother said, was virulently antiblack. "She would put me out like a cat with the garbage," Mom told me once, "if she knew about you."

When my *Frontline* colleague began recounting the stories of these parties at Ravello, I was so struck by the coincidence that I joined the conversation, adding what I knew about the contessa's background from my mother's vivid letters. He was on the verge of asking my mother's name when it struck me like a lightning bolt: I was talking to someone who could identify me and my mother to her best friend.

In midsentence I turned abruptly and walked away, my identity folding into itself. I needed to sort out to whom I could say what. Fifteen minutes into an editorial meeting, I remained silent. Others suggested story ideas; the details flew by me. Uncertainty paralyzed my tongue. Someone was asking my opinion: I stared and shrugged. I couldn't speak. Speak. Speak! I urged myself, as though my tongue were a dog, the list of ideas I had been preparing a bone in front of my mouth.

I had a seat at the table but no voice. My secret upbringing threatened to swallow my entire life.

In the fall of 1995, I was back in Los Angeles. I told my mother I was doing a documentary on biracial kids. I described characters I had read about in Lise Funderberg's book *Black, White, Other.* I told her about the experience of Lisa Jones, Amiri Baraka's daughter, growing up with her white mother while her father explored black nationalism. I told her about the mother of James McBride, who had raised nine biracial children on her own.

Mom remained silent as I told her these stories. She was two steps ahead of me, waiting for me to ask the question.

Mom thought I was leaving for a shoot every day. Instead, I went to the Buddhist community center in Santa Monica. There I spent hours chanting *Nam-myoho-renge-kyo.* The mantra, I had found, helped me sort through the difficult circumstances of my life. As I prayed this time, I wondered, what would happen if I "outed" her? How would it affect Larry's career? My own? Would Mom and I be subjected to hate mail? Would telling this story mean sacrificing my relationship with the Gregory family?

Often Regina came and chanted with me. She advised me to

pray for unity within the family. What I prayed for instead was the courage to ask my mother to go on national television and tell our story.

I began to realize that I could either choose to accept the status quo that had governed my life or choose to change it. Tina Turner, a fellow Buddhist, had once referred to this realization as taking a stand for her life.

Taking a stand meant that I would have to do more than just ask Mom to go public; I would need to question and challenge all the principles that Mom and Aunt Peggy had drilled into me since I was four. I didn't realize that, then; all I knew was that I had to produce a documentary. I had never intended to do the story about "biracial kids." This was a story about our family; its star would be my mother.

After five days of prayer, I arrived home early. Mom was at the market. I turned on the TV, where a drama that coupled race and sex, America's twin obsessions, was just beginning to unfold. The bodies of Nicole Simpson and Ron Goldman had been found brutally stabbed the week before. Police were bringing O. J. Simpson in for questioning.

I thought wryly of the irony: when I was in college, Mom had met O.J. at a party. She had called and told me to get out to L.A. immediately with my sexiest dresses—he was the kind of man she had in mind for me to marry. Mom's choice of marriageable material for me had included the baseball player David Winfield, the boxer Mike Tyson, and Simpson.

I had put her off, protesting that jocks weren't my type.

As I watched the news, I rehearsed the words to convince her—to convince myself—that going public with our story was the right thing to do.

Mom arrived home—and I lost the faith of my convictions.

The next day, summoning the strength of all my prayers, I asked, "Would you be willing to talk, on camera, about why you did what you did and what it's meant for our lives?"

"Yes," she said almost immediately, preempting my list of prepared arguments. She said she had known immediately, when I told her what story I was working on, that I would be asking her to go on camera.

How like a mother, I thought, to know what her daughter wants before she's even figured out how to ask it.

We set the interview date for the end of the following week. It would be just me and my camera, I had promised. No strangers, no crew, no bright lights.

As we started, I was twice as nervous as she. Reporters have a maxim about never doing a major interview without having a fairly solid idea beforehand what the answers will be. Good interviews depend not only upon solid research but upon an element of anonymity, on the interviewee's not knowing quite what to expect.

But my mother knew me better than I knew her. It was not a level playing field.

I needed to do something as unlike me as possible, so I began with a technique I had learned from Leon Dash, an investigative reporter at the *Washington Post*.

"What is your earliest childhood memory?" I asked, hoping to gain an advantage with an opening curveball.

"Gee," she said, hooking one leg around the side of the rocking chair. I could tell that my opening gambit had worked. She sat for a moment, without makeup, facing the sliding glass doors that looked out over Hollywood and South Central L.A. The late afternoon light softened the lines around her eyes and set off her cheekbones. She was seventy-five, but she didn't look much over sixty.

"It would have to be playing with the Indian children on the reservation in Pocatello, Idaho. I remember organizing the other children into a drama group, and we charged the adults a nickel to see our shows. I was 'Nadja, Queen of the Night.' "

I was astonished by the richness of the material in her answer. I knew she had grown up on an Indian reservation, but I'd never heard her talk about playing with the Indian children. I scarcely knew how to follow up.

"How old were you?"

"I was about four or five, I think. My mother used to leave me with Grandma and Grandpa, and I wanted to be with her so badly that I used to make up these other worlds."

"*Granny* left you?"

"Yes. She didn't really want children, I don't think. And I got in her way a lot, so she just used to leave me with my grandparents, her parents."

"Was she married to your father?"

"Yes, but I don't think they were together long. I never met my father until I was twenty-one."

It was difficult to keep up with her. The striking parallels between our lives interfered with my ability to formulate questions. I reconsidered her life's trajectory: the only child of a "wild" mother who had left her daughter in Idaho while she sought movie stardom in Los Angeles.

My mother's entire life, it emerged, had been a quest for acceptance, a struggle to escape the stigma of being born on the wrong side of the tracks. The blueprint for the decisions she would make about her own children seemed, somehow, predetermined.

I could hardly wait to get back home and go through the transcripts.

Alas, there were none. In my anxiety I had forgotten to turn on the microphone. The interview—all three hours of it, filmed in the ocher light of the sun setting over the Pacific—was as silent as a Mary Pickford movie.

I called her back to tell her what had happened and to ask for a retake. At first she agreed, but within the week she reneged. She had been watching the jury selection for the O.J. trial on TV, she said, and it brought back all those fears of being judged by white America.

"He's going to get off, I'm telling you," she said, referring to Simpson, "because the jury will think Nicole got what she deserved. It was just my guardian angel watching out for me when you forgot to turn on that microphone."

I pressed the issue, futilely. She would not be moved.

"You said you wanted everyone to know that your mother was white," she began.

I said no, what I wanted was for her to publicly acknowledge me.

"Well, whatever," she said, as if she didn't understand the concept. "But most people do know. The only ones that don't are Marijen and Buddy. They are my dear, dear friends, and they just wouldn't understand."

I bit my tongue. I had chanted to do this story for healing purposes, not from bitterness. I had prayed that it would close, not widen, the rift between us.

"Was growing up with Peggy so bad?" she asked, in the kind of small voice Aunt Peggy herself might have used.

"This has nothing to do with Peggy," I replied. "This is about us."

She remained silent, as stubborn as I was in the face of her reluctance.

"God, you remind me of myself!" I exclaimed.

"I should. I *am* you!" she retorted.

Her reply irritated me more. I didn't like to think of myself as cowardly, selfish, and self-centered, so concerned about what others would think that I'd deny my own flesh and blood. On the other hand, this tendency to want people to do things my way or not at all, that was vintage Norma.

She shared a story. While in New York recently, she had gone to a dinner party on the East Side. She sat next to an industrialist, a man, she said, who had recently been on the cover of *Time* magazine.

"He was very handsome and well groomed; he looked like Anthony Quinn. We sat next to each other. We had been chatting all night long and getting along fabulously.

"Anyway, he started talking about O. J. Simpson and how Nicole's murder proves that race mixing doesn't work. In other words, that Nicole Simpson got what was coming to her. Anyway, he went on and on, till finally our hostess said, 'Stop that! Norma was married to a black man and has a black child.'

"Well, with that he ignored me the rest of the night. He left the table, and the party, before dessert was even served."

I was skeptical of the entire story, especially since she refused to name "the industrialist." I asked whether it had occurred to her that he might have left because he was embarrassed at having made an ass out of himself.

She sighed as if I understood nothing. "I don't want to be treated like that," she whined. "I want to be treated as who I am, as Larry's wife."

This was where our conversation always came to a dead end. My mother's worldview venerated only married, white women. Her pre-occupation with maintaining that facade had torn our family apart.

As months went by and I exhausted my arguments, I enlisted my brother's aid. Over lunch in Santa Monica, where he spends his summers, we made one last attempt.

"Why should I?" my mother asked again and again. "Why? Who would be helped by it?"

Lary thought for a minute before he answered, making use of both his professorial bearing and the oldest son's knowledge of his mother's soft spots. "Well, I think the country would be helped. We do need to have a large discussion in the United States about our history and the role African-Americans have played in it. That conversation needs to be addressed, this private pain and public face.

"We have it going on in our own family. June has not been accepted—even though you love her and embrace her, you still with-hold that public acknowledgment. I think it would be a good thing if you did this. I think it would allow healing to begin."

My mother began to cry.

"I just don't want to lose Marajen and Buddy," she said. "They're like a father and mother to me."

I noticed an odd, stringent odor and realized in amazement that my mother was perspiring in fear, like a cornered animal. She looked frail, vulnerable, hunched over, an old woman with wispy blond-and-silver hair. Her fingers, gnarled with arthritis, were nervously wringing several bunched-up, wet tissues.

"I was such a bad mother!" she cried. "I never gave you any-thing. What will people think of me? Everyone will hate me!"

Lary and I glanced at each other, then down at our hands, silenced by her deepest fear and our knowledge of its fundamental truth. She had not been a good mother, but she had, nevertheless, managed to give us much.

"You did the best you could," Lary said softly as I reached over and held her hand with my own.

Mom rose and went to the ladies' room to compose herself. Lary looked at me and said, "If she doesn't come around this time, I think we should let this drop. It's too painful." Then, in a deep voice, he intoned, "Oh, the past! The past!"

Aunt Peggy would have said forget all that, it's passed, past history. But I couldn't forget it; the very stories I chose as a documentarian were becoming reflections of my psyche: kids essentially raising themselves on the streets of Roxbury; how the color strata affected politics in Haiti; a mother who had sold her own daughter into prostitution; workers in one state left unemployed when their employer pulled up stakes and moved somewhere else. By documenting these stories about the pain of others, I avoided coming to grips with the pain in my own life. I was afraid that if I ever started crying, the tears might never stop.

Doing my own story had been David Fanning's idea, or so I told myself as progress stalled. He had pulled my story out of me, piece by piece, over many long dinners and bottles of wine. After seven months, I still wasn't committed—I had even produced another documentary during the interim. But since I was spending *Frontline*'s money, I needed to show progress.

While I waited to see if my mother would change her mind about the interview, I went to Philadelphia. I wanted to see the neighborhood in West Philadelphia where my father had lived. Rose Cross, Jimmy's mother, had been no more accepting of his affair with Norma than Granny had.

"He should stick with his own kind," she told my mother when they first met. Thereafter, whenever she visited her son, she brushed by my mother "as if I were a servant in the kitchen," Mom had said. Mom couldn't remember what Rose looked like, but she remembered the sound of the door shutting firmly as my paternal grandmother spent an hour alone with her son.

Rose would have had a long time to consider the nuances of her performance: she had spent her life in other people's kitchens. Before Jimmy's success allowed her to retire, she had worked as a live-in domestic, cooking and cleaning for wealthy whites in downtown Philadelphia.

Jimmy bought her a house in North Philadelphia when he made it big. It was her sole possession, and after his career faltered, she used it to run a speakeasy.

When I went to Rose's neighborhood to shoot footage for the documentary, my grandmother's neighbors took one look at me and said my mother must have been tall. Rose had been a short, round woman. They said she mentioned me but never cared to see me. She considered me and Jimmy's other daughter, Lynda, the bastard children of some miscellaneous white girls her son had been with.

One neighbor asked what I was doing wandering around like a census taker with a cameraman trailing behind. When I told her I was on a search to find my family and wanted to learn about my grandmother, she asked, "So when you find out all that, what will you know then?"

Her question haunted me. I had all but forgotten my conversations with Jimmy from twenty years earlier. I barely remembered Rose's name and couldn't remember my grandfather's name at all.

Slowly, I pieced together a history: My paternal grandmother, a domestic worker named Rose Wilkes—or Wilkins; it was hard to read the writing on her marriage certificate—had married Jimmy's father, Purcell Cross, son of a day laborer, when she was nineteen. The wedding had taken place in her hometown, Ocean City, New Jersey—literally the next town over from Atlantic City. My father had been born there.

Rose's relatives disappeared into the mists of slavery, but I could trace my grandfather's people back to southern Virginia, to a woman named Caroline Cross, who lived in the little town of Lunenburg, one of those small southern towns consisting of a courthouse, general store, and not much else.

Caroline is described as a mulatto in the census. That meant Jimmy already had some white folks in his pedigree, so, as far as I was concerned, Rose Cross had had no call to go acting hincty with Mom about Jimmy sticking to his own kind. Especially because Rose harbored a secret of her own: according to her neighbors, after her marriage with Percy ended, she had lived in a committed relationship with another woman for the better part of twenty-five years.

After a while I saw signs that Mom would relent. She asked to see the earlier interview we had done, the one without audio, then watched all three hours of it, as if she were auditioning herself.

"I'm not unlikable," was her assessment.

She began bargaining with me. She told me that she'd do it after I lost twenty pounds. Immediately, I went on a diet.

Then the magazine *Vanity Fair* called Larry to take part in a cover spread on TV cowboys. The magazine gathered the old TV stars together for a group portrait by Annie Liebovitz. The surviving cast members of *F Troop* were among them.

Mom said she would allow *Frontline*'s cameras to film a sequence with Larry. We didn't discuss what would happen with the footage; maybe she thought—I probably allowed her to believe—that Larry could talk about his "adopted daughter" if she ultimately decided against going on camera.

The shoot took place on the very same Warner Brothers lot where my own ill-fated family photo had been taken with the cast of *F Troop*. As we checked in at the gate, the *Vanity Fair* PR woman asked what the footage would be for.

"I'm Larry's daughter," I said.

"So is his wife your mother?" she asked.

"I'm adopted," I said, the lie rolling off my lips as easily if I were giving a weather report. My coproducer and cameraman, John Baynard, moved from behind the camera's eyepiece and shot me a look. I caught his gaze and held it.

John suspected that I was as reluctant as my mother to do this film, and he was right. I worried about what my colleagues and my black friends would think. None of them knew my life story. I suspected that some of my black friends might consider me a "turncoat" for emphasizing my white ancestry while deemphasizing my "black side," and I wanted to avoid becoming an object of pity.

I had by now exhausted a great deal of *Frontline*'s resources: I had assembled a team, begun searching for archival footage, and spent about eight months looking for intersections between what I knew about my family's story and the history of race relations writ large. Backing out was not an option, not if I wanted to maintain credibility at my job. I had to figure out a way to get Mom to do this interview. I renewed my prayers.

A week later Mom called and said she would do it—as soon as she attended one last party in Palm Springs. She had reconciled herself, she said, to the idea that she might lose her entire circle of friends. "I'm bored with my life," she said. "I want a change."

From the background I heard Larry yell out, "Well, we'll certainly stir up the pot."

On the appointed day, moments before the cameras rolled, she threw me off balance. "You're going to wear your glasses?" she asked. "You're *not* going to go on national television wearing glasses!"

I had been so preoccupied with the prelighting and setting up the shot that I'd forgotten all about the fact that I, too, would be on camera. There was no time now; the crew was set to go, and I was a bundle of nerves. I probably would have poked my eye out trying to put in lenses.

John gave me the signal that we were ready to begin, but before I could ask the first question, Mom interrupted me again. "Where am I discovered, Mr. DeMille?" she quipped.

I missed the reference. "Where are you discovered?"

"Yeah. That was Gloria Swanson's line from *Sunset Boulevard*. 'Where am I discovered, Mr. DeMille?' "

The line is actually "I'm ready for my close-up, Mr. DeMille," but I was struck by Mom's reference to her favorite movie.

Even now, she imagined herself on the brink of insanity for doing what she was about to do.

18. NORMA DESMOND

By the time my mother and I sat down for the second time in February 1996, I had been researching not only my own family history but the history of America's neuroses about skin color, for the better part of two years.

As I began the interview, I felt as though it would be me, not my mother, who would feel exposed—as though the inner workings of my psyche would be revealed on camera through the questions I asked. John wanted me to explore my mother's ambivalence about being a mother, but I just wanted to know her life story.

Two professional cameras, lights, and a four-man crew had taken over my mother's living room. How could I coax her into revealing herself—without revealing myself?

As we began, past and present came together anew with each answer. For instance, I had always wondered where my mother found the courage to begin an affair with a black man. I discovered that those seeds had been planted on the other side of the color line—on the Shoshone/Bannock Native American reservation in Blackfoot, Idaho, where she was raised. In those days there were no blacks in southeastern Idaho—but there was plenty of prejudice. At the general store, the signs said "No Dogs, No Indians, No Mexicans."

Mom said that her only playmates were the Indians and the hoboes, the outsiders of Blackfoot.

"Didn't you have any white playmates?" I asked.

"I didn't like the white children," she said. "Isn't it funny you should ask me that question? I remember I used to get in fights with the white kids in the schoolyard and sock 'em in the nose. The Indian children, they were always so happy to do whatever I said. They let me be the leader."

My mother felt looked down upon by her cousins, the sons and daughters of Granny's eight brothers and sisters. One of them, Faye Bailey, says the family ostracized my grandmother and Norma. My mother thought it was because they found her ugly.

" 'It's a good thing she's smart,' " she remembers her aunt and uncles saying, " ' 'cause she's sure not pretty.' "

I found this hard to believe, as I'd always considered Mom a world-class beauty. She showed me pictures of two female cousins, a brunette and a blonde—wholesome, pretty, blue-eyed American girls. The brunette had her hair bobbed in the style of Clara Bow, the silent-screen actress. The blonde wore hers rolled in front and loose in the back, like Lana Turner or Alice Faye. Mom recalled that they'd been in the Miss America pageant, but when I checked the records, I found no Miss Idaho with the last name of Steffenson. One of them had been Miss Idaho Falls. Annoyed with my punctiliousness, Mom said, "Well, they were pretty enough to have been in the Miss America pageant. They seemed that pretty to me."

I examined the portraits again. They didn't seem that pretty to me. But Mom's feelings of inadequacy were genuine. "I felt like the ugly stepsister at the ball," she said.

Granny seems to have reinforced this sense of inadequacy. My grandmother, June Rose, was the ninth child of Peter and Clara Steffenson. She met Roy Greve, an itinerant railroad worker from Cincinnati, when she was eighteen, and they married in 1920. My mother was born ten months later. Roy Greve would be the first of Granny's four husbands and two long-term affairs, but my mother would be her only child.

"I was like a child that was alone," Mom said. "I would go to school and come home, and my mother would be gone. My grandmother would come up to tuck me in, and I would throw the covers off. I wanted my mother."

During the interview I had little time to react to the particulars of my mother's statements. I tried to compartmentalize myself; June-who-was-conducting-the-interview separated from June-who-was-my-mother's-daughter. The way I was raised made it easy for me to separate one part of my psyche from another. Later, as I absorbed this portion of the interview in the edit room, I could only be thankful that my mother had not run in and out of my life so often that I threw a temper tantrum every time Aunt Peggy tried to tuck me in. It seemed like an awful way to grow up, never knowing where your mother was.

When I went to southeastern Idaho and saw its endless sloping plains of green sagebrush and flat potato fields, I sympathized with Granny's desire to escape. Idaho is beautiful and desolate, its horizons stretching to the majesty of those purple mountains I sang about in second grade, but the farmers who till its soil are tethered to a hardscrabble life.

My Idaho cousins confirmed that as a young man, my great-grandfather had been a trick horseback rider in the circus. Granny, his youngest child, apparently inherited his willingness to embrace risk.

The earliest pictures of Granny show her holding her plain white farmer's dress above her garter with one hand, a cigarette in the other, her head tossed back, laughing. She was about five foot five, with dark hair and a wider mouth than my mother's, but with those same high cheekbones. She boasted about her eighteen-inch waist. She had mastered the Charleston and liked to try out the latest variations at the Pocatello American Legion Hall on Saturday nights. My mother said that for her as a child, those Saturday nights were like magic.

"She used to lock me inside the car while she went inside—" she began.

Being locked inside a car didn't strike me as magical. "She locked you inside the car? How old were you?" I asked.

"Oh, I must have been four or five, I guess," Mom said, as if there were nothing unusual about a young child's being left unattended at night in a locked car. She remembered kneeling against the soft cushions in the backseat, making up stories about the adults as she watched them through the rear window of the car. She remembers the faint sound of music, the ambience of the silent car, the yearning to join the party.

The Indians kept vigil with her, sitting along the curb outside the Legion Hall. They weren't allowed inside either. Occasionally, a group of white boys would leave the dance, drunk on moonshine and the power of whiteness, and pick one to beat up.

My mother remembered that in 1930, when she was nine, Granny left Idaho and resettled in Long Beach, California. There she remarried, but she left Mom in Blackfoot. "During the summer my uncle or someone would take me on the train to California to visit her," Mom reported.

My mother had shuttled between Pocatello and Los Angeles during summer breaks the way I had been shuttled between Atlantic City and New York. I stopped in the middle of my line of questioning as I realized the implication of her statement.

"Did it ever occur to you that you were doing with your own children what had been done to you?" I asked.

"Gee, no," she said. "But now that you mention it, I can see the connection. That's weird, isn't it?"

I pictured my mother, a young girl, indulging her imagination to the clatter of train wheels on the Union Pacific Railroad, the same way I had discovered mine in the patterns of passing cars on the New Jersey Turnpike.

Mom finally moved to Long Beach permanently around the sixth grade. Granny had married a construction worker named Gary Booth, and for a while the family lived in Arizona while he worked on the Parker Dam. Mom even adopted her stepfather's last name, Booth, but as soon as they moved back to Long Beach, Granny's second marriage faltered. She worked in a beauty shop and, when that wasn't enough, played poker and the horses to help support herself and her daughter. "Mother didn't get home until six at night. I used to do all the cooking," Mom remembered.

Some days they lived on onion sandwiches.

"My childhood just went away," Mom said ruefully. "I was always the adult, and Mother was the child in our family. I was always having to point out to her what could go wrong, what we should be doing, where we should be going, what the budget should be."

I had always seen my mother as a competent and indomitable woman. Now, for the first time, I realized she had developed those traits as an overwhelmed child, struggling to compensate for her mother's shortcomings. I had done stories about children like Mom, children who took care of their parents and who vaguely reminded me of myself in the way they shouldered responsibility for the adults around them, but this was the first inkling I had that my mother's childhood mirrored mine in this respect. I was astonished by the way these patterns had repeated themselves.

After World War II, Granny scraped together enough money to open her own beauty salon, The Rio (named after the Carmen Miranda movie *That Night in Rio*). Although it had four stalls, Granny never rented them out. Mom had told me she occasionally worked as the manicurist, but no matter how hard she tried, she said, she never won her mother's approval.

"A daughter with brains was nothing to be proud of. I mean, she wanted a beautiful daughter. She wanted me to be like my cousins, and I wasn't. I mean, everything she wanted me to be, I wasn't," she said, sighing the same kind of sigh I did when talking about Aunt Peggy.

Granny took up with a tall, dogmatic German immigrant named Eric Giewald during the nadir of the Depression. Giewald worked as a chef in a swanky local hotel called the Villa Riviera, making fifty dollars a week—a fortune by the standards of the day. Just as important, he brought home food. Onion sandwiches were replaced by T-bone steaks.

My mother, then thirteen, welcomed his arrival, as it meant that she didn't have to cook anymore. But Eric supported Hitler's Nazi Party, and the home was soon infused with petty rules and displays of superiority. He stopped my mother from visiting her best friend, a Jewish neighbor and classmate—a memory that remained painful for her even after sixty years. He would not let her greet the only black man in Long Beach—the shoeshine man. "Niggers and Jews are not to be spoken to," he told her. "They're lower class."

She began sneaking behind his back in a small but persistent rebellion against his restraint. Surreptitiously, she turned around and waved hi to the shoeshine man as she and her stepfather passed. She had to be home by six; she met curfew, then crept out the window. She was not allowed to date, so she became an athlete, then dated fellow athletes on the tennis court and at the pool. She played in junior tennis tournaments and became an avid swimmer—she was the Pacific Coast Champion in high school. She graduated in 1939.

Then Eric astonished her by asking her to marry him. She said she turned him down, saying, "No, I will always be your little girl."

I was pretty astonished at that myself, especially when she described how Eric had become jealous of her relationship with the man who would become my brother's father, a surfer named Jack May. Jack was older than my mother, in his early thirties. She was eighteen.

"Jack and I just would swim together and talk, and I would get home, like, at seven and eight o'clock, and finally one of these times, when I came in the door, Eric knocked me clear across the room to the other one, and he had beaten up my mother because he said my mother knew this, you know, that I was out seeing somebody else."

I was so focused on the fact that Eric had beaten her and her mother that I didn't hear the words "I was out seeing somebody else" until I screened the tapes later. Mom said she snuck out of the house that night, went to Jack's, and didn't come back for two months. By then she was pregnant with my brother, Lary.

"Eric wouldn't allow me in," Mom told me. "He had been fighting and arguing with Mother. Mother said it was just hell there at the house, because he was yelling and screaming every day. And then finally she told him that I had left him [Jack] and I wanted to come home but that I was pregnant. And anyway, with that I came back, and he was so wonderful to me. He just was an angel."

I confirmed my mother's relationship with Jack May through her cousins, but I wondered what details she might have left out of the story she told me about Eric Giewald—things she would rather forget or things she wasn't willing to say. I was unwilling to pry. During the interview Mom told me that Granny and Eric forced her to move out so that the neighbors wouldn't see the disgrace of her pregnancy. They let her move back in after the baby was born. Less than a month later, Granny called the police and had her grandchild's father arrested. Jack May had worked as a security guard at an army warehouse. While there, Mom told me, he had stolen a typewriter.

Even the sergeant who took the report found my grandmother's action frivolous. "You sure you want to do this?" he asked Granny.

"Yes, he deflowered my daughter!" she answered.

Lary's father went to jail for two years. My mother never saw him again.

I'd always thought that crossing America's racial boundaries had formed the central emotional trauma of my mother's life. But as we talked, I realized that motherhood itself had been equally traumatic— as if the difficulties of her relationship with her own mother, along with her early pregnancy, were events she would spend the rest of her life trying to forget.

"I was a single mother. I've always been a single mother. It's not easy trying to raise a child by yourself," she said. Raising her eldest child, Lary, she said, had been particularly hard. He was not yet a year old when the country entered World War II. Eric was sent to an internment camp for German nationals when the war started, and Granny simply disappeared.

"Disappeared?" I asked, encouraging her to explain.

"Yes, disappeared. I didn't see her for five years. I just had to figure out how to make it by myself."

Mom found out later that Granny had gone to San Francisco, where she ended up living with a Jewish man. During those five years, no one in the family heard from her. When she returned, she explained that she hadn't wanted anyone to know she was living with a Jew.

I had never thought kindly of Granny. She struck me as a cold, dispassionate woman, selfish and self-absorbed, the kind of woman who would gamble away the rent money on horse races, then send her child out to steal food. My brother says I can be harsh because I never knew her. He did.

When Granny returned from her self-imposed exile, Lary was five. She would raise him off and on for the next six years. He remembers her as a funny, smart, good-looking woman who despised the rich and the Republicans—Republicans, she said, cared nothing about the poor. Lary says that in Granny's worldview Negroes were a subclass of the poor: to be pitied and helped, but not socialized with.

That was what passed for progressive politics back then, before Rosa Parks, Lary said.

That's just the way things were.

My mother studied at Long Beach Junior College, then worked as a secretary for the Department of the Navy during the war.

She wanted to be an actor so badly she could taste it. Finally, she went to drama school and seemed to show promise. Her teachers encouraged Granny to come watch her daughter perform.

"When mother came to see those shows," Mom recalled, "she said, 'You're nothing onstage. It's silly for you to even try to be an actress. You can't act.' "

Mom felt crushed. Offered a scholarship to study at the Actors Studio at the New School in New York, she turned it down.

"That was the turning point of my life," she says. "I think I would have had an entirely different life if I had gone. But I couldn't. I didn't believe in myself."

I looked at this self-confident, self-possessed woman in front of me and tried in vain to imagine her as a diffident, shy young woman, a woman unsure of herself and her own talents, uncertain of her own beauty. I couldn't, until I remembered myself at that age.

"Mother's way with bringing me up," Mom said, "was that I—if I were anything at all, I would make a good marriage and would have a man with money. And my career was nothing. In other words, I was not to have a career. And the man was the whole thing. And you took care of the man and cooked for him and did things for him, and you were secondary; you were second place in the world. 'The man is number one. It's a man's world.' And still is."

It seemed that Granny and Aunt Peggy had a lot in common, but where Aunt Peggy had instilled in me a sense of self, Granny seemed to have undermined my mother altogether.

What my mother had really needed in her life, I thought, was an Aunt Peggy.

My mother was nearly thirty when she decided she wanted a career onstage badly enough to leave my brother with Granny and move to New York. By then both of her children—Lary, then eleven, the son of Jack May, and Candie, Larry Storch's daughter—were in foster homes.

Once in the city, she took a room at the Hudson Hotel—in the same building where the *MacNeil/Lehrer Report* offices had been located when I worked there. She got a job in the millinery department of Gimbel's department store. She auditioned. She failed. On several occasions she was locked out of her room for failure to pay rent. Those nights she spent cowering in a corner under the awning of the Ford dealership on the corner of Fifty-seventh Street and Tenth Avenue, across the street from CBS. I knew this part of the story; I had often stared at that doorway on my way to my CBS office, and had even stood there imagining the woman who would become my mother huddled against the door of the car dealership in 1951, hungry and homeless, her possessions left for scavengers on the street.

It was as if she had fallen off the edge of the world, until she found my father and discovered a sanctuary in his laugh.

"Your father was a brilliant, brilliant man," she told me. "I mean, like one of the most brilliant comedians ever. He had the most fantastic gift for being anybody. He would just assume different characters, and he would talk to you as a character, and then you would relate off that character. He was constantly flipping, sort of like Robin Williams, only not quite. Because he wasn't frenetic in any way. He'd just be somebody else for a while. And then *you* would be somebody else, and he was so endearing. And he was—everybody loved him so much, respected him so much."

Living in New York with Jimmy, Mom felt as if she'd finally been freed from the locked car in which she'd lived her life. Finally, she had gained entry to the world of show business, even if it was as the consort of a black entertainer. She found that world of black show business, so foreign from Idaho and Long Beach, fascinating, and she worked hard to blend in.

She soon felt secure enough to send for my brother, who was by then thirteen. "I went to New York, and they were living in a hotel on Forty-sixth between Broadway and Eighth Avenue," Lary recalled.

"I remember for the first day or two, I was calling him 'boy,' and I got a lecture about how this was not appropriate. From then it was almost love at first sight. He took me around to places, introduced me to people. I'd be with all my friends in Atlantic City, and he'd come up and lay a wad of bills on me." Lary swelled with pride, recalling the only father he ever knew, a black man, who gave him the experience of being Somebody.

An unbidden smile comes to my face as I picture Lary, a middle-aged white man with a paunch and thinning wisps of gray hair who is prone to wearing a brick red professor's cardigan, ill-fitting trousers, and rundown Clarks Wallabees, hanging out with black teenagers.

Harold Cromer, my father's partner, remembered Lary well from those summers in Atlantic City. "Lary didn't know if he was black or white," he said definitively when I interviewed him. They lived week to week in a residence hotel in 1953, while my mother supported the family on her meager earnings as a cashier in Gimbel's by day and hatcheck girl at a club on Fifty-second Street at night. The family was unable to find a place to live—or rather, Mom and Lary found places readily enough, until Jimmy showed up.

My brother still gets outraged by one memory from his teenage years. "This one landlord, he was Italian," Lary remembered when I interviewed him for the documentary. He shook his head in bemusement. "He sounded as if he had just gotten off the boat. When he found out there was a black man involved, he said the other tenants would never go for it and we couldn't have the apartment. Then he hastened to add that he's not prejudiced—that some of his best friends are black! And here we were, white people, dealing with this. Blacks deal with this stuff every day."

In Atlantic City, in the basement apartment of Peggy and Paul's house at 407 North Indiana, they were freed from this pressure, if only for the summer. Norma had found the apartment in the local paper. Peggy told my mother she was reluctant to rent to show-business people; she and Paul had had bad experiences. Finally, Mom paid Peggy two months in advance to convince her to let them move in.

Aunt Peggy asked Mom whether she was "passing."

"Passing?" my mother repeated, missing the code, thereby unintentionally answering the question. Yes, Peggy explained. Some very light-skinned colored women—women who often had hair and eyes the color of my mother's—"passed" for white.

That would have delighted my mom—it provided proof that she had indeed become part of the world she longed to join.

The disparate elements of my life assembled in the three-room ground-floor apartment at 407 North Indiana Avenue for several summers between 1951 and 1954. I imagine my mother, her pink toenails gripping pink flip-flops as she crossed the street I would cross without her countless times, walking up to the Italian corner store to buy milk, lamb chops, and eggs, then cooking them on the small electric stove in the tiny kitchen next to the boiler room. I imagine the creak of hinges as my father's hands opened the black wrought-iron gate to the property every night when he left for work, and how he probably came in through the backyard to avoid waking anyone when he returned. I imagine my brother, Lary, keeping Uncle

Paul company at his upholstery shop and helping Aunt Peggy pull weeds from the rich black earth in the front yard.

Aunt Peggy always remembered what Lary told her once while they were working in the garden: "My grandmother doesn't know there are Negroes like you." She recalled it with a wistful tone in her voice, as if she would like to have met Granny, my namesake, June.

My mother had been with Jimmy nearly two years, and during those years show business had undergone a sea change. A new music, doo-wop, had replaced the swing-influenced vaudevillian tunes from the thirties and forties that my father knew so well. A new invention, television, broadcast acts nationwide.

Milton Berle's *Texaco Star Theater* was the most popular program on television. Its success proved an axiom of the era: that comedians made the best show hosts. They were used to dealing with live audiences, they could keep up a lively pace, and they were quick on their feet—a useful thing when dealing with a medium in which Murphy's law could assert itself at any second.

But the same old racial attitudes—straight-out discrimination in some cases, and prejudice in others—kept the doors closed to black entertainers. Black comics—even if they had been salable in the South—just weren't considered acceptable to host a national network TV show. Variety-show producers booked colored singers and dancers but shied away from comics, who might compete with the host.

Stump and Stumpy appeared on Berle's show once or twice doing their song-and-dance routines, and discovered the law of unintended consequences: more people knew of them, but afterward they had to totally retool their act, because millions of viewers had already seen it.

As Jimmy's career began to ebb, his drinking and marijuana use increased. Jimmy had been big time, and he was still a big spender, but now he found himself dependent on the woman he loved in order to survive.

By late 1953 their life together lacked security. Between the lack of money and the racial taunts they faced walking down the street, Mom said, she sensed it wouldn't last.

When she found out she was pregnant with me, Mom's foreign holiday in the Negro world ended. They were in Atlantic City that summer—Jimmy was playing Club Harlem. On Kentucky Avenue, the heart of Atlantic City's black showbiz district, she noticed hostile stares down the long bars in the dark drinking rooms where she had once felt so welcomed.

"On one occasion," she remembered, "Jimmy had me by the arm, and this woman who had been drinking kept making remarks about 'that poor white trash that you're with.' She was loud and obstreperous, but people were just ignoring her. I mean, what else can you do? But then she leapt—she flew out from the end of the bar and started hitting me and calling me poor white trash. 'Get out and leave! You don't belong here!' she said, or something to that effect."

I felt sorry for my mom then, sorry for me inside her womb—the cause of our trouble—and I felt guilty for all the times I have looked at a white woman with a black man and thought similar thoughts. I remembered what my mother's cousin Faye had told me: that in the fifties a white woman would have had to fall off the end of the world to find her haven with a black man.

In the South and at the Supreme Court, the seeds of the modern civil-rights movement had been planted and were growing. But to my mother, isolated in the segregated world of black show business, civil rights and racial equality seemed like ideas from Saturn. The school desegregation case wouldn't be decided for another year, and the Montgomery bus boycott was still four years away.

I considered anew the picture I had seen of Granny in her flapper costume, showing her stockings, cigarette in hand, and the promise of women's liberation it encapsulated, followed by the hope of the New Deal and the moral impulse of World War II. The end of the war had brought hope for world peace and for Negro rights, but by the time I was born in January 1954, those grand social dreams had shattered. Negro rights was a cause associated with Communism, and Senator Joe McCarthy was on a witch-hunt for Communists. The desires of a young man from Philly and a farm girl from Idaho didn't amount to a hill of beans in that world.

"I got to the point I never wanted to go out with Jimmy at all unless it was, you know, to go up to Harlem or something like that," Mom told me. "Because going downtown or, you know, anyplace, if we weren't with the show-business crowd, it was just too embarrassing. I mean, it was awful. It's not like today, where you see interracial couples and you don't think anything about it."

She sought solace and advice from Aunt Peggy.

As an adult I have watched whites stumbling across the racial lines; I've observed their confusion and bewilderment as they confront the hidden codes and thinly disguised contempt from those with darker skin, whom they previously suspected harbored only admiration for them; I have endured their naive questions and responded to those whose hearts seemed open, even if their words emerged clumsy and ill-considered.

So it must have been between Aunt Peggy and my mother. Their friendship was cemented in those months before I was born, when the pieces of my life formed a whole. I can picture the two of them becoming friends: my mother, swelling with me and the questions about what kind of child she would bring into the world, Aunt Peggy, pausing to chat as she made a pitcher of fresh iced tea.

"I used to spend more and more time with Peggy," Mom remembered, "and we used to discuss everything. She was also a dreamer; she wanted to travel all over the world and do things. And we discussed all of those things. I liked her a lot. She was childless, had always wanted a child. And I always thought, Oh, what a wonderful mother she would make."

They discovered similarities in their relationships: Mom was supporting Jimmy; Peggy was basically supporting Paul. And they shared a love of horses. Mom asked intelligent questions; she had a vulnerability about her, and she wanted to better herself—Peggy could see that straightaway. She found Mom genuinely likable.

One day, Mom told me, she worked up the courage to ask Peggy what life was like for a Negro woman.

I can't imagine Aunt Peggy's reaction to such a question, although she had recounted her side of this conversation to me several times when I was young. What was life like for a Negro? That topic consumed all black people during the fifties and sixties. We argued about our condition, talked about how to get around it, over it, or under it, constantly. We wondered whether things would ever change and what we could do to hasten that change along.

I can imagine that Aunt Peggy took her time framing an answer, there in the yellow kitchen, as her white organdy curtains billowed in the afternoon breeze and the petals of her African violets fluttered in the wind.

The world was full of limitations for colored women, she said she finally told my mother, even colored women who were smart and accomplished. Some of the limitations were obvious—look at how Jimmy could get an apartment only on the black side of town, even though he was making good money at Club Harlem—and some limitations were rooted in people's attitudes, in how they considered Negroes inferior.

The biggest difference, Aunt Peggy said, taking a breath and considering her words carefully, lay in the access to opportunities. Norma would always have the chance to make something of her life, because whites had more opportunities. But for Peggy—and for Norma's unborn baby, she added pointedly—opportunities would close off like a shell around an oyster.

My mother said she nodded politely as she listened, but she refused to accept what Aunt Peggy was saying. Of course, she knew Jimmy couldn't play in certain clubs or get work on TV, but if he drank less and worked harder, she was sure he could overcome those career problems. Sammy Davis Jr. was already breaking through, and she thought Jimmy could, too, if he would just update his act. As Peggy rambled on, telling her about the tragedies that befell children who were the products of mixed parentage, she determined that things would be different for me. She had read the stories in

Peggy's stack of *Ebony* magazines about racially mixed children re-jected by both the sides of their families, but she had also seen arti-cles about colored people who were so fair-skinned that most whites couldn't tell they were Negroes. "Peggy kept telling me how hard it would be for you," she told me. "And I'm sure I was polite and nod-ded very nicely, but I didn't believe it. You were going to pass. That's what I decided," she told me during the interview. "You would be born light enough to pass, and I would leave Jimmy and raise you on my own—in other words, this Negro thing would never be a problem."

Throughout her pregnancy, when all they knew about me was the pattern of my turns and kicks on her stomach, they called me Herman.

Fortunately, I was born female.

It was snowing that January when Mom went into labor. They had returned to New York that fall, leaving Lary behind with Peggy and Paul. There was no money—Mom was on welfare. In the snow-storm, she walked to the hospital. She hadn't seen Jimmy for three days. He was on a drinking binge. When he finally showed up at the hospital on January 6, 1954, the day after my birth, Mom told the nurse to send him away.

Was she just angry, or was she worried about the care she would receive once the nurses saw that the father of the baby was a black man? Regardless, my father got past the nurse and burst into the room, making an entrance with his usual flair, a song and dance.

" 'It's Joooon in Jan-u-ary, because I'm in love,' " he crooned in full-out theatrical imitation of Bing Crosby. My mother's heart melted. Even telling me the story forty years later, she smiled at the memory.

"We'll name her June," he said. Mom resisted, because that was her mother's name. Maybe that was my father's point—maybe he thought naming me after my grandmother might repair fences be-tween Mom and Granny. Or maybe, since his mother's middle name was also June, he saw it as a way to bridge the families. In any case, although Mom didn't want to name me "June," Jimmy insisted, and she relented.

On my birth certificate, where race is designated, the nurses listed "white."

"You *were* white," Mom told me. "And so I was very happy. You were the same color as I am, just a shade darker, perhaps. Like an olive, you know, instead of a redhead, which I was."

Every year on my birthday, Mom would describe the first moment she saw me, when the nurses put me in her arms and she held my foot in her palm and saw that it was a miniature version of her foot, and she said that she fell in love with me immediately.

Aunt Peggy came up from Atlantic City with her Rolleiflex to take the first pictures of me when I was six weeks old.

"Isn't it wonderful, Peggy?" Mom told her triumphantly. "She'll be light enough to pass!"

Aunt Peggy looked up as she focused the Rolleiflex.

"They get darker as they get older, honey," she had warned.

I mentioned to my mother that she had always told me that all the good parts of me came from her and the bad traits from my father.

"I never said that," she said.

"Yes you did," I insisted.

"I don't remember that at all," she said. "I've always wanted you to identify with me so much, and I'd say, 'Well, you're just like me.' You know, because I wanted you to feel close to me always, because you didn't live with me, and I wanted that bond. I never wanted that bond broken."

"I don't think it was ever in danger of really being broken," I said, backing down. "I just . . . sometimes it's . . . there's a part of Jimmy that's here, that did not come from you"—I laughed, trying to make the truth easier for her to bear—"and that's the part that I've been pressing you to see. . . . Can you embrace that part of me?"

"Oh, of course," she replied. "Because, you're not . . . I mean, I don't think of you as being part of Jimmy. You're just yourself."

———

My father had almost no work at all during the months after my birth, my mother told me. He spent most of his days in Charlie's Bar, buying rounds of drinks, leaving my mother to pay the tab. Jimmy was a mean drunk, and my mother says she and my brother became the scapegoats for the downward slide of his career. That's when the beatings began.

She told me again a story I had heard often as a child. Jimmy had come home drunk one day and begun beating her. Wearing only her slip and a bathrobe, she picked me up from my crib and tried to run away. He chased her all the way down the steps of the apartment building as she held me against her. We must have been a strange sight bursting onto Thirty-fourth Street in a blizzard. Mom thought she'd surely be safe in public. She stumbled, fell, and, curled with me into a fetal position, enduring his kicks and screams as the patrons of the bar next door gathered to watch.

Whenever I had heard this story growing up, I imagined myself screaming in bewilderment and protest, protected by my mother and trying to protect her as we lay huddled on the snow-covered cement.

But when my mother told this story to me on camera, she added details I had never known. Angry at my father for taking out yet another loan that she would be left to pay, angry that he had come home drunk yet again, she had yelled, "You're just a nigger, and I hate you, and I'm going to leave!"

The word "nigger" hit my ears like bare fists. For a moment my mother was no different from that faceless mass of white people who think all blacks are dirty, poor, stupid, and on welfare. Her words and my reaction hovered in the air between us.

"It was the only time I ever used that word," she tried to assure me.

Unbidden, the thought came: *If I'd been my father, I would have slapped you, too.*

But I did not say it. I had worked so hard to begin this conversation. It was important to hear her out. The part of me that loved her, that felt protective of her, that feared alienating her, made me hush, and as she continued, she ended with another detail I'd never heard: a visual image, the image of men emptying out of the bar on the corner. They formed a circle around her, me, and my father: twelve white men standing in a circle of judgment around a young, beaten-down mother lying on the ground with a baby in her arms. They did not intervene.

"I knew I wouldn't get any help," she conceded, resignation in her voice. "I think had we both been black, maybe they would've helped, you know. But I think they just felt I had it coming in some way."

I wondered whether there had really been twelve onlookers, or whether my mother's memory had invented that jury. "It reinforced my only opinion that I must get out," she ended. "I just had to lay my groundwork very carefully and disappear, so that he never would find me."

It wasn't until after the interview was over, after I had finished the documentary and my mother and I were doing promotional interviews during November 1996, that I learned the means through which she got away from my father.

We had just finished taping *The Tavis Smiley Show*. Mom had not seen the documentary, but she had read the press materials, and she was worried about how she would be portrayed. "Secret Daughter: the story of a mixed-race daughter and the mother who gave her away," the press release said.

"I didn't give you away!" she cried. "You always knew where I was!" She thought I hated her, she had thought my love for her would protect her, but now she could see she had been wrong, and now the world would hate her.

I had been so absorbed by making the documentary that I hadn't even read the press release. I regretted the choice of words, but all I could do was try to reassure her. "I don't hate you," I said, embracing her. "All my life I have tried to *be* you."

"But I was such a bad mother!" she cried.

"You did the best you could," I said softly.

She didn't think so. She was convinced that she had been not only a bad mother but a bad person. It was then that she told me how she both hated Jimmy and pitied him during those last two years, how she felt so trapped that she'd considered suicide but couldn't bear to think what would happen to me and Lary if she killed herself. She had begun, then, to plot her escape. She needed money, but as fast as she brought money in, Jimmy spent it.

Things got so bad that she left Lary with Peggy and Paul for six months and became a prostitute. Jimmy knew what she was doing, and after a while so did my brother. So did Aunt Peggy.

That was the shame buried at the bottom of my mother's dark well of secrets: the fact that she had prostituted herself. It was the reason she had not wanted to revisit the story of her life with my father—because of the way it had ended and what she had done to escape.

It took her eighteen months to save up enough money. She put down the security payment on a new apartment. When she left my father, she left him with a month's rent paid.

My mother couldn't remember when she first brought up the idea of leaving me with Peggy. "I felt that going into a white world would have just been so difficult for you, because you wouldn't have been accepted in so many places," she said during our interview. "I always wanted the best for you, and I thought about Peggy because she was a teacher, she was a very educated woman, and she needed a child. I figured you would just have two mothers."

Maybe it happened during one of her respites in Atlantic City, as I lay asleep on the sofa in the little back room off the kitchen.

"Peggy, how would you feel about taking care of June full-time?" she might have asked.

Catching her breath, Peggy would have fiddled with her diamond ring and wedding band, waiting to hear the rest of what my mother had to say.

"I don't want to give her up totally. I want to be part of her life. In other words, she would live here and go to school with you and come visit me whenever she could."

I imagine Peggy would have wanted to shout "Yes!" immediately.

To have hungered for a child so badly for so long, and now, at fifty, to finally be given the chance, with a little girl she had known since birth. She would have wanted to throw her arms around my mother and shout "Hallelujah!" But I can't know for sure. Aunt Peggy never described that first conversation, and my mother was so matter-of-fact I couldn't read between her lines to Aunt Peggy's emotions.

"Peggy said, 'Let me talk it over with Paul,' which she did. And she called me back in a couple of hours and she said, 'Yes, we will.' "

I do know that Aunt Peggy wanted a clean break, as Aunt Hugh Gregory had suggested. My mother had refused. Aunt Peggy had told me this part of the story with a sigh. "She said she would turn your upbringing over to me, but she wanted to remain a part of your life. And by then Paul and I, who had wanted a child so badly and never had one, had grown to love you so much too, that finally she convinced us everything would turn out all right."

Uncle Paul's main concern was my religious upbringing. He was Catholic, while Aunt Peggy was Episcopalian. Uncle Paul wanted me to go to his church, but my mother distrusted Catholicism. She found Catholics to be repressed and guilt-ridden.

They agreed I'd be raised as an Episcopalian, and the deal was made. There were no formalities and no legal documents. Aunt Peggy and Mommie made what, in earlier times and different circumstances, might have been called a gentleman's agreement.

When we had finished filming the formal interview, I felt as off balance as I had when we started. The cameras were still rolling when my mother told me she thought I was going through all this in an effort to "find myself."

"I don't think I'm looking for myself so much as trying to integrate the pieces," I told her. "I'm tired, every Thanksgiving, of trying to decide am I going to go visit the Gregorys in D.C. or the Mays in Minneapolis, or am I going to come here." Ever since I was a little girl, I had wanted to bring my family together at one time.

"Yeah, but all families are that way," my mother said, refusing to concede my point. "I read that in magazines all the time, you know: 'Should I go to Dad's family or Mom's family?' I mean, you just divvy yourself up. You're not alone in that."

I felt outmaneuvered and silly. "Do you think I'm on a fool's mission?" I asked, suddenly the daughter needing her mother's advice.

"No. No. We'll see what happens," she replied cautiously. "I mean, what do you think this will accomplish? That's the thing."

"Well, you and I will have a closer relationship, I think, as a result of it," I pointed out.

She looked away for a second, then chewed her lip thoughtfully, "Well, we couldn't have a closer relationship on my part. Maybe on yours, maybe you will feel less antagonism to me. I hope, you know, I've made you understand a lot of the way I felt and why I did what I did."

"Do you ever feel guilty that I didn't stay with you?" I asked.

"Oh, yes," she replied. "You know, I had enormous guilt over that. I hope I did the right thing."

Aunt Peggy and the black community of Atlantic City had given me a sense of place and belonging, while my mother had broadened my horizons far beyond that seaside town. I knew, despite all the pain we'd endured, that she had done the right thing.

*I*t was early morning when you woke me. Sunlight breached the frame of the Sleeping Gypsy on the wall. You had told me the lion would guard me, too, from night monsters, and every morning when I awoke, I checked to make sure the lion was still there. That morning the wall reflected the harsh light of early December. Your voice, calling me, sounded more broken than usual. Was there a seriousness in your tone that told me this was not a morning for lollygagging? Were your eyes rimmed with red? Did I ask why you were sad, or was I too absorbed in the daily rituals? Was breakfast that day Wheatena or poached eggs on toast? Did you watch me drink my milk from the cup shaped to fit my little hand, the cup with the cow-shaped handle, knowing it was the last time you would hear me announce "All gone!" when I reached the bottom?

I would have been excited. A trip! A trip meant a bus ride, scenery, new things to see, new things to do! Oodles and boodles of fun! We were going to visit Aunt Peggy and Uncle Paul. It wasn't the first time I'd been there. I'd spent days with them before while you went off on some modeling shoot or another. I don't remember those times; you and Aunt Peggy planned for me not to remember.

Aunt Peggy said a friend drove to New York City, to pick us up and bring us down to Atlantic City in his black Chevy with the New Jersey taxi sign on top and the yellow-and-black logo reversed. Aunt Peggy said it was her friend who brought us down, but it's that damned bus ride we both remember, a collective memory of all the bus rides, through the tunnel, past the graffiti-covered cliffs of Hackensack (who would ever want to live in a place called Hackensack! we laughed), past the railroad bridge, past the gas station to the stark insignia signaling the turnpike, the turnpike leading to another sign, a circle, green and yellow, with the shape of New Jersey on it, the Garden State Parkway, which had no gardens but lots of tolls. We passed Woodbridge and Red Bank and Mullica Township. We counted the tolls, all fourteen of them, while we played "Itsy Bitsy Spider," me singing the words 'cause you always forgot, your hand pretending to be a spider as it crawled up the water spout, falling down, down, down to my ribs and tickling me in my seat till I shrieked with laughter, before we started all over again.

We sang rounds I had learned in preschool. I loved starting a song from the beginning while somebody else was already singing the middle of it; I loved how that made the song sound altogether new:

> Merrily, merrily, merrily, merrily,
> Row, row, row your boat
> Gently down the stream,
> Merrily, merrily, merrily, merrily,
> Life is but a dream.
> Life is but a dream.

After we passed Toms River, we made a turn, and suddenly, even through the closed windows of the bus, we could smell the ocean, smell of marshes and salt conjuring up sand and waves and clamshells. There were pieces of clamshells even in the dark black dirt of Aunt Peggy's front yard.

We pulled in to the grubby granite old bus station, its linoleum floor yellowed with age. It was so much smaller than Port Authority. In front of the station were the cabs: they were regular cars, not yellow cabs like in New York. They sat empty in a line with their motors running, cabbies talking in a group, drinking coffee and smoking cigarettes, waiting for passengers.

We were here, and there was the driver Aunt Peggy sent, Mr. Wilson, in his grubby tweed suit, white shirt, and skinny black tie and brown sweater, his lean walruslike face tucked under a brown Kangol cap, his cab the first in line, us the first passengers from the bus into a cab.

He drove the eight blocks from the Missouri Avenue bus station to Indiana, from yellow to red on the Monopoly board, from the Italian side of town to the colored section, up to 407 North Indiana, where a small wrought-iron gate, the same height as me, protected a big gray house with white shutters.

The gate clanged as we carefully closed it behind us. Up the front walk, up the concrete bottom stair, and up all fifteen wooden ones to the porch, where Aunt Peggy and Uncle Paul were waiting. I flew into Aunt Peggy's arms and gave Uncle Paul a big kiss. Aunt Peggy took out her Rolleiflex, and Mommie and I posed for pictures on the lawn. Two of those pictures I have still—the date, "December, 1957"—one month shy of my fourth birthday. They are black-and-white snapshots, slightly out of focus. I wonder whether they are out of focus because there were tears in Peggy's eyes. I wonder what you were thinking.

Your hair is smartly bobbed at the chin, your face turned away from the camera and focused down on me. You're wearing a princess-style, shin-length coat and carrying a box-style pocketbook. Your heels show off your legs.

In the picture you look down at me (are you smiling? are there tears in your eyes?) and I'm looking at the camera, face framed by the white rabbit trim of a hooded hat that matches the coat and white muff my hands are stuffed into. I have this big smile on my face. I don't know that my life is about change forever, that my olive complexion and short Afro have established a gulf between my Mommie and me that a lifetime of buses, planes, and hair relaxers will not quite undo.

You dropped me off, and the taxi pulled away. You say this is nothing unusual, that it happened plenty of times before, but surely this time was different. Were tears streaming down your face? Was I being held by Uncle Paul? Did I stretch my arms toward you and cry, "Mommie! Mommie! Where are they taking Mommie?" No one *remembers. But sometimes my shoulders ache; ache, it seems, with the pain of reaching for you while someone holds me back.*

Aunt Peggy said I looked cute as a button that day, like a child model. She told me the story of taking a picture on the front lawn of the house at 407 North Indiana—how Mom had posed with me, then Peggy, then Paul, in turn. She told me the story of taking the picture so often that I knew it as well as I knew the story of Christmas. I guess to her I *was* Christmas, her birthday, and all her anniversaries all rolled into one. But I had never understood how I had come to be there until I did a documentary about my own life.

When I started my new life in Atlantic City, my mother said, she was so brokenhearted that she volunteered to work with foster children at Bellevue Hospital.

"It was the most bitterly unhappy period of my life," she remembered. "I erupted in hives. I just didn't think I would be able to live. You were everything to me. Yet I knew it was best for you and it was best for me. It was just one of those situations. Because neither one of us would've had a life."

20. MERCURY

After the documentary aired, many people told me that producing it must have felt cathartic. It didn't. Tearing down my defenses and opening myself to the world was overwhelming, and I found myself in a state of shock. As always when I felt emotionally wounded, I headed south to spend some time with my Gregory cousins. Uncle Monty, the oldest surviving son of Aunt Hugh and Uncle Gum, had died, and we gathered in Washington for his funeral.

At one point Uncle Ernie and Aunt Mignon's youngest son, Greg (who now calls himself Sule), picked up an empty pickle jar and began tapping out a West African rhythm; his older brother, Chico, picked up a spoon and tapped it on the table in accompaniment. Alan, Uncle Monty's youngest, joined in with a gourd; Gina, Uncle Hugh's daughter, picked up a tambourine; I chose some marimbas; others picked up a Senegalese finger harp, spoons; still others raised hands and voices to join our improvisation. We did not need to feel each other out or explain our roles; each just knew that the other's contribution would add to the polyrhythms. The children of Sule and Gina and Hugh and Chico and Monty wandered in and joined us in this beat of life's celebration, our family's triumph over death. The rhythms filled the house; the house itself became a drum, the *terra sancta* of our traditions. We shared a sense, as T. S. Eliot once wrote, "not only of the pastness of the past, but of its presence."

My journey had brought me here, longing for an identity that encompassed all our histories.

———

Even the Gregorys, with all their pedigree, couldn't trace their family line earlier than 1822. My earliest black ancestor appeared in the 1890 census. She's my father's great-grandmother, Caroline Cross.

Caroline lived in southern Virginia, in a town called Lunenburg. She could read, according to the census taker, and she worked as a cook. She had four boys and owned a hundred acres of land. In 1892, she bought another hundred acres. Someone would have had to vouch for a black woman seeking to buy land. Who, the records do not say.

In 1900, the deed for her land had been transferred to the county sheriff, who left it to his son. There is no recorded bill of sale, no record of public auction. I walked around the tract, mostly over-grown by woods, and discovered the foundation of a kitchen, the remains of a chimney. I wondered what had happened to my grand-mother Caroline, whether night riders had come and spooked her off her land or whether she had just chosen to sell it all and move north for better opportunity. Whatever happened, by the turn of the century she and all four of her boys were living in Philadelphia, rent-ing rooms, working as domestics or laborers.

The Cross family continued in those lines of work for three generations.

In Salt Lake City, I dug through the Mormon database, searching for clues about my mother's—about our shared—ancestors. A sign in the Mormon genealogical center in Salt Lake states its goal: to prove the relationship of all humans, a brotherhood of man stretch-ing back to Adam.

I grunted cynically at the idea. Until 1978 only white men were al-lowed to become priests in the Mormon Church. The policy changed when efforts to expand Mormonism met resistance from those who wanted the right to spiritual self-determination, a drive as American as the Pilgrims.

Tracing my mother's maternal grandmother's line, I discovered

William Pierce, a Protestant tradesman who had once served as captain of the *Mayflower*. He plied the waters between New England and the Bahamas in the early 1600s, selling tobacco, cotton—and Native American slaves.

Fifteen thousand Pierce descendants, dispersed from Oregon to Florida, claimed relationship to my mother's Idaho family and, through them, to me. Their sheer numbers penetrated my armor of isolation; their teeming diaspora challenged my notion that by growing up on Atlantic City's Northside I had been separated from the American mainstream. William Pierce's DNA made us kin, no matter how uncomfortable his history made me. Pierce had been a sailor of some renown, holding the record for the fastest trip from Liverpool to Boston in the nation's birthing vessel, the *Mayflower*, but he had also owned—and sold—slaves.

He was killed in a battle with the indigenous people of the West Indies.

Simple justice.

I discovered another relative, John Rogers, a Rhode Island religious zealot of the early eighteenth century. Rogers, an abolitionist, endured public whippings for his refusal to reveal the whereabouts of a slave he had helped to escape.

I was reminded of the former slave Caroline, eking out a living in southern Virginia just after Emancipation.

I was descended from a slave, a slave trader, and an abolitionist. The American Trinity.

The morning after the documentary aired, I received a message that read, "Candace Herman called. Says she was born Candace Booth."

Larry and Norma's child, Candie, their missing daughter, put up for adoption, had emerged from the memories and efforts of forty years to claim us. She told me she had always thought of herself as the unwanted daughter of the well-known TV actor and his wife.

I told Candie her birth certificate had listed her name as Candace June Booth.

At the time I discovered it, I had been taken aback by our shared name and what it said about Mom's longing for Granny's approval. Now the name connected me with Candie immediately, much as our shared smile had connected me and Jimmy's oldest daughter, Lynda, immediately.

Quickly, we exchanged salient facts: Candie had grown up less than four miles from Mom and Larry's house in Los Angeles; she had attended the same high school where my sister-in-law Lany had been head cheerleader. She had admired Lany from a distance. She had attended UCLA as an undergraduate while Lary was pursuing his graduate studies there.

Candie was an elementary-school teacher. She taught fourth-grade bilingual education.

Ten messages from me and Lary awaited my mother that day. "What happened? Why do I have all these messages?" she asked. "Did somebody die?"

I told her we had found Candie, that she was in Los Angeles, and she wanted to meet us. I was unprepared for her reaction. "Oh, June, all of these loose ends are being tied up. It's like everything's resolving. I just feel like I could die!" She choked on her words, then repeated, "I just feel like my life's about to end!"

My mom, the drama queen, I thought at the time.

In January 1997, we gathered at my mother's apartment in New York to meet Candie. Lary flew in from Ireland, where he was on a Fulbright. I came down from Boston. Candie herself, put up for adoption forty-three years earlier, would arrive that night.

As the hour arrived, I checked and double-checked the camera microphone, to make sure it was working.

My mother paced.

My brother, Lary, made small talk.

My stepfather, Larry, sat in a corner and stared out the window. He had been sober for twenty years, but often he slipped into his own little world.

The buzzer rang. "Showtime," Larry said, rising.

We piled out into the hallway like a raggedy line of Fosse dancers.

Mom and Larry's arms and hands were entwined. I couldn't tell whether she was holding him up or whether he supported her.

We waited several times longer than it takes the elevator to travel from the ground floor to the seventeenth. When it arrived, the elevator door slid open, revealing . . . only the elevator man.

"She's in the basement," he explained. "She's upset. She wanted to get some water."

The four of us got into the elevator to go down and fetch her.

Candie was out of sight, but we could hear her, gasping between sobs in a corner of the laundry room. We found her sitting on a small stool, shakily drinking a glass of water.

Mom reached her first and enveloped her in an embrace. As they parted, I felt a jolt of irrational jealousy. Candie looked enough like my mother to be her younger sister. It's not fair—those were my first thoughts. It's not fair she looks so much like my mother, when I, I who have known my mother since I was born, stare in the mirror searching futilely for her likeness.

We rode back up in the elevator.

"You look just like Sally, Larry's mother," Mom said.

Larry stared at his daughter as though she were a vision.

"She looks just like my aunt Esther," he said to me, his voice filled with wonder. "The spitting image. J.B., how can this be?"

In the apartment Candie immediately took me by the hand and led me to the mirror in my mother's bedroom. She wanted to see how we looked alike.

I didn't see the resemblance, but everyone else did. Same eyes. Same cheekbones, a likeness so great that later her own children— my two new nephews and my new niece—would remark on it in the same tones of wonder that Larry had used.

Mom had rented cots for "the kids." At seventy-seven, for the first time in her life, she was spending a night in the same house with all of her offspring. My brother, sister, and I, middle-aged children, piled into the cots at midnight and chatted half the night as if we were teenagers at a slumber party. My brother cracked corny jokes into the wee morning hours, until Candie and I told him to shut up and let us go to sleep.

The next morning, as I wandered into the kitchen, I heard my mother muttering to herself,

"Not his daugher. Not his daughter." She looked up at me angrily. "That's what Larry's mother told me when he refused to pay child support when Candie was born.

"Who else's daughter could she be?" my mother said, as if addressing her dead mother-in-law. *"Look at her! She looks just like him!"*

Candie asked Lary and me why we had been kept while she was given away. Lary and I glanced at each other. After so much time spent reassuring our mother that she had done the best she could, we felt uncomfortable acknowledging degrees of abandonment.

I began to let my hair grow out in its natural state, shaping it into what are called double-strand twists. It resembled corkscrews. I liked the way it popped up every which way. Friends asked whether I planned dreadlocks. No, I said. I had no plan for it; I was just letting it become whatever it was.

My hairdresser, whose name, oddly enough, was Hugh, scoffed at my "natural" hair. He thought I was trying to prove my blackness and downplay my light skin by keeping my hair "kinky and all over the place."

"You wear it like that because you're afraid to be beautiful," he insisted. "You couldn't stand to deal with the reaction you'd get from men, the jealousy you'd face from women, if you took advantage of what God gave you."

He was right. I was always uncomfortable with that Miss America version of myself. Still, I was after a different kind of beauty, a beauty that wasn't dependent on straightened hair and contact lenses. I like the texture of my natural hair. I like its curliness and the thickness of the frizz and the curlicues on its ends. Some days I didn't know what to do with it, some days it felt awkward, but I was learning to accept it, and in the process I was learning to accept some part of myself, long denied.

My mother had always been so healthy that none of us could believe the diagnosis that came after Memorial Day of 2003: colorectal cancer, metastasized. Months left, even if chemotherapy worked.

It had been seven years since the broadcast of the *Frontline* documentary "Secret Daughter." After it aired, a strange thing had happened: my mother's conservative friends—including the contessa—the ones to whom she had most feared revealing the truth, had embraced her, while some of those she expected to be most tolerant had never spoken to her again—not because she had an out-of-wedlock child with a black man but because she'd left that child to be raised by others. The world had changed since 1954—in ways that neither of us had anticipated.

The documentary won several awards. I was glad for the recognition, but that wasn't what was so important to me. What mattered was that the family had been brought together and that I finally understood the fractal geometry of my life: more than a set of linear relationships, my family extended beyond bloodlines and included relatives I didn't even know. I had reunited my mother and her husband with their long-lost daughter.

For me personally, the documentary brought a measure of resolution: I married the jazz musician I had met ten years earlier at the Lickety-Split, a man the color of milk chocolate who refuses to let me seal myself in my solitary world. From time to time, he works in the same club where my father and his chums used to hang out.

In 2000 I left *Frontline* and began teaching at Columbia University's Graduate School of Journalism in New York.

Mom had sold the house she and Larry bought in California and also moved to New York. She had developed a relationship with Candie and her children and even with Lary's children, whom she had always held at arm's length because they reminded her of getting old.

She was not ready to die. She was just getting ready to live; the chemotherapy only hastened her decline.

The frame of her bones emerged as her flesh dissolved. At first I found her bony frame beautiful, a well-constructed scaffold for the shapely woman she had been; then it went further, and she became a skeleton waiting for death to claim her.

The day before she died, she told me she had watched the documentary only once, seven years earlier, as it aired. "It felt like a searing, white heat on my eyeballs," she said. "I could never watch it again." That night she held my hand so tightly I struggled to disengage myself.

She passed away on August 26, 2003—eight weeks after the diagnosis, just before school started. The intimacy that developed between us during the last two months of her life, when I visited her daily, made her absence particularly painful. Friends told me I could hold her memory in my heart, but I couldn't—my heart felt rent in two. The pain of missing her filled the space where our secret used to be. I began teaching, but my heart wasn't in it. I continued living because that is what children are born to do. The rhythms of life—rising in the morning, commuting to work, eating lunch, sleeping at night—became a painful austerity. For the first time in my life, I wished that I had children of my own, to take my mind off my own grief.

There was no way to celebrate the end of such a life. Although I desperately wanted to bring her whole family together, there was no way to make it happen.

My mother had wished to be cremated. Candie, who was raised Jewish, and Lary, who had converted to Judaism, said it was against Jewish custom. Larry said his good-byes in the funeral home. So we decided to have a memorial service for her later, and I went alone to the mausoleum, driving a rental car behind the hearse.

As Mom was returned to ash, I sat before the Buddhist altar and remembered her as she looked during a trip we took to Italy in 1970, when she wore a smashing teal and fuchsia batik ensemble with a flared skirt and a wrap bodice, simple tan sandals, her auburn hair in a casual flip. The Italian men had gaped as we passed. I remembered her years later, sitting in her kimono on the wrap-around terrace of her New York apartment, drinking her morning coffee and combing her pet Abyssinian cat, Elsa. She'd adopted Elsa from the pet shelter. In Mom's last years, she'd also adopted younger women who reminded her in some way of herself: the dental technician who wanted to become a comic actress; the Colombian house cleaner who had fled a lousy relationship and was raising her six-year-old daughter alone; the Thai artisan who made beautifully hand-crafted jewelry and sold it at the flea market; the dancer in Larry's touring company whose guilelessness reminded her of how she was in those years before the world taught her its lessons.

It was if as, by nurturing these women, she could nurture an alternate version of her own life. I chanted for her to be reborn in her next life as someone who would make a difference.

That was the last thing she had said to me: "I want to come back as a good person. I want to change the world."

Michael, my brother's oldest son, had scheduled his wedding in Minneapolis for the week following Mom's death. Lary and Lany planned a family memorial for Mom to be held the day afterward, but Larry Storch, incapacitated by grief, wouldn't travel.

At the service they talked about my mother's meaning in their lives; I sat stone-faced, heartbroken that I had failed in this last attempt to bring the pieces of my mother's life and mine together. She had deteriorated so fast that I hadn't even had time to let any of my Gregory cousins know what was going on. Mom had just met all of them, finally, at my own wedding two years earlier; now she was gone.

Everyone thought the Minneapolis service was a fitting tribute, but I didn't. There was no party. No fun. No ethnic food. No music. No stars.

The next week Larry and I held another memorial for Mom in the apartment that had served as the epicenter of her life in New York. We hung Christmas lights throughout the house. We bought platters of food and comfy chairs. Had I been able to figure out how to fit them into the space, I would have hired a mariachi band.

Fifty people squeezed into the apartment. They included some

actors and comedians, and many "gypsies"—dancers from the chorus lines of shows Larry had done, along with set designers, prop
managers, and pit musicians. Lary and Lany came—but not their
children. Candie and Candie's two older children came—but not her
husband or their youngest.

As Larry's colleagues and friends asked which of us was which, I
made light of the situation. "Mom believed that nothing should
match, including the fathers of her children." That got a big laugh.
It was the kind of statement Aunt Peggy would have called
inappropriate—not to mention at a funeral—but among a showbiz
crowd, it was the hit line of the night.

One crisp blue Thursday, maybe two months after Mom had
passed, I headed to the dentist. My mother had recommended him,
but visiting his East Side office meant crossing so many memories:
retracing the steps along West Sixty-seventh Street we had walked
every day when I was a child, walking through the park, passing the
playground where my mother had brought me to play. Tears filled
my eyes most of the way.

Crossing Madison Avenue, I caught my breath. A woman was
approaching me, and she looked familiar: the almond-shaped
eyes slightly askew, the prominent forehead, the high cheekbones—
I started, and I stared. Mom? I drew closer, my heart skipping beats.
Then, as I stepped up onto the curb, I saw the beige tint in the skin
and blinked.

It was my own reflection I had seen in the window; the woman I
thought was my mother—she was me.

FOR THE BEST IN PAPERBACKS, LOOK FOR THE

In every corner of the world, on every subject under the sun, Penguin represents quality and variety—the very best in publishing today.

For complete information about books available from Penguin—including Penguin Classics and Puffins—and how to order them, write to us at the appropriate address below. Please note that for copyright reasons the selection of books varies from country to country.

In the United States: Please write to *Penguin Group (USA), P.O. Box 12289 Dept. B, Newark, New Jersey 07101-5289* or call 1-800-788-6262.

In the United Kingdom: Please write to *Dept. EP, Penguin Books Ltd, Bath Road, Harmondsworth, West Drayton, Middlesex UB7 0DA.*

In Canada: Please write to *Penguin Books Canada Ltd, 90 Eglinton Avenue East, Suite 700, Toronto, Ontario M4P 2Y3.*

In Australia: Please write to *Penguin Books Australia Ltd, P.O. Box 257, Ringwood, Victoria 3134.*

In New Zealand: Please write to *Penguin Books (NZ) Ltd, Private Bag 102902, North Shore Mail Centre, Auckland 10.*

In India: Please write to *Penguin Books India Pvt Ltd, 11 Panchsheel Shopping Centre, Panchsheel Park, New Delhi 110 017.*

In the Netherlands: Please write to *Penguin Books Netherlands bv, Postbus 3507, NL-1001 AH Amsterdam.*

In Germany: Please write to *Penguin Books Deutschland GmbH, Metzlerstrasse 26, 60594 Frankfurt am Main.*

In Spain: Please write to *Penguin Books S. A., Bravo Murillo 19, 1° B, 28015 Madrid.*

In Italy: Please write to *Penguin Italia s.r.l., Via Benedetto Croce 2, 20094 Corsico, Milano.*

In France: Please write to *Penguin France, Le Carré Wilson, 62 rue Benjamin Baillaud, 31500 Toulouse.*

In Japan: Please write to *Penguin Books Japan Ltd, Kaneko Building, 2-3-25 Koraku, Bunkyo-Ku, Tokyo 112.*

In South Africa: Please write to *Penguin Books South Africa (Pty) Ltd, Private Bag X14, Parkview, 2122 Johannesburg.*